Thomas Hardy

A Collection of Critical Essays

For Nilima and Apoorva

Thomas Hardy

A Collection of Critical Essays

Edited by

Subhash Chandra

PRESTIGE

Published by
Prestige Books
3/28, East Patel Nagar
New Delhi 110 008

1999

ISBN: 81-7551-037-4

Photo Typesetting by
Pivot Computers
Delhi 110 006
Ph. 3981867

Printed at
Chaman Offset Printers
New Delhi 110 002

Contents

Acknowledgements

The editor and the publisher gratefully acknowledge their indebtedness to the following for granting permission to use the copyright material:

NOVEL: A Forum on Fiction (vol. 16, no. 2, Winter 1982). Copyright NOVEL Corp. (c) 1988. Reprinted with permission.

The Centennial Review and the author for the essay, "Angles of Vision and Questions of Gender in *Far from the Madding Crowd*."

ARIEL and the authors for the essays, "Passion and Flood in *Far from the Madding Crowd*" and "Hardy's Poetry of Transcendence."

English Language Notes and the author for the essay, "Sale and Sacrament: The Wife Auction in *The Mayor of Casterbridge*."

E.L.H. and the authors for the essays, "Nature and Paganism in Hardy's *Tess of the D'Urbervilles*," and "*Jude the Obscure*: Reading and the Spirit of the Law."

The Victorian Newsletter and the author for the essay, "The Thing Signified in *The Dynasts*: A Speculation."

Contributors

Suman Bala, S.B.S. College, University of Delhi

Charlotte Bonica, University of Pennsylvania

William E. Buckler, New York University

Subhash Chandra, S.B.S. College, University of Delhi

Leonora Epstein, University of California, Los Angeles

Geoffrey Harvey, Bulmershe College of Higher Education, England

Lewis Horne, University of Saskatchewan

Deepshikha Kotwal, University of Jammu

Arti Mathur, P.G.D.A.V. College, University of Delhi

K.B. Razdan, University of Jammu

Ramon Saldivar, University of Texas, Austin

V.P. Sharma, School of Correspondence Courses, University of Delhi

G.R. Taneja, R.L.A. College, University of Delhi

Judith Bryant Wittenberg, Simmons College, Boston, Massachusetts

Thomas Hardy: Then and Now

SUBHASH CHANDRA

Thomas Hardy was born on June 2, 1840 in the village of Higher Bockhampton near Dorchester. England was then in the throes of Industrial Revolution. Chartism, a reform movement, was stirring (also frightening) many people. However, the Dorset countryside at the southwest corner of the island (which appeared as Wessex in Hardy's novels) appeared to remain placidly changeless and unaffected by the turbulence of history or technology. Of course, the rural and traditional Dorset, steeped in old country ways, rituals and speech, could not remain entirely untouched by the winds of change for long. When Hardy was seven years old, Dorchester saw its first railroad and then all through the second half of the century, the countryside was invaded by new machines, new men. These slow incursions into the tranquil world of the countryside—a world of charm, peace and social unity—are reflected as a major theme in the fiction of Hardy. Wessex in the novels betrays signs of division, because in real life, Hardy witnessed how Dorset was moving away from the possibility of an organic culture.

Hardy is unmistakably a "personal writer," particularly as a poet and to only a slightly lesser degree as a novelist. His world largely contains his own fortunes and his emotional reactions to his fortunes. Undoubtedly, the personal experiences and events are transformed into artistic material, because Hardy's avowed purpose was not confessional but artistic. Besides, the transmuting operation of time has worked upon the private experiences which go into his art, because these experiences come from far back in his life. Hardy possessed the Wordsworthian power to recollect the emotion in tranquillity—a power to exhume an emotion even after decades and the emotion remained as fresh as when it was interred.

As a boy, Hardy was of "an ecstatic temperament," and danced "the endless jigs, hornpipes, reels, waltzes and country-dances" to the tunes his father played on the violin. *Under the Greenwood Tree* contains the details of Hardy's association with Stinsford String Choir. Though Hardy denies that there was "family portrait in the tales," the tranter's house is recognizably the Hardy's at Higher Bockhampton, and old William Dewy, Reuben

Dewy, Dick Dewy, and Michael Main occupied the same seats and played the same instruments as Thomas Hardy senior, Thomas Hardy junior, James Hardy, and James Dart in 'Mellstock' church gallery.

Besides being playful, Hardy was also noticed as a bright, shy and sensitive boy vulnerable to pain who became the favourite of the lady of the manor, Julia Augusta Martin. She, Hardy would later recall, was "passionately fond of him" and his own feeling towards her was "almost of a lover." Some crucial events overtook Hardy's boyhood and youth which decisively shaped his psyche and formed his perception of the human condition. A shock which cast a gloomy shadow on Hardy's mind was the sight of a child labourer, dead of starvation, under a hedge. The narration by his father of the hanging of a young boy, to whose feet weights had been tied to ensure a speedy death, left a deep scar on Hardy's mind. Hardy witnessed the execution of Martha Brown at Dorchester country gaol for the murder of her husband at Birdsmoorgate, near Broadwindsor, on August 9, 1856. Two or three years later, he watched through a telescope a convict in Dorchester being hanged to death:

> At the moment of his placing the glass to his eye the white figure dropped downwards, and the faint note of the town clock struck eight. The whole thing had been so sudden that the glass nearly fell from Hardy's hand. He seemed alone on the heath with the hanged man, and crept home wishing he had not been so curious. (F.E. Hardy, *The Life of Thomas Hardy* 1962)

These two executions remained embedded in Hardy's memory and contributed to the story and final scene of *Tess of the d'Urbervilles*. However, none of these childhood traumas in the form of social violence can be regarded as the only source of the darkness of spirit which seems to permeate Hardy's work. Probably the change which made him regard human experience as a string of disaster and mischance, took place after his boyhood.

It was at Issac Last's school, where Thomas got enrolled that he first became conscious of the possibilities of serious intellectual work. He started studying Latin and after a while could read Virgil, whom he continued to love for the rest of his life and Lucretius with whom he shared temperamental affinities. Thomas was a hard-working sincere boy who won prizes for his studies and acquired the habit of self-education which remained with him till his death. However, at the age of sixteen, he was taken out of school and put under the charge of John Hicks, who was a Dorchester architect. It was with John Hicks, who was a kind man, with a profound knowledge of the classics that Hardy's lifelong absorption with church architecture (especially Gothic) began.

While living in Dorchester, Hardy befriended two important personalities who acted as catalysts in his turning to literature and the intellectual life. Reverend William Barnes, a dialect poet and philologist, was the first one who served in several ways as an excellent model for Hardy's creativity. It was Barnes who instilled in Hardy the confidence that the life of obscure country people could also become an inspiring subject for writing poetry and that the local speech could be recorded in verse exactly as it took place among people. However, Hardy's introduction to the modern thought was brought about through his contact with Horace Moule, a young man whom Hardy met in Dorchester. Hardy was persuaded by Moule to read *Essays and Reviews*, which was a powerful and influential collection of polemical studies. This book was published in 1860 by a group of dissident churchmen and critical dons and constituted a scathing attack on the entrenched dogmas of the Church of England. Interestingly, it was through Moule that Darwin's *The Origin of Species* was brought to Hardy's notice and this book proved still more damaging to his faith. As a result, Hardy turned into a sceptic and gave up his idea of preparing for the church forever. Hardy had begun to write poetry even as he was studying architecture with Hicks. But till this time, he had no ambition to turn to literature as his career and, therefore, in 1862, he went to London to pursue his study of architecture on more advanced lines. He got a place with Arthur Bloomfield in Adelphi Terrace and stayed there for the next five years until 1867. During these years in London, Hardy, in a sense, completed his education. He worked hard and conscientiously at architectural drawings during the day and in the spare time visited the museums and art galleries and read extensively. He read widely the Greek tragedians as also such recent and contemporary English writers as P.B. Shelley, Robert Browning, Walter Bagehot, Charles Robert Darwin, T.H. Huxley, A.C. Swinburne, Herbert Spencer and John Stuart Mill.

Darwin dealt a severe blow to the world of conventional Christianity and confirmed Hardy's belief that pain and cruelty are essential elements of human existence. Spencer was responsible for teaching him that "the Power which the Universe manifests to us is utterly inscrutable." The roots of Hardy's later notions about the Immanent Will or Emergent Consciousness also go back to Spencer. However, Hardy was goaded to open disbelief by Huxley and Mill according to whom the universe is unsponsored and contains neither moral quality nor an inherent purpose. Hardy's quest was not for a system with which to replace Christian theology. In fact, Hardy ardently desired philosophical props which could become instrumental in maintaining the ethical discipline and human solidarity in a frigid universe as conceptualized by the sceptics. Huxley and Mill influenced Hardy more powerfully and directly than Darwin and Spencer. Huxley maintained, "There is no alleviation for the sufferings of mankind except veracity of thought and wisdom, and the resolute facing of the world as it is." In his fiction, Hardy too, projected the view that one must face the world as it is, and in a way echoed Huxley: "If a way to the Better there be, it exacts a full look at the Worst." Hardy's keen admiration of Mill as a man of rectitude and courage made him absorb Mill's philosophy more deeply. William Rutland, in his study of Hardy's intellectual development (*Thomas Hardy: A Study of His Writings and Their Background* 1954) attempts to bring out the similarities between their thought by juxtaposing two passages—a key passage from Mill with one from Hardy. In his "Essay on Nature," Mill is critical of the "natural theologians" who uphold that "all the suffering in the world exists to prevent greater" suffering. According to Mill it is

> a thesis which . . . could only avail to explain and justify the works of limited beings, compelled to labour under conditions independent of their own will; but can have no application to a Creator assumed to be omnipotent, who, if he bends to a supposed necessity, himself makes the necessity to which he bends. If the maker of the world *can* all that he will, he wills misery, and there is no escape from the conclusion.

We find a partial echo of Mill's ideas in a letter Hardy wrote in 1902:

> Pain has been, and pain is: no new sort of morals in Nature can remove pain from the past and make it pleasure for those who are its infallible estimators, the bearers thereof. And no injustice, however slight, can be atoned for by her future generosity, however ample, so long as we consider Nature to be, or to stand for unlimited power. The exoneration of an omnipotent Mother by her retrospective justice becomes an absurdity when we ask, What made the foregone injustice necessary to her omnipotence?

There is similarity in the line of thought of Mill and Hardy but with the difference that while Mill's views are expository in nature, Hardy personalizes and moulds his thought "to the possibility of creative use."

Hardy was determined to be a poet by the time he reached London. He wrote a large number of poems during his stay in London and sent them to literary magazines. However, the editors invariably sent them back. A look at these poems shows that his literary style had already been formed by the time he attained the age of twenty five. He began imitating, like every young poet, the great writers of the past—in his case Wordsworth and Shakespeare. But several poems bear Hardy's own unmistakable stamp "The Ruined Maid," and "Hap," for instance, exhibit his characteristic philosophy and typical tone.

The years Hardy spent in London may have been fruitful for him, but he was not happy there. He felt himself to be "among strangers and strange things," and though he accepted with ease the radical views of the city's intellectuals, he could not bring himself to reconcile to the city's mode of life. His diary for 1865 contains an entry: "My 25th birthday: not very cheerful. Feel as if I had lived a long time and done very little." Sometimes, he did meet his friend Moule, but by and large he was gripped by a feeling of loneliness and was shocked by what he saw of squalor, vice and human misery among the richest in the world.

Hardy had begun to feel physically weak and ill and mentally depressed. He felt repelled by the business of getting on in the world and thought that he had had enough. He returned to Dorchester in 1867 and took up architectural work at Mr. Hicks's office, but now working part time. Simultaneously, he began to write a novel, *The Poor Man and the Lady* which contrasts the trivialities of fashionable London life with the naturalness of the country. In July 1868, Hardy sent the novel to Macmillan's. While the publishers admired a good deal of the novel, they rejected it on the ground that it was too uneven to be printed. Hardy then tried Chapman and Hall whose reader, George Meredith, advised Hardy to abandon social satire and to try something more popular in the style of Wilkie Collins. *The Poor Man and the Lady* was never published in its original form, but about ten years later it was partly drawn on for the short story, "An Indiscretion in the Life of an Heiress." Some of the radical passages were removed from the story which, however, gives a fairly good idea of the style of young Hardy. Much better writings were to come from Hardy's pen in later years, but even his first crude attempts at prose fiction were admired by many distinguished literary men.

The result of Meredith's advice was quite as sensational as Collins's fiction, as Hardy completed *Desperate Remedies* which was published in 1871. The novel is a murder and mystery story, a melodramatic work, quite below the level of *The Poor Man and the Lady.* Nonetheless, some sections of the novel foreshadowed Hardy's genius. In 1870, Hardy had met a young woman, Emma Lavinia Gifford, during a journey to Cornwall on an architectural assignment and was attracted by her "aliveness," her interest in books and her vivacity. She reciprocated Hardy's love and they got married in 1874 after a prolonged engagement. The union was a happy one for some time. While Hardy was steadily busy with his writing, his wife acted a sympathetic helper, though they both keenly felt the absence of children. When Hardy became famous as a writer and his wife got ambitious, their marriage ran into serious trouble. Hardy was still on cold and distant terms with her when she died in 1912. Emma and Hardy had known a young woman, Florence Dugdale, who had been at Max Gate since 1912, organizing the household and protecting the aged author from the intrusions of the stream of visitors. Hardy married her in 1914. After fourteen fitful creative years, which saw the publication of *Late Lyrics and Earlier* and the completion of the first draft of *The Famous Tragedy of the Queen of Cornwall* in 1923, Hardy breathed his last in 1928. His ashes were buried in Westminster Abbey. The pall-bearers included the Prime Minister, the Leader of the Opposition, and several other celebrities of the time.

The first review of *Desperate Remedies* appeared in *Athenaeum* (No. 1) and *Morning Post* (13 April 1871) and *Spectator* (No. 3). While *Morning Post* commented on its obvious imitation of Wilkie Collins, it regarded the book as a success of its kind. However, the review in the *Spectator* severely attacked the morality of the novel.

Hardy's creative oeuvre began to attract critical attention before it had been ten years with the public, as essays summing up his achievement started appearing. The *New Quarterly Magazine* (October 1879, No. 17) published a perceptive survey, suggesting that *The Return of the Native* signified a new departure and had in it a more conscious purpose. A full account of Hardy's works upto and including *The Trumpet Major* was published in 1881 in the Nonconformist *British Quarterly Review*. This survey also considered *The Return of the Native* as the highest achievement of Hardy and dealt, in detail, with Hardy's women characters. Havelock Ellis quoted it in his comprehensive essay in the *Westminster* for April 1883 (No. 24). Ellis's essay constitutes a detailed study of Hardy's works and closely explores the psychology of the heroines. Also for the first time a connection with Schopenhauer is made. According to Ellis *Far from the Madding Crowd* marks Hardy's most outstanding achievement and believes that perhaps Hardy may not repeat the artistic excellence and power of this novel. Coventry Patmore's essay, reviewing *The Woodlanders* in the *Contemporary Review* (No. 30) ranges widely, referring to the novel only nominally, while J.M. Barrie's account of the novel in 1889 in the same journal (No. 33) happens to be more comprehensive. Barrie emphasizes for the most part the flux in which the rural life of Hardy's times is caught and draws parallels with George Eliot and Richard Jefferies.

When Hardy had been writing for about twenty years, the general discussions began to proliferate around 1890. Hardy's power of landscape, his humour, the antipathy of the women readers of Hardy towards his works and the frequent comparison with Meredith are taken note of by Gosse in his article in the *Speaker* for 13 September 1890 (No. 34). *Tess* gets included in W. Minto's account in *Bookman* in December 1891. Minto rates Hardy higher than George Eliot, pointing out nonetheless that Hardy's penchant for psychological analysis and scientific language might have made him a little less popular. A sensible but undistinguished general summary of Hardy's career was given by Janetta Newton Robinson in the *Westminster* for February 1892 (CXXXVII, p. 153) and a popular appreciation of Hardy, "The Genius of Thomas Hardy," was contributed by Frederick Greenwood to the *Illustrated London News* for 1 October 1892 (p. 431). Hardy's work got noticed in America, too, where John A. Steuart included Hardy in his *Letters to Living Authors* of 1890. William Sharp's essay "Thomas Hardy and His Novels," appeared in the New York *Forum* (subsequently reprinted in his *Papers Critical and Reminiscent* in 1912). Sharp finds Hardy an incomparably finer artist than Zola and focusses on Hardy's realism and masculinity, his Englishness and his unsentimental pathos. According to Sharp, *The Return of the Native, The Woodlanders* and *Tess of the d'Urbervilles* rank among the best of Hardy's novels. W.P. Trent wrote a full and judicious critical survey of Hardy's career achievement in the *Sewanee Review* (No. 46) in 1892. While Trent is intensely critical of *The Mayor of Casterbridge* in which he does not see Hardy's characteristic artistic genius at work, he ranks *Tess* first, then *Far from the Madding Crowd* and third *The Return of the Native*.

Several articles, surveying Hardy's work as a whole, appeared in the early years of the twentieth century. Edward Wright, in his twenty-four page essay for the *Quarterly* (No. 68) for April 1904, commends Hardy for his insight into country life and peasant character. He compares Hardy to Euripides, but criticizes Hardy's later works in which the novelist is found to be a "sentimental materialist," a "misdirected force." F. Manning, in his interesting essay, "Novels of Character and Environment," in the *Spectator* (No. 73) is critical of Hardy's didacticism. He does not regard *Tess* and *Jude* as outstanding works, in terms of art, their peculiar merits notwithstanding, but considers *The Return of the Native* a fuller representation of life. A general essay by Charles Whibley in *Blackwood's* (No. 74) gives a fair idea of Hardy's critical standing at this time, and records that "never since the Georgics have the industries of the countryside been turned to literary account with so fine a sense of their enduring importance." Against this background, Hardy sets dramas "tense and simple, like the dramas of Sophocles." Hardy's flaws of style are found to be inconsequential and a greater future as a novelist is prophesied for him than as a poet.

One notices proliferation of critical evaluations of Hardy's works in

American periodicals from 1900 onwards in the form of general surveys. W.D. Howells's book *Heroines of Fiction* contains two chapters on Hardy. A discussion of Hardy's tragic pessimism and "cosmic irony" is contained in P.H. Frye's *Literary Reviews and Criticisms* (1908) in an essay entitled "Nature and Thomas Hardy." Mary Moss wrote an exhaustive essay, commenting on all the novels of Hardy in the Boston *Atlantic Monthly* in 1906 (XCVIII, 354), in which she observes, "he [Hardy] bridges the gulf between poetry and science. He holds fast to romance without slurring or ignoring the facts of the actual life." A brief sketch of Hardy's life and summary chronological survey of his works constitute the subject of W.L. Phelp's article in *Atlantic Monthly* (No. 72) which was reprinted in his *Essays on Modern Novelists* in 1910. A distinction is drawn by Phelps between the pessimism of the earlier novels which he terms as "a noble ground quality," and "the merely hysterical and wholly unconvincing" didactic pessimism of *Jude the Obscure*. However, Phelps admires Hardy's uncanny intimacy with nature. A significant essay was contributed to the *North American Review* for January 1914 (no. 75) by Harold Williams. In this essay the Wessex novels are especially focussed on and regarded not simply as representations of village manners, but as tragedy, embodying the unity of the individual with universal life. *The Woodlanders* is considered the typical achievement while *Tess* is placed in the most distinguished position in relation to the other three novels, viz., *Far from the Madding Crowd, The Return of the Native* and *The Mayor of Casterbridge*. Approximately forty years later, these very fine tragedies were selected as being central in Douglas Brown's study of Hardy's novelistic output.

Amongst the full-length studies of Hardy, which had begun to appear as early as 1894, Lionel Johnson's *The Art of Thomas Hardy* (re-issued in 1923) with a chapter on Hardy's poems, remained by far the best work for many years. It deals, inter-alia, with the principal characters of men and women, and his concept of tragedy, especially as it is translated in *Tess*. The book raises a number of significant critical issues, obtrusiveness of the critic's own personality notwithstanding. Annie Macdonell's modestly ambitious descriptive survey also got published in 1894 and served as an important critical document at the time. F.O. Saxelby's *A Thomas Hardy Dictionary* was one of the important books which appeared in the early 1900s. Academic studies of Hardy's work began to get published by 1911. Helen Garwood's *Thomas Hardy: An Illustration of the Philosophy of Schopenhauer* and F.A. Hedgcock's *Essaie de Critique: Thomas Hardy penseur et artiste* blazed the trail of serious critical studies. Hardy came to be considered an established man of letters and a great tragic artist comparable to Sophocles and Aeschylus with the publication of Lascelles Abercrombie's

Thomas Hardy: A Critical Study (1912).

Criticism from now onwards turned into a reaction against the solemn adulation of Hardy, focussing more closely on poems instead of the novels. At the same time the critical appraisals pointed out the faults, awkwardnesses of style and the dated elements in Hardy's writings.

Modern criticism finds Hardy's work as mixed in quality. The upheaval of the 1914-18 war made Hardy's writings appear less subversive than they were thought to be in the nineties. In an age when Lawrence and Joyce were accepted and when Conrad and James were sought to be re-discovered and re-evaluated, Hardy's world of Wessex came to be neglected. Nonetheless, the old-fashioned comprehensive exposition of Hardy's creative output continued to be made. A relevant example of this type of criticism is to be found in H.C. Duffin's *Thomas Hardy*, first published in 1916 and revised in 1937. Vernon Lee (in her influential critical work on Hardy, *The Handling of Words*, 1923) continued further the early criticism of style by analysing a passage from *Tess*. T.S. Eliot's *After Strange Gods* (1934) contained some characteristically sharp perceptions but constituted a perverse judgment of Hardy's work. It should, however, be noted here that Eliot later implicitly retracted his damning evaluation by allowing his book to go out of print.

During Hardy's lifetime, the most fervent criticism of Hardy concentrated on the aspect of morality in his works. Upto and including Eliot's *After Strange Gods* critics were largely concerned with Hardy's pessimism, his view of God, universe and marriage. *Tess* and *Jude* came in for trenchant criticism on account of their immorality. The virulence of some of the attacks made Hardy flinch. He became almost ill to find himself at the centre of the greatest literary scandal for years and wished he had never been born. What caused acute anguish to Hardy was that even his wife Emma, who had constantly inspired and supported him in his creative endeavours, was against him. She went to the extent of attempting to stop the publication of *Jude*. Hardy felt so deeply hurt that after the publication of *Jude* in 1895, he decided to give up writing fiction and his thoughts turned to poetry which he had always wanted to write and which he had been writing for the last thirty years. His first collection, *Wessex Poems*, came out in 1898. Hardy began work on *The Dynasts*, an epic drama in blank verse in the early years of this century. *The Dynasts* was published in three volumes, successively in 1904, 1906 and 1908. It describes what happened to Europe at the time of the Napoleonic war. Though Hardy's poetry has not received the attention it deserves, Middleton Murry's essay in *Athenaeum* in *Aspects of Literature* (1920) praised Hardy's poetry. F.R. Leavis offered a perceptive analytical evaluation of the few poems which he found to be great in his *New Bearings in English Poetry* published in 1932 and later in *Scrutiny* in 1952. Publication of Hardy's biography, *The Early Life of Thomas Hardy* and *The Later Years of Thomas Hardy* in 1928 and 1930 by F.E. Hardy (the biography was actually written by Hardy himself in an attempt to give the world a standard autobiography) introduced biographical approach in Hardy criticism. Over the years critical works appeared which made use of the biographical details to elucidate and interpret Hardy's writings.

Post-Eliot phase of Hardy criticism is marked for attempts to rehabilitate Hardy and make him academically respectable. Several critics insisted on the formalities and symmetries of Hardy's fictional structures, highlighted the faithful realism of Hardy's representation of Dorset and valorized the seriousness of his "philosophy," even though these critics tended to be apologetic about the eccentricities and audacities of Hardy's imagination. A most decisive step in the direction of rehabilitating Hardy was the comprehensive, unpedantic summing up of Hardy's oeuvre in the special and brilliantly edited Centennial issue of *The Southern Review* in Summer 1940. This number constitutes an important landmark in the history of Hardy criticism inasmuch as even after more than two decades Albert J. Guerard used four essays in his anthology on Hardy from this Centennial issue.

For a few years after the Centennial number of *The Southern Review*, Hardy criticism remained in the low key. One reason for this was that this special number covered a large ground concerning Hardy's thematic thrusts, philosophical predilections and social, moral and ideological stance, in addition to commenting on Hardy's style and technique. Yet another factor for a comparative inactive critical attention has been that Hardy does not lend himself easily to the methods of the New Critics, the Formalists, or the explorers of psychic underground and delvers into archetype. This, however, does not mean that Hardy suffered from complete neglect. The critical response during the fifties and sixties has not been a stream, but certainly it has been a significant, perceptive and steady trickle, which kept Hardy very much in the canon of English literature. A crucial landmark in Hardy's evaluation is that of David Cecil whose book, *Hardy the Novelist* appeared in 1943. Cecil, while admiring Hardy's "sheer intensity of creative imagination," regards him as "the last English writer to be built on the grand Shakespearean scale." Albert Guerard published a full-length study of Hardy in 1949. Since then the most influential and notable study has been Douglas Brown's *Thomas Hardy*, published in 1954 and revised in 1961. Brown's book is remarkable for introducing a typical element in modern Hardy criticism. It establishes a strong sense of the relationship between Hardy's work and the social and economic history of the rural England in Victorian age. John Holloway's *The Victorian Sage: Studies in Argument* (1953) and R.L. Purdy's bibliographical work, *Thomas Hardy: A Bibliographical Study* were important publications of the period. D.H. Lawrence's most brilliant and also the most perverse work, "Study of Thomas Hardy," written during the first World War, was reprinted in *D.H. Lawrence: Selected Literary Criticism* edited by Anthony Beal in 1955.

The sixties saw the publication of some insightful works on Hardy. The main stumbling block for the Victorians acknowledging the worth of Hardy's work was his "pessimism" or rejection of the idea of Providence. To a certain extent, this obstacle has remained for some of the modern critics and readers because it is generally assumed that Hardy invariably looks on the black side of things. The only book that deals adequately with this whole question and which serves as an excellent corrective to conventional works on Hardy is Roy Morrell's *Thomas Hardy: The Will and the Way* (1965). *Providence and Mr. Hardy* by Lois Deacon and Terry Coleman published in 1966 revealed for the first time to the world Hardy's affair and engagement to Tryphena Sparks, a cousin from his mother's side. The reasons for the affair not culminating into marriage are not known, but it is believed that Tryphena served as inspiration for Hardy to create not only the heroine of *Jude the Obscure*, but also some parts of the novel. Irving Howe in his *Thomas Hardy* (1966) takes note of the "severe critical attack" on Hardy during the preceding few decades and launches a vigorous and impressive effort to emphatically defend Hardy, concluding that he [Hardy] continues to live as a "writer." Howe admits that Hardy is problematic, but then goes on to argue that it is for this very reason that Hardy can be discussed almost "as if he were a contemporary, in a way that most of the contemporaries cannot." Llewelyn Powys's *Some Memories of Thomas Hardy* (1969) presents typical personal reminiscences of the writer. Kenneth Marsden's *The Poems of Thomas Hardy: A Critical Introduction* (1969) points out the similarity between Wordsworth and Hardy in respect of the process of composition of their poems from remembered experience. Poems composed in this manner usually evidence conspicuous fidelity to the peculiar experiences which served as the source of their inspirations. According to Marsden, Hardy's poetry is "intensely personal," and one can appreciate the poems by a little "sympathy" and "understanding" for the persona which speaks in them and some cognizance of the "spiritual" from which the author writes. A most valuable addition to Hardy criticism is F.B. Pinion's *A Hardy Companion* (1968) which deals with all that Hardy ever wrote, including his stories, poems and drama and illuminates Hardy's creative achievements by considering them in relation to their background. In 1969, Ellen E. Titterington wrote *Afterthoughts of Max Gate* which sketches Hardy as a stubborn, authoritative, old writer who at times displayed a sense of humour. E.J. Stevens published his *Hardy as I Knew Him* in 1969 which is expanded from a talk given by him for the BBC on 16 August 1938, in which he points out the suitability of Hardy's novels for adaptations as plays.

In the early seventies, J.I.M. Stewart adopted biographical approach in his book *Thomas Hardy: A Critical Biography* (1971) to throw light on Hardy's fiction, poetry, and drama. Another definitive work which got published in 1972 is Merryn Williams's *Thomas Hardy and Rural England* which attempts to place Hardy in his social context. Williams also wrote *A Preface to Hardy* in 1976 which is a most readable and positive study of Hardy's prose and verse. Williams offers "a variety of scholarly approaches to her subject to demonstrate the depths of his [Hardy's] power to release tragic emotion and universal humanity within the closely studied visual realism." As opposed to Stewart's biographical approach and Merryn Williams's historico-biographical perspective, Lance St. John Butler in his *Thomas Hardy* (1978) concentrates only on Hardy's texts, believing that great literature is to a large extent self-explanatory to the reader, if he attends carefully to what the writer says. Hardy's poetic drama, *The Dynasts* did not remain unnoticed. A significant evaluative work, *Hardy's Poetic Vision in "The Dynasts": The Diorama of a Dream* was published by Susan Dean in 1977. Some other valuable books, which added to the corpus of Hardy criticism in the seventies were *Thomas Hardy: The Poetry of Necessity* (1975) by Richardson James; *Hardy: The Tragic Novels* (Casebook, 1975) by R.P. Draper; *The Genius of Thomas Hardy* (1976) by Margaret Drabble; *A Commentary on the Poems of Thomas Hardy* (1976) by F.B. Pinion; *Thomas Hardy: His Career as a Novelist* (1971) by Michael Millgate; *Thomas Hardy and British Poetry* (1975) by Donald Davie; and a biographical work, *Young Thomas Hardy* (1975) by Robert Gittings.

Hardy continued to engage critics' attention and critical works on his writings came out periodically. Emphasis was laid on Hardy's psychological presentation of his characters by Rosemary Summer in her *Thomas Hardy: Psychological Novelist* (1981). Hardy's modernity and social criticism in his creative works were highlighted by C.H. Salter in *Good Little Thomas Hardy* (1981). A perceptive Indian response to Hardy's fiction was published by Noorul Hasan in 1982 under the title *Thomas Hardy: The Sociological Imagination*. Hasan highlights Hardy's inability to make sense of the world and points to Hardy's scepticism. While on the one hand Hardy presents ordinary people as being capable of self-renewal, he is pessimistic in his portrayal of the breakdown of the old agricultural order; the indifference of the universe to pain and death. The Indian response to Hardy has not been confined to his fiction alone. Manas Mukul Das wrote an illuminating study of Hardy's poetry, *Thomas Hardy: Poet of Tragic Vision* in 1983, analyzing not only the form of his verse, but also bringing out the inherent tragic dimension of Hardy's philosophy in the context of the poems. Michael Millgate wrote Hardy's biography entitled *Thomas Hardy: A Biography* in 1982 and the same author edited another significant work, *Thomas Hardy: The Life and Work of Thomas Hardy* in 1984. Hardy's concern for the language, his fascination with words, where he found them and how he found them is explored in Ralph W.V. Elliott's book, *Thomas Hardy's English* which came out in 1984. John Goode presents extraordinarily subtle and original readings of Hardy's novels in his work *Thomas Hardy: The Offensive Truth*, published in 1988. Goode does not attempt to render Hardy's novels more palatable by ransacking the texts for a message of social hope. Goode's Hardy is the dark and bitter Hardy. A most useful annotated bibliography was published by R.P. Draper under the title, *An Annotated Critical Bibliography of Thomas Hardy* in 1989.

The nineties saw a spurt in Hardy criticism. The famous Hardy scholar, F.B. Pinion published his *Hardy: The Writer* in 1990. Some of the important studies of Hardy in 1990 include G. Beningfield's *Hardy Landscapes,* S. Berger's *Thomas Hardy and Visual Structures*, D.L. Collins's *Thomas Hardy and His God*, R. Chapman's *The Language of Thomas Hardy*, P. Ingham's *Thomas Hardy*, K.Z. Moore's *The Descent of the Imagination*. That Hardy has come to arouse intense critical interest in the present day's scholars is evidenced by the publication of two anthologies of his writings in 1990; *Thomas Hardy: Selected Letters* edited by Michael Millgate and *Thomas Hardy's Personal Writings; Prefaces, Literary Opinions, Reminiscences* edited by Harold Orel. The woman question is taken up by R. Morgan in *Woman and Sexuality in the Novels of Thomas Hardy* (1991). In the same year T. Johnson published A *Critical Introduction to the Poems of Thomas Hardy*. Critical response to Hardy in 1992 was relatively more prolific. Several significant studies appeared in this year. Rosemarie Morgan published an informative book, *Cancelled Words: Rediscovering Thomas Hardy*. Morgan studies in depth the manuscript of Hardy's first great novel, *Far from the Madding Crowd*. The MSS throws new light not only on this particular novel, but also on the whole of Hardy's work. Some other studies on Hardy in 1992 include Charles Lock's *Thomas Hardy*, C.E. May's *Thomas Hardy*, M. Millgate's *Thomas Hardy* and also *Testamentary Acts*, F.B. Pinion's *Thomas Hardy*, J. Fisher's *The Hidden Hardy*.

The Hardy criticism continues to proliferate. Several useful full-length studies got published in 1993. These were S. Gatrell's *Thomas Hardy and the Proper Study of Mankind*; G.R. Steel's *Sexual Tyranny in Wessex*; M. Willams's *A Preface to Hardy*; J.P. Ward's *Thomas Hardy's Poetry*; Margaret R. Higonnet's (ed.) *The Sense of Sex: Feminist Perspectives on Hardy*; Dennis Taylor's *Hardy's Literary Language and Victorian Philology*. The factors responsible for giving a fillip to the critical encounters with Hardy have been, firstly the changed world-view which sees the world as disjointed, disintegrated and absurd and secondly, a subversive perception of the entrenched ideological creeds that were rated high in the Victorian social and philosophical milieu. The modern and postmodern self finds himself besieged by debilitating forces. Traumatized and baffled by the constrictive elements in his environment, man's predicament today remains the same as Hardy put his fictional personae in. In fact, Hardy was ahead of his times, like any true artistic genius, and the very factors, which elicited negative or even destructive responses in his own time, have come to be regarded as his strong points, making him relevant to today's intellectual ethos. Though Hardy's appeal is universal, since his protagonists wrestle with the life-denying forces with all their might, in order to carve a comfortable niche in the turbulent seas of human existence, very much in the manner of the Greek tragic heroes, he has remained a particular favourite with the Indian readers and syllabus-makers alike for obvious reasons. His novels, being the embodiments of the Immanent Will and the inscrutable (often malevolent) functioning of Fate come close to the characteristic Indian sensibility. The Indian students of Hardy find it easier to comprehend and respond to him as any Indian village and its inhabitants, with their rustic humour and fund of native wisdom, could easily be substituted for Wessex.

Early Hardy Novels and the Fictional Eye

JUDITH BRYANT WITTENBERG

Late in his life, Thomas Hardy told a correspondent about his traumatic memory of an event that occurred when he was sixteen: "I am ashamed to say I saw [Martha Brown] hanged, my only excuse being that I was but a youth, and had to be in the town at that time for other reasons. . . . I remember what a fine figure she showed against the sky as she hung in the misty rain, and how the tight black silk gown set off her shape as she wheeled half-round and back."[1] At about the same time, Hardy recorded in third-person from a similar memory of another hanging he witnessed not long thereafter, watching through a telescope from the heath near the family cottage in Higher Bockhampton: "The sun behind his back shone straight on the white stone facade of the gaol, the gallows upon it, and the form of the murderer in white fustian, the executioner and officials in dark clothing and the crowd below being invisible at this distance of nearly three miles. At the moment of his placing the glass to his eye the white figure dropped downwards and the faint note of the town clock struck eight. . . . He seemed alone on the heath with the hanged man and crept homeward wishing he had not been so curious."[2]

Hardy's verbal reconstruction of these pivotal scenes from his adolescence, specific versions of which would recur in his first published novel and in two of his last three, have a number of striking elements in common: the persistence in the mind's eye of a highly charged moment from the past with overtones of sexuality; the definition of the quality of light, either diffused, as in the first example, or strongly centered, as in the second; attention to colors and outlines in the recreated scene; and emotional interaction between the viewer and the viewed, in which the sight is seen through and colored by an affective lens—in these cases, that of excitement and shame.[3]

These hanging scenes, and numerous other such scenes in Hardy's *Life* and fiction (the *Life* being essentially a narrative text not unlike the novels) are instances of "the voyeuristic moments," the moment in which the seeing subject and the seen object intersect in a diegetic node that both explicitly and implicitly suggest the way in which the world is constituted in and through the scopic drive. In using the term "voyeuristic moment," I am deliberately invoking J. Hillis Miller's discussion of what he calls the "linguistic moment" in the Victorian portrayal of nature—the moment in which language interrogates itself, revealing itself to be an inaugurating force.[4] Because seeing *precedes* saying in psychic development, the linguistic moment has its necessary prologue in the voyeuristic moment: as Jacques Lacan has pointed out, the subject is released from its entrapment in the dialectic of identification engendered through its visual discoveries of the mirror state by and into language.[5] Thus the eye, the seeing subject, is antecedent to and formative of the I, or the speaking subject. This precept is relevant to Hardy's fiction, which linguistically enunciates the way in which knowledge is acquired and in which the I-world dialogue is carried on by means that are predominantly specular. Thus his work has an important relationship not only to the various eye-centered aesthetic concepts of his own era, but to almost three centuries of philosophical and psychoanalytical theories of perception.

Voyeurism, with its overtones of sexual perversion, is, of course, a problematic term to use in conjunction with an effort to come to terms with the implicitly self-interrogating fundamentals of a fictional oeuvre such as that of Thomas Hardy, so long treasured for its apparent mimetic qualities, its evocation of Dorset folk and heath and woodland. Yet though the term in its literal sense can be applied to the psychology of many of Hardy's characters, as Albert Guerard first suggested,[6] and to his spectatorial narrator, as J. Hillis Miller, David Lodge, and others have pointed out,[7] it also has an important metaphoric application in describing Hardy's epistemology and in placing his work in the historical continuum of art, literature, philosophy, and psychoanalysis. Hardy himself said, in his 1888 essay on "The Profitable Reading of Fiction," that "a writer . . . looks upon the world with his personal eyes," and he called "erroneous . . . the assumption that a novel is the thing and not a view of the thing."[8] The terms "eyes" and "view," as Hardy uses them here, refer both to physical vision and idiosyncratic opinion—which cannot, in actuality, as E.H. Gombrich tells us, be separated[9]—or sight and in-sight, which are at the deepest level the same.[10] It is the viewing, with all its implications, that constitutes the voyeuristic moment so fundamental, both technically and thematically, to Hardy's fiction.[11]

Though Hardy's concern with sight-related issues had its origin in his personal psychology and formative experiences and manifested itself artistically in a highly individualized form, it had some of its general roots in developments in Western philosophy beginning in the seventeenth century. After Descartes had posited the mind-world dichotomy in his germinal work, the *Second Meditation* of 1642, creating the Cartesian split that was to so profoundly affect later thinkers, philosophers in England began to explore the resulting issues, including the problems of defining thc precise nature of the interaction between mind and world, raising questions and proposing hypotheses that would eventually be as important to psychoanalysts as they were to other philosophers. By the end of the eighteenth century, Lockean empiricism, Berkeleyan subjectivism, and Humean scepticism had elaborated in various ways upon the compelling problems of epistemological definition in a Cartesian universe and collectively posited a world in which the seeing "eye" was the point of origin for the knowing "I," however uncertain the constituents of the "I" might be.

But if the seventeenth and eighteenth century English philosophers had much to say about what would be recognized as the more or less normative functions of the eye, folklore and mythology were full of tales that revealed a problematic, even destructive, role of the eye in sexual situations. So Noah's inquisitive son, Ham as punishment for seeing his father drunk and naked, was given black skin and his offspring cursed with servitude; while the legendary Tom of Coventry, peeping through the shutters at the naked Lady Godiva, was punished with blindness, his name becoming synonymous with "voyeur." Even as the philosophers presented seeing as useful and necessary, advocating, in the face of grave uncertainties about all other elements in the universe, a sort of scopo-epistemophilia, folk literature warned of its dangers, implicitly urging a tempered scopophobia—one source lists at least seventy categories of looking taboos that can be found in that literature.[12]

Psychoanalytical theory has been much concerned with both aspects of seeing, the normative and the aberrant. Freud saw a basic drive to see as fundamental to the instinct for knowledge that begins to manifest itself in a child between the ages of three and five, and as basic to the process of awaken desire for the love-object during later sexual development, stating that "visual impressions remain the most frequent pathway along which libidinal excitation is aroused."[13] (Gotthold Lessing cites the legend noted by Pliny that suggests that the visual arts also had their origin in desire, being part of efforts by the daughter of Dibutades to retain a visual trace of her departing lover.[14]) Freud's modern disciple, Jacques Lacan, fixes a crucial visual moment even earlier, the *stade du miroir* that occurs between the ages of six and eighteen months, when the child discovers the image of himself in a mirror—an Other, a more perfect self that will eventually give rise to an ego-ideal, or superego. Lacan designates the mirror stage "a drama" in which is disclosed both "libidinal dynamism" and an "ontological structure of the human world."[15] Thus, for Freud and Lacan, seeing is absolutely pivotal to the normal process of establishing the self-in-relation-to-the-world and of discovering sexual desire.

Of course, when these processes are deformed in any way, then seeing becomes a perversion. A child whose normal impulse to see exposes him to a traumatic sight, such as that of a "primal scene" (sexual intercourse between his parents), may forever after deal with the resulting anxiety by becoming a peeper, one who repeatedly views similar scenes for the purpose of achieving a belated sense of mastery and overcoming the helplessness he felt during the first experience, or who views scenes that have in some essential way a difference from the original one and thus serve to reassure him that there is/was in fact no danger. Because no sight can fully engender the sense of mastery or reassurance for which the voyeur is striving, he often develops an insatiable need to look again and again. Such obsessional visual curiosity often has an active sadistic component which is displaced, reduced from action to observation,[16] and accompanied by the tendency to exhibitionism.

The voyeuristic impulse, in either its normative or perverse form or somewhere along the continuum between the two, plays an important role in the production of a work of art and in the varying levels of subsequent response to it. Obviously, the working painter, is the artist most concerned with exploring the visual elements of his world, with seeing and seeing into, but the writer, too, has an experience that is more or less voyeuristic. In an essay on Hardy, John Fowles referred to "the benign psychosis of the writing experience,"[17] and a psychoanalyst has suggested that the basic drive behind that "psychosis," the journey into the imagination, is voyeuristic. He defines the imaginative process as "the purified successor to infantile peeping." Furthermore, once the writer has created his text, he becomes an "exhibitionist" before his readers, thus transforming a voyeuristic procedure into an exhibitionist defense.[18] His readers in turn become, as it were, voyeurs "seeing into" and absorbing the poetic discourse, which becomes not only pleasurable but reassuring in its creation of order and meaning; among these readers the most inquisitive or voyeuristic are the critics, whose peeping into the text is not only penetrating but repetitive as they return again and again to discourse until they have "uncovered" all the meaning which they are after—somewhat more obsessional form of the normal voyeurism of the average reader, who looks at a text but once and usually in a superficial manner. Roland Barthes, speaking of "the trebled, the infinite perversity of the critic and of his reader," suggests that the reader of criticism is the voyeur of a voyeur (of the initial voyeur, the writer).[19]

Clearly the issue of "peeping" is central in a general way to the processes of creation, reading, and criticism; it also has a number of more specific manifestations. Efforts to discuss and define the stances from which a narrative text is conducted, for example, are usually preoccupied with "point-of-view," those various "observers" we know as the narrator and individual characters. Boris Uspensky has suggested that the very structure of a text may be described by investigating the various points of view and the relations between them.[20] The text is thus not only comprised of but essentially defined by the intersection of a posited series of "voyeurs"; the seeing eye becomes a constitutive force. This more or less figurative concept has, of course, a quite literal application to the later fiction of Henry James, where the use of a limited point of view demands that within the text information be received primarily through peeping and its aural correlative, eavesdropping, and to the work of Thomas Hardy, where not only most of the characters but the narrator seems almost pathologically voyeuristic, reduced to the passive and visual absorption of sense data.[21] The fiction of Hardy, like that of James, thus represents an arena where all the post-Lockean and psychoanalytical theories of seeing inform, even dominate, the basic presentation of the narrative text.

The recurrence of the voyeuristic moment in Hardy's fiction was, to a large extent, produced by an unusual confluence of personal bent and cultural climate. His own proclivities, events that happened to him as a child, his occupational training, occurrences in the world of art and literature just after the mid-nineteenth century—all combined in an intricate way to generate in Hardy the compulsion to reproduce and to explore in his fiction again and again the instants in which the seeing self, in a moment marked by visual and emotional intensity, interacts with the seen world. Hardy recreates those instants in a way that engenders in the reader the fear and pleasure of seeing and of being seen, even as it interrogates the nature of the interchange between the self and other.

II

After five years of working for an architect in London, during which Hardy enlarged his awareness of visual techniques by repeated visits to art galleries and museums, even as he began to write poetry, he returned to his family home at Bockhampton because he felt his "health become much weakened." Not long after, he started working on his first novel, *The Poor Man and the Lady*, which was never published in its original form and the manuscript of which Hardy ultimately destroyed. In his next four novels, *Desperate Remedies, Under the Greenwood Tree, A Pair of Blue Eyes*, and *Far from the Madding Crowd*, written beginning in 1869 and published at the rate of one a year from 1871 through 1874, Hardy depicts again and again versions of the crucial and disturbing voyeuristic moment in which so many of his psychological and epistemological concerns are expressed. The novels vary in a number of ways, most markedly in tone and in the adroitness with which Hardy manipulates his materials and develops his characters, but all of them are love stories having at their center the same basic constellation of characters—a young woman and three suitors who vie for her hand with relative degrees of success or failure. First love, with its component of awakening sexuality in which the eye plays such an important role, was an appropriate subject for Hardy—full of splendor and darkness, desire and fear—and his use of a triangle of competing males with a female at its center allowed him to create an intricate array of scenes in which seeing and its emotional ramifications play a crucial part.

Critics agree that *Desperate Remedies* and *A Pair of Blue Eyes*, published in 1871 and 1873 respectively, are the weaker of the first four novels. Among their more striking flaws is a preponderance of melodramatic, even macabre, scenes that are insufficiently prepared for characters and inadequately integrated with other elements of the narrative. Nevertheless, the generally eruptive nature of these scenes, part of Hardy's larger failure to fully control his material in these novels, makes them fascinating psychologically if less than completely satisfying aesthetically. Here Hardy gives us a close and often startling look as the basic materials, occasionally in a somewhat "raw" state, from which most of his strongest work was fashioned. Thus these flawed early fictions, like his last published novel, *The Well-Beloved*, have an intriguingly direct relationship to his personal obsession and life experiences. Their artistic problems reveal the manner in which Hardy was struggling to make fictional use of elements such as the theme of visual trauma and the compulsion to peep and to eavesdrop, along with knowledge he had acquired during his architectural training and the time he spent in art galleries.

Desperate Remedies, despite the weaknesses engendered by Hardy's efforts to please the publishers who had rejected his previous novel, and by his inexperience, is of special interest, for behind the sensational plot Hardy carries on what is essentially a forum devoted to a discussion of the varying roles played by sight in the acquisition of knowledge and in the complexities of human relationships. Eyes here play an explicit role as a defining characteristic—the major clue in the detection of the false Mrs. Manston is her eye color—and, as in all of Hardy's novels, eyes are a crucial narrative device for the accretion of essential information. Vastly more important, however, as a key to some of Hardy's most vital concerns is the depiction in dramatized form of a whole array of major sight-related issues augmented by the narrator's discursive consideration of problematic aspects of those issues.

Many such topics here, as in most of Hardy's fiction, are centered on the major female character and present themselves during the efforts of various males to fulfill their desire for her. For example, the problem of making character assessments on the basis of visual data is referred to in the responses of Ambrose Graye to the appearance of the "first" Cytherea, later Miss Aldclyffe, when the narrator comments that "a mere distinguishing peculiarity, by catching the eye, is often read as the pervading characteristic," soon adding that love "at first sight" is an event whose blissfulness is "only eclipsed by its hazardousness." (37-38)[22] When Cytherea Graye enters a few pages later, she immediately becomes "an interesting subject of study for several neighbouring eyes," and after the description of her which follows, the narrator cautions that "to attempt to gain a view of her—or indeed of any fascinating woman—from a measured category, is as difficult as to appreciate the effect of a landscape by exploring it at night with a lantern—or of a full chord of music by piping the notes in succession." (41-42) This very same topic is treated poetically in "Eunice," which appears late in the novel and in which Hardy cites the challenge of achieving even "hazy portraiture" of a woman because of the "aspect's changeful rays" and "sweet transition" that make of her a "pictured melody and not a set contour." (310) Using an analogy with two key sense-responsive elements, light and music, the narrator suggests the difficulty of creating a portrait at once static and moving through time and space, also implying that defining through sight is both necessary and inadequate. Thus Hardy's narrator, in the pages of his first published novel, tacitly discusses the essential of his novelistic method—the effort to make living pictures, produced from and addressed to sight—and admits the near-impossibility in some cases of achieving that goal. His fundamental technique is simultaneously asserted and interrogated.

If sight itself is a problematic, though crucial, sense, some of its functions are even more problematic. Although Hardy uses sight generally in Lockean terms as the locale for the intake of sense data which the mind integrates to produce knowledge, much of that knowledge, in a novel such as *Desperate Remedies*, proves to be profoundly disturbing to its recipient. Hardy's novels are full of instances in which characters inadvertently see things that disrupt first their emotions and then their lives, but there is perhaps no more extreme example of this than the well-known early scene of *Desperate Remedies*. Cytherea's idle glance out of a nearby window during a Shakespeare reading presents her with an "illuminated miniature," a "sky-backed picture" of unmitigated horror, when she sees her father fall to his death from the scaffolding on a church spire where he has been at work. (43-44)[23] The scene contains elements present in Hardy's recollection of those two supremely traumatic sights from his own adolescence, the hanging he witnessed in his teens—the sharp contrast of black and white, the careful placement of the point of station (i.e., the distance of the spectator from the nearest point of the "picture"),[24] the presence of specifically located sunlight, and the powerful reaction of the seer to the seen. The Hardyan narrator designates it as a moment of initiation for Cytherea, as the hangings had perhaps been for Hardy himself, saying that it was the instant at which she stepped into a "labyrinth" along whose mazes she was to struggle for the next two years. The narrator also offers some explicit commentary about the capacity of the psyche to make association and to displace painful memories onto related objects: "Emotions will attach themselves to scenes that are simultaneous. . . . Ever after that time any mental agony brought less vividly to Cytherea's mind the scene from the Town Hall windows than sunlight streaming in shaft-like lines." (44)

Seeing in this case clearly has disastrous consequences for the seer, though for Cytherea it proves to be largely financial (poverty) and social (orphanhood), with only a general sense of vulnerability attesting to its potentially grave psychic impact. Hardy was either unable or unwilling to explore the specific nature of the long-term psychological effects of such a trauma on his character, even though the body of his fiction persistently reveals the effect of a similar trauma upon him. Shortly after the disturbing sight of her father's death, Cytherea and her brother are described as eagerly viewing a landscape "with children's eyes," (50) which may signify either that she has been able to repress memories of the prior view and to return to a state of visual innocence or that Hardy had given little thought to the nature of her post-trauma sight responses. Interestingly, Hardy conjoins many elements of the first scene in a later one, where Cytherea is again inadvertently present at the death of a father, her namesake's, although what she actually sees is the posthumous activity, which she views without comprehension. Instead, she overhears the death throes of Miss Aldclyffe's father in a moment that reveals the way Hardy presents eavesdropping as a correlative of peeping. Though Cytherea ponders on the likeness of Miss Aldclyffe's bereavement of her own, she again evinces no deleterious effects.

Both scenes, however, create in her a vulnerability to the gaze of others and an active fear of being seen, the first explicitly, the second implicitly. After the death of Cytherea's father and Hocbridge's discovery of her poverty, the young men of the town begin to stare at her "with a stare unmitigated by any of the respect that had formerly softened it." (47) As the town "watch[es] and whisper[s]," Cytherea and her brother decide to "drop from the sight of" all those who now gossip freely, leaving "scarcely a trace." (47-49) Her newly acquired sensitivity to being stared at is one way a descent on the social scale often manifests itself in a Hardy character (and perhaps in many inhabitants of small towns), but its element of felt sexual violability seems faintly pathological.

This response pattern takes a more extreme form after Cytherea's unwitting presence at the second death scene, which occurs while she is in bed with Miss Aldclyffe in that peculiar proto-lesbian episode which has puzzled most Hardy readers and critics. There is undeniably a sexual component in the interchange that occurs between the two women just before Mr. Aldclyffe dies, and although Hardy makes no overt link between that scene and Cytherea's subsequent fearful, guilty response to the gaze of Aeneas Manston, its similarity to her previous response to the gaze of the town offers grounds for the speculation that such a connection exists. If so, the relationship of death and sexuality to peeping/eavesdropping and a guilty fear of being seen is a significant one.

Certainly there is in all of Hardy's fiction no more overtly sexual depiction of the male gaze as a weapon that threatens vulnerable females than in the portrayal of the eye of Aeneas Manston. The first moment Cytherea glimpses him, she feels "his eyes are going through me," and those eyes, "penetrating and clear," seem to pierce her whenever she comes within range of his vision. (153-54) Manston's eyes associate him with the devil, for he can look directly at lightning without blinking, and if, as Hardy's narrator asserts, "men love with their eyes," (68) there is little question that Manston's eye-centered "love" is demonically sexual.

Frightened of his gaze, a fear augmented at one point by her susceptibility to his organ-playing (surely Hardy meant no double entendre), Cytherea makes anguished efforts "to get rid of the look" and feels safe only when "hidden from his view." (158-59) Pursued by his burning eyes and pressured from other quarters, Cytherea capitulates, agreeing to marriage, but when she discovers on her wedding night that he is already married, her first impulse is "to escape from sight." She resolves not to "meet Manston's eye alone." (271-72) During Manston's subsequent pursuit of his reluctant bride, Cytherea has the appalling experience of seeing him peep through a window at her, then break in and attempt to take her sexually by force. From first to last, Manston's penetrating eyes are for Cytherea terrifyingly sexual, yet, even as she shrinks away, she is clearly drawn to them, and to him, as if he were "some fascinating panther or leopard." (162) Appropriately, Manston's death has explicit links both to that of Cytherea's father and to those witnessed by the adolescent Hardy. He hangs himself and is discovered "with the early sun a-shining in at the grating upon him." (373)

Like many other elements in *Desperate Remedies*, whether they take the form of melodramatic incident or tempered discussion by the narrator, Cytherea's pursuit by the man of "desirous eyes" says much that is significant about the fundamental and complicated role of the eye, as Hardy understood it intellectually, from his reading and picture-viewing, and as he experienced it emotionally, from occurrences in his own life. Moreover, the presence of the gatekeeper, who reveals to Owen Graye some crucial details of Miss Aldclyffe's early life that he obtained by peeping through a partition at her, may indirectly tell us something about the compulsion to narrate that can conceivably be induced by memorable sight-centered experiences. The gatekeeper has possibly been burdened by his voyeuristically-acquired knowledge, for he attempts to communicate it incoherently, while asleep, and coherently, upon awakening, after which telling he is apparently relieved, like the Ancient Mariner, and falls into a peaceful sleep.

This brief passage, which supplies some necessary data to the narrative, also in some sense serves as a little parable about innocent voyeurism, ensuing unacknowledged guilt, and the need for catharsis through narration. It perhaps tells us about some of the unconscious motives that—along with his consciously developed interest in visual matters revealed in the narrator's recurrent discussion of such matters—impelled Hardy to turn to novel-writing. The compulsion to see, the interest in how seeing leads to or fails to lead to knowledge, and the impulse to recreate living pictures that at once rehearse the experience and explore its many facets are central to Hardy's first published novel and undoubtedly lay behind its creation. Novel-writing was, as Hardy reveals in this early work, for him at once a desperate remedy and a deliberate exercise.

In *A Pair of Blue Eyes*, published two years later, Hardy again makes use of numbers of overt biographical elements, this time centered around his blossoming courtship of Emma Gifford, and again presents some highly dramatic scenes whose artistic flaws to some degree demonstrate the intensity with which Hardy contemplated visually-based emotional experiences, even as he attempted to explore them intellectually and narratively. *A Pair of Blue Eyes* is perhaps the early Hardy novel which has the greatest number of explicit autobiographical components and evinces, temporally, the most direct relationship to a period of Hardy's life. That it also contains a fair amount of unconscious autobiography, along with discursive and dramatized treatments of eye-centered issues, tells us a good deal about the way in which all these matters were linked in Hardy's psyche as well as in his intellect.

Significantly, Hardy uses the word "eyes" in the title of this revealing novel and begins his narrative by describing the manner in which Elfride Swancourt's eyes are "a sublimation of all of her . . . there she lived." (35)[25] In the next paragraph, the narrator compares her eyes to an autumn sky and notes the way in which the viewer looks into rather than at them: "These eyes were blue; blue as autumn distance—blue as the blue we see between the retreating mouldings of hills and woody slopes on a sunny September morning. A misty and shady blue, that had no beginning or surface, and was looked into rather than at." (35) Stephen Smith later teases Elfride but tacitly reinforces the narrator's early emphasis by listing her eyes first in a catalogue of the things he loves most about her. If eyes are Elfride's focal quality, her suitors' eyes are equally important as a means of admitting and then imprinting upon their "mind's eye" memorably moving (in both of its meanings) pictures of her.

The use of such terms as "moving picture" or "living picture" is quite deliberate here. It is erroneous to speak too emphatically of the "paintings" in Hardy's novels in that he is as interested in using his verbal tools to capture human action and the changing effects of light and alternations in perspective as he is in fixing fully static moments. Moreover, a dominant defining quality of the heroines in Hardy's early novels is the litheness with which they move, so that underlying even the most seemingly static Hardy scene is the sense in which it is just on the point of changing; often one can discern a whole series of individual "frames," as on a strip of film.[26] Stephen early sees Elfride in what becomes "her permanent attitude of visitation to Stephen's eyes," (48) in profile bending over the piano, backlit by a candle which makes an aureola of her loosened hair. This visual moment contains movement, for during its brief course Elfride looks rapidly at Stephen and back at her music, even as the look on her face changes from one of archness to one of sadness. Early in Henry Knight's romance with Elfride, he also sees a striking picture of her, like that of Stephen's in being full of light and motion. Knight views her on the terrace, where the setting sun

> flooded her face and heightened the bright rose colour of her cheeks to a vermilion red. . . . The ends of her hanging hair softly dragged themselves backwards and forwards upon her shoulder as faint breeze thrust against or relinquished it. Fringes and ribbons of her dress, moved by the same breeze, licked like tongues upon the parts around them, and fluttering forward from shady folds caught likewise their share of the lustrous orange glow. (174-75)

The intrusive Hardyan narrator often uses such scenes, as he did in *Desperate Remedies*, to offer deliberate comment on their effects on the viewer. "Every woman who makes a permanent impression on a man is usually recalled to his mind's eye as she appeared in one particular scene, which seems ordained to be her special form of manifestation throughout the pages of his memory," (48) says the narrator, just before Stephen sees his "picture." The narrator thus revealingly compares visual memories to the pages of a book in a way that tells us, as did the gatekeeper's story in *Desperate*

Remedies, about the crucial linkage of seeing, remembering and narrating that is obviously behind some of Hardy's creative impulses. *A Pair of Blue Eyes*, like *Desperate Remedies*, contains other discursive commentary on visual issues bearing only indirectly on the narrative at hand but serving as an indication of Hardy's continuing rumination on the general subject. The earlier novel contains an intriguing scene in which Manston suddenly sees a passing train without realizing what it is, so that it appears as a collection of initially unrelated components registering themselves on his retina. In *A Pair of Blue Eyes*, John Smith interestingly details a series of visual imprints, alternating them with mind-introduced reasoning that leads him to the conclusion that the person approaching him is his son.

But if in this novel, as in the earlier one, sight, considered in the abstract, offers the narrator and the characters a fruitful topic for discussion, it also plays a compelling and often destructive role in the narrative itself. Knight recalls the ancient philosophers who "used voluntarily to deprive themselves of sight to be uninterrupted in their meditations," (318) and for Knight as well as the other central characters, seeing and its invoked responses provides a troubling entryway into the labyrinth of life. Elfride is the first to experience a sight-engendered crisis when she accidentally sees on a blind the shadow of Stephen putting a shawl around an unknown woman and then kissing her. The view is sufficient to distress her but insufficient to enlighten her.[27] That shadow on the blind is paradigmatic of the many Hardyan scenes (seens) in which the knowledge acquired by looking is incomplete but deeply disturbing.

Yet there are many other occasions in Hardy's fiction when knowledge similarly acquired is more complete but equally disturbing. The sight-sensitive Stephen first appears in the novel with "eyes rigidly fixed in advance, an inbred horror of prying forbidding him to gaze around," (41) but eventually he is driven to spy by his difficulties with Elfride and thus discovers the disturbing news of her fickleness in a "strongly illuminated picture" of her intimacy with Knight in the summerhouse. He peeps through the lattice work to see Knight's arm stealing around Elfride's waist and becomes "shattered in spirit and sick to his heart's centre." (246-47) The "death" of Stephen's innocent faith in her and in their love, along with the "death" of his friendship with Knight, is underscored by an accompanying real death, that of Lady Luxellian. Stephen soon has even more disturbing knowledge forced upon him in the highly visual and melodramatic scene in the Luxellian vault, when he directly encounters Elfride and Knight together and learns of their engagement. The moment is pictorially precise for the characters as well as the reader, "a scene which was remembered by all three as an indelible mark in their history," and it contains most of the elements present in similarly traumatic scenes of the fiction of this period—the presence of death, the stark contrast of black and white, and the careful placement of light, both natural and artificial:

> The blackened coffins were now revealed more clearly than at first, the whitened walls and arches throwing them forward in strong relief. . . . The white daylight on his right side gleamed faintly in, and was toned to a blueness by contrast with the yellow rays from the candle against the wall. (265)

Hearing of the engagement, Stephen feels "the intense cruelty of his fate," (268) and the encounter ends with a painful glance between the former lovers:

> To Elfride the intense agony of reproach in Stephen's eye was a nail piercing her heart with a deadliness no words can describe. With a spasmodic effort she withdrew her eyes. (269)

These disturbing moments recall the striking scene at the beginning of *Desperate Remedies*. Mr. Graye's terrifying and mortal fall reappears twice, in altered form, in *A Pair of Blue Eyes,* accompanied by the explicit sexual component that was absent from or only tacitly present in the scene in the earlier novel and these scenes are more fully integrated with the development of the characters and the plot. The first takes place on the tower of Endelstow Church, when Elfride, in the company of Knight, willfully walks along the parapet and nearly falls to her death before Knight, springing forward "with a face of horror," seizes her "as in a vice." (177) Her "falling" in love with him and her eventual "fall" from innocent bliss are both portended by this scene, while her bleeding wrist foreshadows her loss of virginity (which, in the eyes of society, may already have taken place during her elopement with Stephen) and her corpse-like paleness her ultimate death.

Knight experiences a similar but even more dramatic fall in the well-known scene on the Cliff without a Name, heavy-handedly linked with the previous fall by Elfride's comments that "This is the moment I anticipated when on the tower." (219) Major elements of Hardyan trauma are there—the black cliff and black sea with its white border ("his funeral pall and its hedging," [224] the narrator laboriously points out), the setting sun that casts "a splotch of vermilion red upon a leaden ground," (225) and the presence of eyes in the trilobite fossil "regarding" Knight and causing time to close up "like a fan." (222) Hardy adds some overt sexual elements that suggest that the sort of fate which awaits Knight once he is off the cliff is not so different from that lurking on the rocks below. He has previously revealed an overly intellectual, anti-physical attitude toward romance, and the sea below, moaning and "rubbing its restless flank" against the cliff, (224) seems only an exaggerated augury of the nearly naked Elfride who rescues him by removing her underwear—and eventually appears sexually sullied in his eyes. His fear of death is evidently but an extreme version of his fastidious distaste for the more passionate forms of physical contact. Hardy manages to infuse the scene with terror, as it is happening, and, retrospectively, with somewhat satirical foreshadowing.

Hardy goes to some trouble to point out the comparative relationship of Knight and Stephen as suitors (the third suitor Lord Luxellian, is offstage for most of the novel). "Stephen fell in love with Elfride by looking at her: Knight by ceasing to do so" (199); Knight loves "philosophically rather than romantically," (200) which is Stephen's method. And both meet desperate failure, Smith because of his social class and his tendency to self-abasement that awakens Elfride's capriciousness, Knight because of his puritanical failure to accept Elfride's womanliness; their belated pressing of their suits and discovery of her death serve as punishment to both inadequate modes of loverhood. Hardy's courtship of Emma Gifford may have motivated him to muse in this half-comical, half-melodramatic way upon the terrifying prospects implicit in the full commitment to romance that leads men subconsciously to bring about failure upon the eternal elusiveness of woman, not only as an object to be defined visually but to be possessed. *A Pair of Blue Eyes*, like his other works of this pre-marital period, depicts an array of male characters focused on a central woman. Hardy's mingling of satire and melodrama in his treatment of the men in his 1873 novel seems related to his evincing both detachment and sympathy in his portrayal of the frustrated suitors, Gabriel Oak and William Boldwood, in his next novel, *Far from the Madding Crowd.* Such dual-faceted approaches may well have been occasioned by Hardy's desire to contemplate his own prolonged suitorhood in a balanced fashion.

There is some suggestion that Hardy might have intended this novel as a *kunstlerroman*, had he been able to break away from his persistent preoccupation with the role of sight in knowledge and personal trauma, for both Knight and Elfride are writers and Stephen is an architect who also sketches for personal pleasure—all representing aspects of Hardy himself. Knight early says that "it is only those who half know a thing that write about it. Those who know it thoroughly don't take the trouble," (148) suggesting that some sort of lack in life is what impels art, while those who live fully have no need to create. He later reflects on the need for concentrated energy to prepare a full volume instead of short articles and reveals his notebook of jotting, "disjointed and disconnected," (186) which he uses as a source for his writing, as did Hardy. But nothing is made of these materials with their potential for a dramatization of the growth of an artist or the complexities of the life-art relationship.

Late in the novel, the narrator comments about Smith's unconscious and repeated portraits of Elfride that reveal his feelings for her: "The hand, like the tongue easily acquires the trick of repetition by rote, without calling in the mind to assist at all. . . . Young men who cannot write verses about their Loves generally take to portraying them." (352) That stress on unconscious repetition in art and on the need to transmute felt desires into artistic form does more than describe Stephen's desultory sketches; at some level it provides a key to the whole of Hardy's art, full as it is of unconscious but revealing recurrences that signify an impulsion to portray elements that originate in powerful emotions. In subsequent novels, Hardy would enrich his narratives in a variety of ways so that the meditations on the dramatization of the complex role of seeing in both normative and pathological experience would never be quite as crudely dominant as they were in *Desperate Remedies* and *A Pair of Blue Eyes*, but virtually every novel would contain significant version of the "voyeuristic moment" and would rehearse again and again the manifold psychological and epistemological implications of such moments. Hardy's concern with visual matters thus goes far beyond the realm of technique; it has import for not only the inception and meaning of his fiction but also its relevance to aspects of philosophy and psychoanalytic theory.

NOTES

1. Lady Hester Pinney, *Thomas Hardy and the Birdsmoorgate Murder 1856* (Beaminster: Toucan, 1966), p. 2. [*Monographs on the Life, Times and Works of Thomas Hardy*, no. 28.]
2. Florence Emily Hardy, *The Life of Hardy* (London: Macmillan, 1962), pp. 28-29.
3. Hardy's concern with outlines as well as with color, light, and affect combines the allocentric (objective) and auto-centric (subjective) aspects of seeing. Many artists tend to be preoccupied with one or the other. See Ernest G. Schachiel, *Metamorphosis: On the Development of Affect, Perception, Attention and Memory* (New York: Basic, 1959), pp. 107-11.

4. J. Hillis Milller, "Natural and Linguistic Moment," *Nature and the Victorian Imagination*, ed. U.C. Knoepflmacher and G.B. Tennyson (Berkeley: University of California Press, 1977), p. 450.
5. Jacques Lacan, "The Mirror Stage as Formative of the Function of the I as Revealed in Psychoanalytic Experience," *Ecrits*, trans. Alan Sheridan (New York: Norton, 1977), pp. 1-7.
6. Albert J. Guerard, *Thomas Hardy: The Novels and Stories* (Cambridge: Harvard University, 1949), pp. 114-16.
7. See, for example, J. Hillis Miller, *Thomas Hardy: Distance and Desire* (Cambridge: Belknap Press of Harvard University, 1970), pp. xiii, 7; David Lodge, "Thomas Hardy and Cinematographic Form," *Novel*, 7 (1974), p. 250.
8. Reprinted in *Thomas Hardy's Personal Writings*, ed. Harold Orel (Lawrence: University Press of Kansas, 1966), pp. 110-25.
9. E.H. Gombrich, *Art and Illusion* (2nd ed., New York: Bollingen, 1965), pp. 60, 64, 299-301.
10. Rudolph Arnheim, *Art and Visual Perception* (Berkeley: University of California Press, 1954), p. 31.
11. See Tom Paulin, *Thomas Hardy: The Poetry of Perception* (Totowa, N.J.: Littlefield, 1975), which treats some of these issues as evinced in the poetry.
12. Stith Thompson, *Motif-Index of Folk Literature*, I (A-C) (Bloomington: Indiana University Press, 1955), pp. 510-14.
13. *The Standard Edition of the Complete Works of Sigmund Freud*, trans. James Strachey (London: Hogarth, 1953), VII, p. 156.
14. Gotthold Lessing, *Laocoon* (1766), trans. Edward Allen McCormick (Indianapolis: Bobbs-Merrill, 1962), p. 12.
15. Jacques Lacan, "The Mirror Stage . . ." p. 2. Jean Piaget says that, beginning at age four weeks, an infant has a "need to look," that objects are "an aliment for the activity of the glance." *The Origins of Intelligence in Children*, trans. Margaret Cook (New York: International Universities Press, 1952), pp. 63-66.
16. Otto Fenichel, *The Psychoanalytic Theory of Neurosis* (New York: Norton, 1945), pp. 347-49.
17. John Fowles, "Hardy and the Hag," *Thomas Hardy after Fifty Years*, ed. Lance St. John Butler (London: Macmillan, 1977), p. 29.
18. Edmund Bergler, *The Writer and Psychoanalysis* (Garden City, N.Y.: Doubleday, 1950), pp. 90-94.
19. Roland Barthes, *The Pleasure of the Text* (New York: Hill and Wang, 1975), p. 17.
20. Boris Uspensky, *A Poetics of Composition* (Berkeley: University of California Press, 1973), pp. 130-43.
21. See David Lodge, "Thomas Hardy and Cinematographic Form," p. 250; J. Hillis Miller, *Thomas Hardy: Distance and Desire*, pp. xii, 7; Norman Page, *Thomas Hardy* (London: Routledge and Kegan Paul, 1977).

22. This and subsequent page citations refer to the New Wessex Edition of *Desperate Remedies* (London: Macmillan, 1975).
23. See Norman Page, "Visual Technique in Hardy's *Desperate Remedies,*" *Ariel*, 4 (1973), pp. 65-71, for a thorough discussion of the types of visual devices Hardy uses in the novel. The visual components of such scenes, says Page, force the reader to give them closer attention.
24. The term used by Aaron Penley in what was probably one of Hardy's guidebooks, *The Elements of Perspective* (London: Winsor and Newton, 1851), p. 9. Many architects now refer to this as "the station point."
25. This and subsequent page citations refer to the New Wessex Edition of *A Pair of Blue Eyes* (London: Macmillan, 1976).
26. See David Lodge, "Thomas Hardy and Cinematographic Form," pp. 246-54, and Joan Grundy, *Hardy & the Sister Arts* (London: Macmillan, 1979), pp. 106-33 for discussion of the filmic quality of Hardy's fiction.
27. The woman proves to be his mother, not a true rival. Or is she? When Stephen tells Mrs. Smith that he's in love with Elfride, she responds, "Whatever do you want any woman at all for yet?" (110) A typical maternal remonstrance, perhaps, but Stephen bears similarities to a later Hardy character, Clym Yeobright, whose closeness to his mother makes her a disruptive third party in his romance.

The Incongruous and the Inevitable: Hardy's Vision of Life in His Major Novels

K.B. RAZDAN

Thomas Hardy's major fiction glows with the sombre radiation of a melancholy philosophy. The works of the great novelist's second phase, *The Return of the Native, The Mayor of Casterbridge*, and those of the last stage, *Tess* and *Jude*, all reflect a failure of youthful hope, of dream-like aspirations and mythic struggles. The protagonists of these works, Clym Yeobright, Michael Henchard, Tess and Jude, cumulatively project a world, a life-view that hovers between the dream and the nightmare, desire and pain, agony and ecstasy, finally metamorphosing into an existential hell. These violent oscillations of mood in the fictional cosmos of these works, project a view of human existence as moulded by certain unforeseen and unpredictable forces. What are these forces, these mysterious elements that diabolically and with a sustained perversity thwart humans at every step of their lives? Be it Henchard or Yeobright, Tess or Jude, what emerges with a kind of metronomic clarity is the realization on the part of the reader that in the lives and careers of the above cited protagonists, Hardy presents an unnerving dissonance between man and his environment.

The environmental factor is represented by the vast, inscrutable and menacing forces and objects of Nature. An almost unsettling and demonic portrayal of Nature forms an important element in Hardy's vision of life. Nature and a brutal and remorseless fate it unleashes to ensnare and defeat humans, endows some of the great works like *The Mayor of Casterbridge, The Return of the Native* and *Tess*, with an apocalyptic vision of life. Like a canker at the heart of a beautiful flower, Nature lurks behind the bushes, ready to spring upon the unsuspecting human individual: the Forest in *Tess*, and Egdon Heath in *The Return of the Native*. Unlike Wordsworth, Hardy did not embellish Nature with motherly mysticism or regard it as the incarnation of a spirit. For him the phenomenological environment was far from being all beauty and goodness. Nature did have its beautiful aspects, but the aspects of cruelty, indifference and caprice far outweighed everything else. In this respect, Hardy's vision of life resembles that of some of the modern and post-modern American novelists like Nathanael West, Kurt Vonnegut, William Burroughs, Joseph Heller and Thomas Pynchon.

Comparison with these American novelists wouldn't be illogical at all; in fact such an exercise would be interesting and revelatory. In all novels, whether English, American or European, "the internal fiction is usually of primary interest," and "the primary interest is in *dianoia*, the idea . . . and the conceptual interest may be called thematic."[1] The best translation of *dianoia* can be 'theme' and in Hardy's major protagonists like Henchard, Yeobright, Tess and Jude, the thematic interest triumphs over fictional interest. In case of Henchard and Clym Yeobright, the central figures in *The Mayor of Casterbridge* and *The Return of the Native*, respectively, as well as in the roles of Tess and Jude, we discover two main tendencies vis-a-vis Hardy's interpretation of human life: "a comic tendency to integrate the hero" (or the heroine) with society, and "a tragic tendency to isolate"[2] the protagonist from everything that might nourish and harmonize, invigorate and rejuvenate the spirit, mind and soul of the human individual. The separateness of the Hardy protagonist, thus, only contributes to the distinctness of the author's vision. In a purely modernistic sense, Hardy's philosophy of life. which emerges out of the cumulative spectrum formed by the lives of his fictional personages, is intrinsically existential, and it is the existential pattern of experience that forms the crux of the major novels. It may be Henchard's act of *hubris* (the ancient Greeks called *hubris* as the sin of excess) in selling off his wife at the village fair, his confrontation with Donald Farfrae and relationship with step-daughter Elizabeth-Jane, and eventual wretched end in a lonely and desolate hut or Clym Yeobright's fateful 'collision' with Eustacia Wye and the dismantling of his self and being, courtesy Egdon Heath, but it is always the same tragic aspect of human existence: man is a mere toy, a plaything in the hands of the inscrutable, malicious and malevolent forces rampant in the universe. The fair, innocent, virtuous and goddess-like Tess, suddenly in the sinister forest, falls prey to the brutal animalistic lust of Alec d'Urberville. Her engagement and marriage to Angel Clare turns into a nightmare. Angel, himself a sinner, abandons the victim Tess, the honest and scrupulous wife who, on the wedding night, confesses to her husband the affair with Alec. In the case of Jude it is plain horror all the time. Jude Fawley is entangled by the enchantress the *haetara* type woman Arabella Donn, a mere female animal, and after being remorselessly deserted by her falls in love with his cousin Sue Bridehead, a vivacious intelligent young school teacher. Jude oscillates between these two women, is finally inveigled back by Arabella and dies miserably. In this last novel of his, Hardy perhaps got repulsed by the horrors of his own creation and turned away from novel writing to poetry.

In the portrayal of human character, and in the depiction of events and happenings, Hardy's imagery as a component of his vision of life comes close to being archetypally demonic, a characteristic of the ironic mode in which he writes. As novels of character and environment *The Mayor of Casterbridge*, *The Return of the Native*, *Tess* and *Jude the Obscure*, depict a set of helpless, struggling and pathetic humans lost in "a world of the nightmare and the scapegoat, of bondage and pain and confusion,"[3] in which the divine "largely personifies the vast, menacing, stupid powers of nature."[4] The machinery of fate is administered "by a set of remote invisible gods, whose freedom and pleasure are ironic because they exclude man."[5] Most of Hardy's protagonists (especially Henchard, Clym Yeobright, Tess and Jude) are nothing but modernized and displaced versions of the scapegoat, the sacrificial victim who is to be sacrificed to strengthen certain invisible forces, forces which we may define as God, gods, fate, accident, chance, coincidence, even the bizarre and the grotesque in a mechanical and hopeless universe. The Greeks called the sacrificial victim, the scapegoat, as *pharmakos*, and the terms can as well be applied to the main figures of Hardy's major fiction comprising the novels of character and environment. Michael Henchard, Tess and Jude, do become *pharmakos* personages in whom love, in conformity with a demonic human world, develops into "a fierce destructive passion that works against loyalty or frustrates the one who possesses it."[6] Permeating Hardy's world, especially the rural countryside in which most of the protagonists function, are the familiar symbols of the demonic: the sinister landscape, the sinister garden, the tree of death, and such images as crosses, scaffolds, and the sinister whirlpool. Thus, a kind of a secularized myth forms an integral aspect of the vision of life and existence, that crystallizes out of the lives of Hardy's major protagonists.

Here, it won't be inappropriate to quote the words of Jung:

> The experience that furnishes the material for artistic expression is no longer familiar. It is a strange something that derives its existence from the hinterland of man's mind—that suggests the abyss of time separating us from pre-human ages, or evokes a super-human world of contrasting light and darkness. . . . The value and force of the experience are given by its enormity. It arises from timeless depths; it is foreign and cold, many-sided, demonic, and grotesque. . . . The disturbing vision of monstrous and meaningless happenings that in every way exceed the grasp of human feeling and comprehension. . . . But the primordial experiences . . . allow a glimpse into the unfathomed abyss.[7]

Infusing Hardy's complicated plots, "his loving descriptions of place and person, his webs of interrelated lives,"[8] is this "disturbing vision" conveying a dramatized sense of the demonic. Coming back to *Jude*, this demonic and apocalyptic view of human life and destiny evolves into "a full and definitive statement on evil and mischance and self-destructiveness, on the social and cosmic absurd."[9] The life and action of Henchard as well as Jude convey not only a more austere aesthetic of the modern novel, but also illustrate the afflictions that are eroding human society and civilization in the present century as well. A rudderless society fosters only a dismal faith, the anxieties of sexual maladjustment, social unemployment and a chronic *angst*. The persistent sexual destructiveness of both Jude and Sue, a total and encapsulating vision of weakened vitality and enervating despair, all these can be identified by the reader as factors dominating contemporary man's own existence. In the case of Henchard and Clym Yeobright, the same kind of analogy operates: both these heroes inhabit a world of "perverted or wasted work, ruins and catacombs, instruments of torture and monuments of folly."[10] Egdon Heath in *The Return of the Native* becomes the presiding monstrous deity which overlooks, controls, manipulates and finally executes the fatal blow against puny, lost, confused, and helpless humans. Here, Hardy's vision of life and living seems to have its own organic growth. Initially we are made to realize that something intrinsically weak and poor in man goes anytime haywire and initiates a process of destruction, a process which takes place in a society held together by a kind of molecular tension of egos. Next, what follows is the 'fall,' the protagonist's (and that includes the heroine as well) acts of excess as desperate measures to find fulfilment, individual, sexual, and social. This connotation becomes more relevant in the personages of Henchard and Jude, pathetic denizens of a sinister human world in which relationships become base and perverted and a dystopian matrix governs the lives and fortunes of the leading characters.

In the opening paragraphs of *The Mayor of Casterbridge*, we get an account of Henchard and his wife walking together in a late summer evening, approaching the large village of Weydon-Priors in Upper Wessex. Both husband and wife go on plodding in a listless and dazed manner, and the first inkling of Hardy's philosophically melancholic vision of life comes in these words describing the facial expression of Henchard's wife:

> When she plodded on in the shade of the hedge, silently thinking, she had the hard, half-apathetic expression of one who deems anything possible at the hands of Time and Chance, except, perhaps, fair play. The first phase was the work of Nature, the second probably of civilization.[11]

A total absence of conversation during the walk, followed by "the atmosphere of stale familiarity," already foreshadows the inevitable, the lethal blow of Time, Chance, and Nature when Henchard auctions off his wife in a state of inebriation. What can be more grotesque and bizarre than a husband selling off his wife? Henchard and his wife are an incongruous combination and the inevitable has to follow. Even lovers become incongruous in Hardy's fictional cosmos and eventually are swallowed by the 'abyss' of existential anomie and alienation: Clym Yeobright and Eustacia Wye, Jude and Sue Bridehead, and Jude's affair with Arabella Donn. In all these man-woman combinations, the principal energy becomes the energy of futility and a fierce destructive passion governs the mind of the personages involved.

Take the case of Tess, the young and vivacious lass of the d'Urbervilles, a countryside rural nymph who after being entangled by a Satyr (Alec), becomes from a 'maiden,' a 'maiden no more.' Hence again, fate and chance catch Tess unawares and she hasn't a ghost of a chance of escaping the inevitable. Stepping out of her mother's door to try her fortune at Alec's Trantridge poultry farm, Tess little knows the calamity that eventually befalls her. Alec ensnares her in the sinister forest and dogs her persistently like a genie. Hardy's vision of existential human predicament becomes the metaphor of fiction as well. And the metaphor is "not simply one of disorder; it is also reductive. It creates meaning by referring to an autonomous dream, an arbitrary and personal truth."[12] This is seen when we have a look at some of the words in the letter Tess writes to Angel Clare, a letter of agony, and longing for a dream that had been wronged:

> Angel, I live entirely for you. I love you too much to blame you for going away. . . . Do not think I shall say a word of sting or bitterness. Only come back to me. I am desolate without you, my darling, O, so desolate! . . .
>
> How silly I was in my happiness when I thought I could trust you always to love me! I ought to have known that such as that was not for poor me. But I am sick at heart. . . .
>
> If you really cannot come to me will you let me come to you? I am, as I say, worried, pressed to do what I will not do. It cannot be that I shall yield one inch, yet I am in terror as to what an accident might lead to, and I so defenseless on account of my first error. . . .
>
> Come to me—come to me, and save me from what threatens me!
>
> Your faithful heartbroken Tess.[13]

Here, in this letter, what we get is a pathetic, desolate and desperate cry from a human being in distress. A typical happening in a world, a society dominated by cruelty and outrage. This is Thomas Hardy at his pessimistic best. The author's fatalistic orientation of Tess's life reflects in turn a fact which is quite startling: *Tess* as a novel becomes a novel of destiny in which the heroine meets defeat on her own terms. She tries to run away with Angel after killing the monster Alec, the flight is hopeless across Salisbury Plain and Tess is captured at Stonehenge. The pattern of Hardy's fiction here is contained and self-reflexive. The life and tragic end of Tess pose a vital question vis-a-vis Hardy's own stance: is Tess a rebel or a victim? Rebel or victim, she is at odds with her environment. Her energy is the energy of defiance, and her aggressions are directed against herself (the victim) or against the world, a demonic human world (the rebel). In either case, Tess remains an alien to society (in the post-seduction phase), a misfit.

In Hardy's vision of life, necessity also becomes an interesting and intriguing factor. For Henchard, Clym Yeobright, Tess, and Jude, necessity evolves and becomes "an inner compulsion, purposeless and self-destructive. It is spiteful of itself."[14] All the above mentioned four protagonists of Hardy's fictional cosmos maintain an illusion of choice though choice brings no victory. The action of time "is one of ironic and eternal recurrences—Sisyphus at his boulder—but the end is always the same: discomfiture. This is 'demonic' time."[15] Being the inhabitants of an existential hell man creates on earth, Henchard, Tess and Jude in particular present through the collective spectrum of their lives a scene of bondage, frustration, and absurdity. They become the archetypes of existentially ironic man, symbols of the incongruous irony of human life. As parts and components of Hardy's theme and vision, these personages transcend the limits of verisimilitude. For instance, we go back to the bizarre incident of Henchard shaking loose from his wife and thereby, discarding that drooping rag of a woman. A violation of human dignity takes place, and an intimate relationship is made subservient to the cash nexus. Yet it should be understood that Henchard does not sell his wife out of greed or monetary considerations. He does it because he is supremely dissatisfied with the drabness of life and is driven towards an act that will proclaim his defiance and disgust. A perpetual tension between self and living producing total alienation for the victim-hero constitutes the other interesting facet of Hardy's existential vision. After he realizes what he has done, Henchard tries to locate Susan for a long time and with every passing day, the quantum of alienation and *angst* increases.

In the case of Jude, the novelist's vision assumes more lethal and emasculating connotations. The paradigm of form here, as in the case of Henchard and Tess, is suggested by the pattern of encounter, the "shifting, straining encounter of the rebel-victim with destructive experience." Jude and Henchard, along with Tess, represent a socially approved norm in the early phases of their lives, yet fate and chance will it otherwise: the experiences of these principal personages in Hardy's fiction become destructive bordering upon the apocalyptic, and an altered apprehension of the self defines the character, the personality and the thought process of the hero. All this conforms to, and forms a part of, Hardy's darkening view of life. An excessive accumulation of disaster in the major novels may tempt the reader to link it to some kind of a vague metaphysics. Such an exercise would only be futile in determining the precise contours and connotations of the novelist's social or existential vision. Why? The reason is simple. Hardy remained a Christian to the extent of believing that purpose does course through the universe, though the universe may itself seem to be absurd and mechanical. Yet, the brakes are applied here and Hardy never gives the impression that this purpose can be kind or benevolent or the attribute of a particular divine being. An obsessive concern in *The Mayor of Casterbridge, Tess, The Return of the Native* and *Jude the Obscure*, is to make the plots and the personages involved convey an oppressive fatality without positing an agency determining the course of fate. The agency remains unseen, mysterious, inscrutable inconceivable, ruthless and melancholy. Such is the energy, the force, the vehemence of the vision displayed that sometimes it seems that in his passion to bend plot to purpose, Hardy is plotting and conspiring against his own characters.

Tess and *Jude* move the time of their action closer to the time of composition, and express more clearly what Hardy called 'the ache of modernism.' The concept of change or new and altered time may not be here "that strange disease," as Matthew Arnold defined modern times, yet as a part of his vision of life, the depiction of modernity in the late novels comes as a warning sign: the paradise had been lost and human existence towards the close of the nineteenth century had already become dystopian and dehumanized.

The consistently dark view of life expressed in the major novels earned Hardy the label of a pessimist, a label he firmly rejected insisting that he was an 'evolutionary meliorist.' The epithet indicates that the great novelist was a product of the age of Darwin, and his journey from youthful orthodoxy to adult scepticism reflects a representative quality. Misunderstandings and confusions have been there in the tendency to regard his novels as offering a philosophy or a system of ethics. Hardy was indeed much more than being a simple countryman or a rustic story-teller. Darwinism which dethroned man from being the apex of creation and made him a recent unimportant sport of nature, left its trail of bitterness in the mind of every intellectual and creative artist. To compound this source of distress, the struggle to liberate himself intellectually left Hardy with a life-long increment of sadness. He now became determined "to depict the universe in terms of a mechanistic determinism,"[17] yet so strong was the resistance felt towards the theory of Organic Evolution by his heritage of Christian indoctrination, that Hardy "fell back at times into a kind of gnosticism, a view of life as predetermined by bad intentions without a discernible figure or force actively intending, or at least a view of life as predetermined by bad luck."[18] Logically thus, it should not be difficult for the reader to understand why this prolific writer, taught to believe in God's benevolence, or at least to depend upon His attentiveness, should have in an age of industrialization, dehumanization and Mammon worship, felt in his mind a sediment of cruelty, pain, indifference and intense dissatisfaction, necessary byproducts of the struggle for existence. The remorseless advance of scientism in the second half of the nineteenth century, instilled in many writers the feeling that there is no good in knowing when the thing one knows best is how little can be done with knowledge. Hardy himself, like his Clym Yeobright and Jude Fawley, knew that reflective men would be hopelessly committed to a life of ideas, yet the metamorphosis of consciousness which modern life enforces upon men would make the situation, existentially and creatively, painful, distressing and finally gloomy. This is the crux of Hardy's apparently pessimistic and nearly apocalyptic view of life. Needless to say that the development of consciousness as a corollary to modernity, would certainly create, and does create even now amongst most of us, an intense dissatisfaction with the limits and frustrations of consciousness. What then is the net result? The same we view in Henchard, Clym Yeobright and Jude and finally Hardy himself: torpor and weariness with the mind entangled in its own motions, perpetually in orbit around a vague and nebulous centre. Those fated for thought have perhaps no choice but to suffer. What "we gain by science is, after all, sadness, as the Preacher saith," and this is what Hardy finally assumed to be true.

In *Far from the Madding Crowd, The Return of the Native, The Mayor of Casterbridge* and *Tess*, the forces of Fate and Destiny incarnate themselves in two forms: as chance and as love. Chance becomes the most typical and repetitive instrument of existential execution. A running battle between man and Destiny is witnessed throughout the major novels. Destiny being an inscrutable and malicious agency, men are unable to predict its machinations and blows. Even the past of the characters becomes a scourge for Fate to whip-lash the helpless protagonists of Hardy's fictional cosmos. Past actions are all related to love. Fate, thus gets chiefly incarnated as love: all Hardy's novels are love stories. Love becomes the catalyst, the predominating motive which propels and activates the characters. Cast into a deep and dark abyss in the form of an unsatisfying and brutal world, man thirsts and pines for happiness. Happiness finally becomes, metaphorically as an existential symbol, a mirage, an ever-receding horizon on the firmament of man's consciousness and awareness. Love, as a prerequisite for happiness, becomes eventually a blind, irresistible power, capturing humans with relentless fury and metronomic regularity: Bathsheba, Gabriel Oak, Eustacia Wye, Tess, and Jude, all are love's victims. The heroines are especially touched with a characteristic pathos, perhaps Hardy knew that the passiveness and frailty of a woman makes her more vulnerable to dependence on fate. As representatives of mankind, women in Hardy's novelistic universe remain the victims of superhuman forces.

Though Hardy wrote only about country people in nineteenth-century Wessex, the life of Wessex is implicitly a part of the life of entire mankind, the whole human race. Paradoxically, the spectrum of Hardy's human drama is as vast and mind-boggling as its scope and setting look confined. The Emersonian "en-masse," and the Shakespearean "as flies to wanton boys, so are we to the gods/ they kill us for their sport," are both ironically and intrinsically contained in Hardy's existential perspective on the human race.

NOTES

1. Northrop Frye, *Anatomy of Criticism* (Princeton: Princeton University Press, 1957), 52.
2. *Ibid.*, p. 54.
3. *Loc. cit.*
4. *Loc. cit.*
5. *Loc. cit.*
6. *Ibid.*, p. 149.
7. Carl Jung, *Modern Man in Search of a Soul*, translated by Dell and Baynes (London, 1933), qtd. Richard Carpenter, *Thomas Hardy* (London: Macmillan, 1976), p. 36.
8. Richard Carpenter, p. 36.
9. Albert J. Guerard, ed., *Hardy: Collection of Critical Essays* (New Jersey: Prentice Hall, 1963), p. 1.
10. Northrop Frye, p. 147.
11. Thomas Hardy, *The Mayor of Casterbridge* (London: Macmillan, 1960), p. 2.
12. Ihab Hassan, *Radical Innocence: Studies in the Contemporary American Novel* (Princeton: Princeton University Press, 1961), p. 32.
13. Thomas Hardy, *Tess of the d'Urbervilles* (London: Macmillan, 1961), pp. 378-79.
14. Ihab Hassan, p. 32.
15. *Ibid.*, p. 32.
16. *Ibid.*, p. 30.
17. Norman Page, *Thomas Hardy* (New York: Routledge and Kegan Paul, 1977), p. 23.
18. Richard Carpenter, p. 33.

Hardy's Rustics Reconsidered

G.R. TANEJA

Hardy exploited his close familiarity with the countryside and the ways of life and manners prevalent there in the very first novel that he published in 1871.[1] When Clerk Cricket is shown in *Desperate Remedies* holding forth on a wedding that is being postponed, "it might be put off; putten off a thing isn't gotten rid of a thing, if that thing is a woman," and, if "God A'mighty sends bread as well as children . . . 'tis bread to one house and children to another very often," one can detect a note of authenticity and freshness in Hardy's rendering of rustic sentiments even so early in his literary career. One might even say that this is an aspect of his art that he did not learn and perfect as he proceeded in his career. Nonetheless in his later novels he makes more varied use of it and shows greater sophistication in its handling.[2] But he knew his rustic characters from the start and he knew them well, indeed. If dialogue is one of the many means in his novels through which the rustic characters are given life and vitality, Hardy's handling of the rustic dialogues can be profitably compared with words that he puts into the mouth of "non-rustic characters." The superiority of his rustic dialogues—with their supple, lively, and genuine idiom—is easily established over the artificiality of conversation among other characters in his early work.[3]

Many and varied, indeed, are the roles and functions that the rustic characters perform in Hardy's different novels. While a significant role played by them is to impart a necessary balance to the otherwise dark and tragic view of life projected in the novels, they perform various other functions to suit the artistic and thematic requirements of the novels. That they appear in each novel as a homogeneous group, turns them into a chorus and Hardy utilizes their group-character and their collective response to the major events and actions to help achieve a perspective and an objective viewpoint from a source whose sympathies are not directly involved. They thus become a source of additional information for the readers to appreciate the motives of the major characters and significance of the events. They often symbolize a vanishing way of life, a phenomenon threatened with extinction, even destruction, and, in this context, constantly present a contrast to the "non-rustic" upperclass characters. Quite often they are responsible for channelizing the development of action in a particular direction. They are sometimes used to heighten the effect of actions in the novels. They are a source of humour and, as the embodiment of the comic spirit, offer a corrective to the view of Hardy as essentially pessimistic and gloomy. Their quiet and primitive life-style contrasts ironically with tempestuous events in the novels and the stormy passions of the main characters. Above all they are a triumph of Hardy's art of characterization.

In fact Hardy's rustics are a part of the folk material which is a necessary aspect of Hardy's aesthetics and which constitutes the underlying structure of the novels of Hardy. Hardy in a sense wrote in the "traditional," as opposed to the "literary," mode. An appreciation of this aspect of Hardy's aesthetics tends to explain some of the peculiarities that have alway troubled the readers of Hardy: his illogical plotting and abundant use of chance and coincidence, for instance.

Not only does the nature of the functions of rustic characters vary from novel to novel, their importance in terms of the total structure of the novels, too, is never the same.

In *Under the Greenwood Tree* the bucolic tale of Mellstock Choir gains in focus and attention at the cost of the love-story of Fancy Day and Dick Dewy. The rustic characters with their quaint habits and peculiar mannerism of speech vie with their urban counterparts for the readers' attention. As the village choir, they are to be replaced by an organist, and their primary anxiety is to be allowed to sing their Swan-song on a significant occasion, not on "some nameless paltry second-Sunday-after or Sunday-next-before something." Hardy develops these characters in a variety of situations. We first meet them at the house of Dick Dewy where they have assembled to prepare for their performance the next day. We see them "going on rounds," caroling at Christmas, in the church, at their leisure, at the party given by Dick's father and finally when they visit the Vicar. Their individual fortunes thus dominate the better part of the novel and later in the novel when the story of Fancy and Dick gains prominence, they perform other functions of a chorus.

In *Far from the Madding Crowd* the rustic group is one of the best developed groups, but performs comparatively a minor role. They function as a chorus and comment on the major events, provide background information, anticipate the action in some cases, and, as symbol of changeless, stable community, provide a contrast with the stormy passions of the major characters. Essentially comic as they are, they enliven many a moment in the novel.

In *Return of the Native* the rustic characters are much more functional. They are involved more directly into the action of the novel. Charley arranges for Eustacia to join the mummers and later prevents her from committing suicide. Susan Nunsuch's son, Johnny, sees Mrs. Yeobright going away without being permitted to enter thc house of her son and later tells Clym about it. Christian loses the money entrusted to him by Mrs. Yeobright for Thomasin and Clym and indirectly becomes responsible for Mrs. Yeobright's death. The dramatic manner in which Eustacia's death is immediately preceded by the burning of her effigy, and earlier Susan Nunsuch's pricking of it with a needle in the church suggests that Hardy wants us to see a connection between Eustacia's death and these actions.[4]

In *The Woodlanders* the rustic characters again function as a chorus which Hardy utilizes more for a commentary on, and analysis of, actions and characters rather than for direct participation or influencing the main action. The timber-workers offer shrewd comments on Fitzpiers and Mrs. Charmond, reflect on the loneliness that envelops the figure of Marty and offer proverbial comments on marriages in general.

The rustic characters thus not only perform different functions in each novel which are not of equal importance, they are in each novel a different group of people. Each group is strongly differentiated from the rest. In *Under the Greenwood Tree* it is mostly the members of the choir. In *Far from the Madding Crowd* it is the farm-labourers seen at work, or occasionally settled at Warren's Malthouse. What binds the chorus in *Return of the Native* is the geographic fact of their proximity to Egdon Heath. In *The Woodlanders* it is the timber-merchants. In *The Mayor of Casterbridge*, the rustic group, being in a city, is in a way more urban and, therefore, appears to be more worldly-wise. What renders each group of characters a unified and homogeneous group is their common concern with the fluctuating fortunes of the major characters, the essential oneness of the inherited wisdom with which they react to the world around them, and the same soil to which they all belong.

Within each group each member of the rustic community is individualized by sharp and skilful strokes of Hardy's art. Michael Mail is "a bowed and bent man who carried a fiddle under his arm, and walked as if studying some subject connected with the surface of the road." Robert Penny, the book- and shoe-maker, walks "with his face fixed on the north-east gates of heavens before him, so that his lower waist buttons came first and then the remainder of his figure." Elias Spink, on the other hand, "walked perpendicularly and dramatically." "Henery" Fray insists on his way of spelling his name. Joseph Poorgrass is a very bashful man with a "saintly profile" who blushes when he sees beautiful women, and who once addressed an owl as "Sir." Jan Coggan is "Crimson man with Specious countenance, and a private glimmer in his eyes." Robert Creedle believed that as green slugs "lived on cabbages, so they must be made of cabbages. . . . God forbid that a live slug should be seen on any plate of victuals that is served by Robert Creedle."

To a certain extent almost all the rustic characters are given individual traits and are made memorable on account of personal eccentricities of speech and mannerism. When Hardy sets out to describe one of his rustic characters, he takes great pains to draw portraits of the characters in very great detail and with vivid strokes. The point of view of the reader—as well as that of the author—when observing a "portrait" or rustic "scenes" is that of an observer facing a painting. For a heightened sense of life that Hardy succeeds in imparting to them, he exploited the painters' method of vivid visualization. His diction, too, is often borrowed from the painter's register. *Under the Greenwood Tree* was published with the sub-title, *A Rural Painting of the Dutch School*. Joan Grundy points out how Hardy's descriptions are often, though in words, set pieces like paintings and, in his numerous descriptions in *Tess*, for instance, she finds "an Impressionistic sensibility at work."[5] Yet, despite an individualizing trait a rustic character generally remains an integral part of the group to which he belongs.[6] Occasionally a minor rustic character is given prominence and is made to function more actively and meaningfully outside the regular functions of the group.[7] Such a character is given stronger mark of individuality. He is shown to have more than a special habit, peculiar mannerisms and speech habits. Such a character often reappears at various points in the narrative. Joseph Poorgrass in *Far from the Madding Crowd* and Christian Cantle in *The Return of the Native* can be classified in this category. In *The Woodlanders* Charley is such a character. Not only does he help Eustacia join the mummers but also prevents her suicide. His adolescent love for Eustacia, though a minor episode, is lovingly told. He appears again at the end after the death of Eustacia.

It has perhaps been rightly remarked that Hardy's rustic characters are neither types nor individuals but "universals." If we instantly recognize the rustics of Hardy (as we do the soldiers of Kipling, for instance) as being essentially the Hardy characters as also the rustic characters of all times and all places, it is, one must maintain, on account of this element of universality. It gives them the oneness of the group as well as the vitality of individual characters. It is significant to note that the projection of the rustic characters as a community suits Hardy's purpose, and he deliberately avoids placing excessively individualized characters among them.

Hardy's apparent commitment to the idea of total futility of all human endeavour does not derive from any cynical contempt for man himself. Even when a Tess is driven to misery and crime, an Eustacia left unfulfilled and frustrated till the very end, a Giles condemned to inch towards death for no apparent justification at all, Hardy's tragic view of the universe in the ultimate analysis does not foster hopelessness and a sense of void and nothingness. His tragic novels invariably end on a note of an ultimate affirmation of life. A doomed Hardy character is not denied the human dignity that Swift would not grant his "pernicious odious vermins"; nor is the man portrayed as an infinitesimal atom as in the existential world of Sartre and Camus and the Theatre of the Absurd. The President of the Immortals remains forever unrelenting; the unfulfilled Intention thwarts all human effort towards fulfilment; "happiness" is "but an occasional episode in an otherwise painful drama of human life"; and chance, change and caprice become keys to the mysteries of Hardy's universe.[8] The essential genuineness of human existence and unmistakable conviction of the value, worth and validity of human life remains among the fundamental convictions that emerge from the novels of Hardy.

What, among other factors, reveals Hardy's essential humanity, his tolerance, understanding and acceptance of the erring mortals, his feeling for the supremacy of life, even at the cost of individual life—is the minor characters, as noted earlier, that are an essential feature of almost every Hardy novel. The rustic characters play, as we shall see later, a significant role in the total context of the novels and it reveals them as integral to the total design of Hardy's novels—thematic, structural, and archetypal. In confronting the tragic moment and the ensuing chaos and despair with the stability, continuity and hope and the affirmation of the fundamental values of life that they may symbolize, they add a necessary dimension to the novels as tragedies. After the tragic death of Giles, for instance, the rustic chorus in the last chapter of *The Woodlanders*, with quiet wisdom and a social objective stance, uphold the promise of continuity. Compared to the major characters whose life-long, frenzied search for peace and happiness through love merely ends in futility and failure, the rustic characters give the impression of curious self-sufficiency: no sense of inadequacy or incompleteness tortures them as it tortures Eustacia, for instance.

Almost invariably in the novels of Hardy the rustic characters stand for a way of life and are deliberately contrasted with the upperclass characters and *their* values, ways of life and behaviour. In this context an upperclass character is an "outsider." The world of Little Hintock, Dorset or Bath, Mellstock and Egdon Heath is a world of stability, time-honoured norms and values that are deeply rooted in the soil and the rustic characters are imbued with the wisdom of the ages. When an outsider moves into the rustic community, he upsets the very balance of life of the community and this later leads to a tragic situation. A conflict between a way of life that has walked hand in hand with time and the ways of the new world; between the simple elemental passions of the peasants, labourers and workers, and the towering passions of the psychologically complex, even neurotic characters; between past and present—one might say, is one of the major concerns of most

Hardy novels. One must here point out that Hardy's role as a champion of the "common" man and a critic of the contemporary society tends to get over-emphasized. But there is of course no doubt that Hardy's attitude in this context reveals a degree of ambivalence.

But an upsetting of the state of natural balance in which the rustic community exists, is often caused by a member of the community who is partly if not wholly responsible for the ensuing tragedy. Thus, the "insider-outsider" is more of an outsider because he is usually more educated than other members of the rustic community. He is not only open to outside influences, but perhaps on account of his awareness of the distinct character of the two ways of life is vulnerable to the banal influence of the sudden change that through him, affects the rustic community.

The prominent outsiders who affect the rustic community include characters such as Troy—who had been educated at Casterbridge Grammar School, and was a clerk to a lawyer, and then a sergeant in the Eleventh Dragon Guard. He was a stranger to the world of *Far from the Madding Crowd.* He falls in love with Fanny and then Bathsheba. Eventually he wrenches the very frame of life of this community and is responsible for much of what follows. In *The Woodlanders* it is Fitzpiers and Mrs. Charmond who bring about the disaster that overtakes some of the major characters that inevitably affects the minor rustic characters, too. The vicar in *Under the Greenwood Tree* falls in this category.

Grace, Fancy Day and Clym may be considered as the "insider-outsiders" whose doings affect the rustic community even though they are unsympathetic to the rustics themselves. These characters are not strictly outsiders but expose the community to the influences that they bring with them from outside.

It is interesting that such a rustic character usually stands in a transitional position and becomes the centre of a conflict in which both sides claim him or her.[9] An attempt to find roots on the part of such a character while trying to remain loyal to both sides not only generally does not succeed, but results in a sense of alienation and deracination. In *The Woodlanders* Grace's awareness of the outside world through her superior education clashes with her allegiance to her father and the old world order he symbolises. She is rendered unhappy and suffers largely on account of having to make drastic decisions that involve making choices put forward by her conflicting desires.

The rustic characters are usually old and middle-aged men. Sometimes, rarely though, we come across a woman among them such as mother Cuxson in *The Mayor of Casterbridge* or Grandmother Martin in *Two on a Tower.*[10] Such characters go to work, earn their livelihood and pursue various other chores. But to appreciate in depth the shifting hues of the chiaroscuro of life and human nature seems to be their primary interest and intention. Their sense of humour and a cynical eye, proverbial wisdom and a mellow crustedness that mark their personalities let them stand aloof from the surroundings. They are concerned yet detached. An untoward happening, a death or a disaster merely confirms their wisdom or occasionally adds to it. These occurrences do not affect them. It is with remarkable detachment and stoic disinterestedness, then, that they reflect on what concerns them most, the actions of the major characters and their implications in the novels. They judge the doings of others and are just in their judgements—more than just, they are hard, sometimes even unjust. Their detached coldness precludes sympathy and therefore mercy. When a character suffers on account of his own actions, they do not lament or offer pity but merely take note of the nemesis that befalls such a character. This brings them close to their counterparts in the Greek drama.[11] In thus observing the world and commenting on the deeds of men they perform the true function of a chorus. In *Far from the Madding Crowd* when Bathsheba decides to do without her bailiff, we hear:

> A headstrong maid, that's what she is—and won't listen to no advice at all. Pride and vanity have ruined many a cobbler's Dog. Dear, dear. When I think o'it I sorrows like a man on travail.

To Oak, who is keen to know about her, they give information about Bathsheba's parents:

> "I knew them a little," said Jacob Smallbury; "but they were townsfolk, and didn't live here. They have been dead for years. Father, what sort of people were misses's father and mother?"
>
> "Well," said the Malster, "he wasn't much to look at; but she was a lovely woman. He was fond of her as his sweetheart."

Such comments and observations do not merely enlighten the reader; they are meant for other characters in the novel too. Eustacia thus overhears about Clym's return, his education and—a typical Shakespearean device—learns about other Benedictine possibilities: "I say, Sam, she and Clym Yeobright would make a very pretty pigeon-pair—hey?"

And they ask questions, providing opportunities for major characters to explain their motives. Clym tells a group of them, "I thought our life here was contemptible. To oil your boots instead of blacking them, to dust your coat with a switch instead of a brush," and that he had decided to give up his way of life in the city. Having learnt about Clym from Clym himself, they as usual go on to reflect:

> "He'll never carry it out in the world," said Fairway. "In a few weeks he'll learn to see this otherwise."
>
> "'Tis goodhearted of the youngman," said another. "But for my part, I think he'd better mind his business."

Similarly, we learn from the group talk in *The Woodlanders* about Grace's mother and Fitzpiers learns from the peasant about Mrs. Charmond's intended visit again.

Often in their comments they tend to assess and measure the import of the events and actions in the larger contexts and thus provide social commentary and evaluative comments that "place" the action in proper perspective and to a degree condition our response to the work as a whole.

The pessimistic view of life that Hardy projects in his novels has given him the reputation of a grim and solemn writer. The exuberance and spontaneity of humour in the novels of Hardy has generally not been given due importance.[12] The comic element as found in the dialogues, episodes and incidents in the rustic characters must surely have been one reason for the popularity of Hardy's novels.[13] Externally the comic element derives from the peculiarities of speech and diction and behaviour. Wit sometimes functions as irony:[14] sarcasm, hyperbole, and paradoxes abound. Humour tends to reveal itself in the varied aspects of the situations involving rustic characters in various episodes. The essential human nature is revealed, and wit and irony tend to add to it a corrective critical dimension.

The action in *Under the Greenwood Tree* is essentially comic and it is the rustic humour that predominates here (as in the other novels of Hardy). There is a whole host of characters who are delightfully humorous: Grandfather William with his face like the sunny side of a ripe ribstone-pippin; Geoffrey Day with a wife whose "doom it was to be nobody's wife in wide universe. But she made up her mind that she would, and did it twice over. Doom? Doom is nothing beside an elderly woman"; an eccentric Mrs. Day who insists on doing spring cleaning on the day of Fancy's wedding; and of course Thomas Leaf who keeps sinking into oblivion.

There are similar comic incidents and episodes in other novels. Almost never is there a trace of grossness in any humorous episode. The gentle, sombre touches of humour deepen our sense of tragedy, and are often reminiscent of the comic episodes in Shakespeare's tragedies. The only fit match for the gravediggers of Shakespeare is perhaps Jan Coggan in *Far from the Madding Crowd* who goes to bring back the body of Fanny and her child.

Oak reproaches him for wasting time on the way.

> "Nobody can hurt a dead woman," at length said Coggan, with the precision of a machine "All that could be done for her is done—she is beyond us: and why should a man put himself in tearing hurry for lifeless clay that can neither fear nor see, and don't know what you do with her at all? If she would have been alive I would have been the first to help. If she now wanted victuals and drink, I'd pay for it, money down. But she's dead, and no speed of ours will bring her to life. The woman's past us—time spent upon her is thrown away: why should we hurry to do what is not required? Drink, shepherd, and be friends, for tomorrow we may be like her."

Despite the highly realistic portrayal of the rustic characters with their essential rootedness in the note of earthy common sense and traditional proverbial wisdom, there is an unmistakable aura of glamour about them: "the faintest atmosphere of poetry laps them round"; perhaps a degree of idealization saves the rustic characters from degenerating into grossness or vulgarity.

But the romanticization of these characters need not be assumed to give them the status of Hardy's mouthpiece. Hardy's complex and philosophical view of life is embodied in richly wrought works of art and such simplistic devices are foreign to Hardy's art. About the rustic characters, Hardy himself seems to have had no illusions. They for him do not constitute a Utopian-Arcadian world or any golden age whose passing away he seeks to lament. The heartless elimination of a way of life is something that Hardy surely seeks to draw attention to. The depopulation of the countryside, resulting in the destruction of a stable community and a traditional society was to him a deeply regrettable phenomenon and he depicted it in *Tess.*[15]

The world of Hardy, then, is a changeless world. What makes up the past of Wessex is a long continuum punctuated by births and deaths, marriages and rituals, customs and superstitions. The slow rhythm that marks the life of the rustic community is disturbed by the rooting out of the apple tree and the pulling down of a wooden cider house is the mark of "stirring times." They speak the voice of history—"history-in-process"—and their rambling narratives and gossip record the personal, social and intellectual history of the times.[16] But in the novels of Hardy they do not merely carry the burden of the novelist's philosophy, world-view or a message. They enrich the works of Hardy as a powerful metaphor, emobodying within them the essence of the creative impulse, and, most unobtrusively, perform the poetic function of channeling our response to the vital centre of Hardy's art.

NOTES

1. Hardy was brought up in a peasant community and had, among his close relatives, carpenters, cobblers, labourers, bricklayers, fan servants, journeyman joiners, servants and teachers. His maternal grandmother was a yeoman farmer's daughter and his father an artisan and a self-employed mason, though later he built up a small business and at one stage employed eight men and a boy. See Robert Gittings, *Young Thomas Hardy*, ch 2. W.J. Dawson writes (*The Makers of English Fiction* [1905]): "The secret of Hardy's unique power in rendering rural scenes, is that they are essential to himself. They are part of his own blood and fiber. They belong to his heritage as peasant and woodlander, and are expressive of his temperament." Later David Cecil similarly felt that "brought up in a peasant community, [Hardy] can only successfully vitalize characters of a peasant-like simplicity. This cuts out the Knight-Angel type." But Cecil, as Wotton remarks, made it sound like a major disqualification; see *Towards a Materialist Criticism* (Goldenbridge, Ireland: Gill & Macmillan, 1985), p. 152.
2. Hardy's dialogue was criticized by many early reviewers. The Warton Professor of English at Oxford remarked that Jude and Sue talk like an Ibsen translation. Others constantly referred to his oddities of style, "monstrous paraphrases" and "specimens of the worst 'penny-a-liner's' language"; "people talk as no people talked before"; "over-academic phraseology." Edmund Gosse wrote: "Sue and Jude talk a sort of University Extension jargon that breaks the heart." (*Cosmopolis*, January 1896, p. 69) The speech of the rustic characters was faulted even more vehemently by the early reviewers of Hardy. R.H. Hutton found their wit and 'intellectual' banter and their biblical wit quite incredible: "George Eliot never confuses her own ideas with those of her dramatic figures, as Mr. Hardy seems to us so often to do." (*Spectator,* no. 8, December 19, 1874, p. 1598) *Spectator* [no. 16] noted that they frequently lapse into educated speech. A reviewer in the *Blackwoods* (March 1879) commented: "He never serves himself with a plain phrase, if he can find anything more far-fetched; and even those humorous peasants who used sometimes to remind us of Shakespeare's gravediggers and Dogberrys begin to talk like books—Mr. Hardy's books, that is to say." 'Britten' wrote in the *Athenaeum* (November 18, 1882, p. 658): "We must still take leave to doubt whether one Dorsetshire village ever produced quite so many Touchstones at one and the same time."
3. To a certain extent Hardy's rustic dialogues remained superior even in his later works.
4. Liddy, Bathsheba's maid, is another character, in *Far from the Madding Crowd*, whose small act encouraging Bathsheba to send a valentine to Boldwood, in fact, is to a great extent wholly responsible for the tragedy that engulfs Boldwood.
5. As also by Hardy's highly vivid descriptions which were appreciated by

Hardy's early reviewers. An anonymous reviewer in *Spectator* (April 22, 1871, p. 482): "[Hardy] has, too, one other talent of a remarkable kind—sensitiveness to scenic and atmospheric effects, and to their influence on the mind, and the power of rousing similar sensitiveness in his readers." See also Joan Grundy, *Hardy & the Sister Arts* (London: Macmillan, 1979), p. 61.

6. Of course, in each novel there are important minor rustic characters who do not formally belong to *the group*. Not all the rustic characters in *Under the Greenwood Tree*, for instance, belong to the choir. Creedle in *The Woodlanders* is not a timber worker.
7. Characters like Diggory Ven and Marty South perform such a function but they are better classified as secondary characters. Moreover, they are too deeply individualized to be able to form part of a group.
8. Cf. George Wotton: Hardy's perception of the purposelessness of existence determined his tragic view of life as well as his 'resignation,' his acceptance of the inevitable and, like Shakespeare, he regarded the 'manifestation of a purposeless world as tragedy of an insignificant, petty and hopeless nature." (p. 158) Wotton's quotation is from Helen Garwood, "Thomas Hardy: An Illustration of the Philosophy of Schopenhauer." (1911)

   But see Lawrence J. Serzyk, "The Coming Universal Wish Not to Live in Hardy's 'Modern Novels,'" *Nineteenth-Century Fiction*, 26:4 (March 1972), pp. 419-35. See also William Clyde Brown, "The Ambiguities of Thomas Hardy," *Notre-Dame English Journal: A Journal of Religion in Literature*, 15:3 (1983), pp. 85-103. Brown argues that in his later poems Hardy expressed the possibility that the blind, amoral universe, universal power might reform. David Lodge notes that in *The Woodlanders* Hardy offers a Darwinian view of nature as harsh and competitive, and a pastoral view, which reveals nature as responsive to "the heart that loves her." See John Bayley, "The Love Story in *Two on a Tower, Thomas Hardy Annual*, 1 (1983), pp. 60-70. Frank Giordano remarks ("A Reading of Hardy's *A Set of Country Songs* [*Victorian Poetry*, 17, 1/2 (1979), pp. 98-107]) that there is more humour and less tragedy in Hardy than one might anticipate. In fact in his verse Hardy rejects the constraints of "realism" which results both in illusion as well as disillusion. In lyric poetry Hardy revelled in the freedom that he found from having to indulge in cause-effect exercises that most of his novels tended to be. See, for an excellent analysis, Margaret Mahar, "Hardy's Poetry of Renunciation," *English Literary History*, 45, 2 (1978), pp. 303-24; also T.B. Tomlinson, "Hardy's Universe: *Tess of d'Urbervilles*," *The Critical Review*, 16, pp. 19-38.
9. These characters obviously do not belong to the class that is being considered here.
10. But otherwise Hardy's novels have generally been considered as "woman-centred" and have proved fertile ground for feminist critics. See Patricia Ingham, *Thomas Hardy* (Feminist Reading Series; New York: Harvester Wheatsheaf, 1989).

11. Some of the major novels have been analyzed on the lines of Greek tragedies and a great deal of emphasis has been placed on the role of the minor rustic characters in this context. See for instance, Richard Benvenuto, *The Return of the Native* as a Tragedy in Six Books," *Nineteenth-Century Fiction*, 26:1 (1971), pp. 83-93; Duane D. Edwards, '*The Mayor of Casterbridge* as Aeschylean Tragedy," *Studies in the Novel*, 4, pp. 608-18; and Lawrence J. Starzyk, "Hardy's *Mayor*: Anti-traditional Basis of Tragedy," *Studies in the Novel*, 4, pp. 492-607.
12. See Bryn Caless, "Hardy's Humour," *Thomas Hardy Annual*, 3 (1985), pp. 111-28. Caless argues that Hardy's humour is most potent when his emotional involvement with a character leads to the latter's realization of the incongruity of the situation.
13. I have found no evidence, specially in the reviews of Hardy's novels, that he was given any recognition for these qualities. See *Hardy: The Critical Heritage* (Lonodn: RKP, 1963). The novelist and critic and admissions tutor Antonia Byatt at University College, London, compiled a popularity index of writers ("fun and not statistically rigorous"): "Figures show shifting fashions in the reading habits of our brightest young people who are going to read English at the University. Hardy fared better" than, say, Nobokov and Updike. See Philip Howard, "Bronte up, Pinter down, Golding dashes in," *The* [London] *Times*, January 4, 1982, p. 1.
14. Cf.: "To check her tears she turned, and seeing a book in window-bench, took it up. 'Look Marty, this is Psalter. He was not a religious man; but he was pure and perfect in his heart. Shall we read a palm over him?' 'O yes, we will, with all my heart!' Grace opened the brown book, which poor Giles had kept at hand mainly for the convenience of whetting his penknife upon its leather covers." *The Woodlanders*, ch. xlxxx.
15. It is an error to identify "the greatest delineator in prose of rural England" with the one who inherited the Marxian mantle as Raymond Williams (*The Country and the City* [London: Chatto & Windus, 1973] and Merryn Williams, *Thomas Hardy and Rural England* [London: Macmillan, 1972]) attempt to do. Hardy's concern in his novels is less with the state of contemporary agriculture than with "the vast and changeless setting" which forms the backdrop to the human drama Hardy focuses on. See, for a detailed discussion, Arthur Pollard, "Hardy and Rural England," *Thomas Hardy Annual*, 1 (1983), pp. 33-43. See also Rosemary Sumner, "The Experimental and the Absurd in *Two on a Tower, Thomas Hardy Annual*, 1 (1983), pp. 71-81 and Donald Baker, "Thomas Hardy: Prophet of Total Theatre," *Comparative Drama*, 7, pp. 121-34. Baker attempts to show that Hardy anticipated Artaud's multi-media symbolistic style of theatrical production.
16. See Samuel Hynes, "Hardy's Historians," *Thomas Hardy Annual*, 5 (1987), pp. 102-18.

I am grateful to Prof. David Baron (Acadia University) for his comments on an earlier draft of this paper.

Angles of Vision and Questions of Gender in *Far from the Madding Crowd*

JUDITH BRYANT WITTENBERG

One of the more controversial issues in recent Hardy criticism concerns his attitudes toward and fictional treatments of women. For example, in a 1975 article, Katharine Rogers says that, although "Thomas Hardy repeatedly shaped his characters and plots to show his sympathy with women and his awareness of the disadvantages society laid upon them, . . . if we look beyond Hardy's conscious intentions to such things as repeated themes, incidental comments, and subtle differences in the presentation of analogous male and female characters, we find evidence that he could not altogether overcome the sexual stereotypes of his culture."[1] Despite the fact that critics are unlikely to reach any consensus on this topic in the near future, it remains a fruitful one. Readerly awareness of Hardy's ambivalence on this particular subject provides a useful avenue to understanding the sort of larger dialectic that gives his best fiction much of its tension and power. This essay will examine one aspect of Hardy's method—his preoccupation with sight-centered matters and their relationship to his depiction of women and their problems in *Far from the Madding Crowd*—and the way in which it embodies a dialogue having both philosophical and psychoanalytic implications that places Hardy's work in a larger context.

I

Perception and its role in both intellectual and emotional development has been important to thinkers other than aesthetic theoreticians such as E.H. Gombrich and Rudolph Arnheim.[2] Several English philosophers, most notably John Locke, George Berkeley, and David Hume, all of whose works Hardy was familiar with, had, by the end of the eighteenth century, elaborated upon the compelling problems of epistemological definition in a Cartesian universe and collectively posited a world in which the seeing "eye" was the point of origin for the knowing "I." Later psychoanalytic theorists, some of whose work Hardy anticipates in intriguing ways,[3] such as Freud, regarded the drive to see as fundamental to the instinct for knowledge and as basic to the process of awakening desire for the love-object during later sexual development.[4] Thus the eye becomes throughout life, particularly for males, one of the important erotogenic zones.[5] Seeing can also, of course, lead to trauma and thence to neurosis or perversion.[6]

While much of Hardy's fiction is informed by post-Lockean and psychoanalytic theories of seeing, *Far from the Madding Crowd* (1874), his fourth published novel and the first great work of his career, represents a culmination of his treatment of the various visual preoccupations that are evident in all the work of his early period. Persistently and complexly present in the text are several thematic and technical elements arising from Hardy's concepts of the individual eye as the inlet of sense knowledge and as a sexual force, of the way in which one's sense of self is essentially created in perceptual moments, and of the collective eye as the locus of moral judgment; moreover, Hardy relates such issues in intriguing ways to questions of gender and control. Though these elements are clearly subordinated to the story, they underlie both its basic assumptions and its presentation.

The early pages of the novel serve in this respect as a paradigm both of the entire work and of all Hardy's fiction of this period, compressing an extraordinary number of sight-centered components into our introduction to Gabriel Oak and Oak's meeting with Bathsheba Everdene and linking them to crucial aspects of male and female roles. They constitute a rich exemplification of Hardy's conception of the complex role which vision plays in life and in the fiction-making process. Several physical points of station (i.e., the distance of the spectator from the nearest point of the "picture" he sees), each with significant implications, are juxtaposed in these opening pages, the first of them, that of the narrator, being the most important to this and all of Hardy's fiction. The spectatorial narrator begins by offering a Halsian portrait of a ruddy, smiling Oak that obviously applies to the general as well as the specific instance, going on, in a confident, somewhat amused tone, to describe Oak's behaviour, character, and religious views, contrasting the limited "mental picture formed by his neighbours" with the things available to the notice of "thoughtful persons," (2) among whom the narrator obviously belongs.[7]

Oak's point of view is the second one offered and the second in importance. Hardy shifts us to him, "glancing over the hedge" in a typical voyeuristic moment of the benign variety. He sees Bathsheba preening on her wagon and judges her as vain, remaining himself seemingly unaroused, but the more libidinal moments of peeping which immediately follow are portended by the cat who "affectionately survey[s] the small birds around." Women are often identified with birds in Hardy's fiction (as in much earlier writing in English), and the cat's gaze, though idle, is unquestionably predatory, like the male gaze.

Although there is no overt sexual component in Oak's second instance of peeping at Bathsheba, its basic nature is implied by the narrator's comment that "he saw her in a bird's eye view, as Milton's Satan first saw Paradise." (14) The invocation of one of the most sexually destructive voyeurs in English literature suggests what sort of unconscious motives underlie Oak's voyeuristic impulses. Although when he next peeps through the loophole of his hut at Bathsheba behaving in a strikingly unconventional manner on her horse, he is described as merely amused and astonished, he has obviously been aroused, for shortly afterward he looks at her "proportions," Hardy's euphemism for her figure, "with a long consciousness of pleasure." (19) Hardy's narrator comments on the sexuality involved—"Rays of male vision seem to have a tickling effect upon virgin faces in rural districts"—while Oak himself seems to become aware of the violating penetration of his gaze, guiltily, withdrawing his eyes from Bathsheba "as suddenly as if he had been caught in a theft." (20-21)

In a moment with similar implications, farmer Boldwood's sexual awakening from long years of celibacy is revealed in a phrase about his using his gaze in a penetrating way: "[He] had never before inspected a woman with the very centre and force of his glance." (134) Here, as in the depiction of Aeneas Manston's forceful eye in *Desperate Remedies*, Hardy is quite explicit in his treatment of the eye as a substitute sexual organ and of seeing as not only a prologue to but also a displaced form of sexual possession of the female. That Hardy was far more candid in his treatment of sexual matters than his Victorian contemporaries has long been acknowledged; by examining Hardy's recurrent depiction of the male gaze, we can see that candor was of an extraordinary range.

How deeply disconcerting Oak's gaze is to Bathsheba is made clear by her response. She blushes deeply, her blush signifying embarrassment and possibly some unwitting form of tumescence, and she later refuses to look at him, apparently feeling "that Gabriel's espial had made her an indecorous woman." Her sense of vulnerability manifestly has a social as well as a sexual component, for, as Hardy's narrator points out, "as without law there is no sin, without eye there is no indecorum." (21) Here, as throughout the novel, we are shown how the awareness of being seen by some form of the collective eye, the location of moral-social judgements, engenders anxiety and prompts action that ranges from efforts at self-control to rash alternations of plans. So Sergeant Troy's fury at being publicly kept waiting at the altar by Fanny Robin leads him to cancel their wedding and, in effect, to destroy her life.

Though Troy's anger at being seen in a humiliating moment precipitates the central tragedy of the novel, it is usually Bathsheba who, like many of Hardy's heroines, evinces the sensitivity to being seen and subsequently to being judged, that is a direct consequence of the sense of vulnerability. During her first appearance in the cornmarket, she is appalled by her awareness of "eyes everywhere!" (104) Then in one of her early intimate conversations with Boldwood (it occurs, perhaps significantly, shortly after he loses his ocular "virginity" and turns his gaze upon her), she becomes "afraid they will notice us." (146) In a similar moment of intimacy with Troy, she says to him anxiously, "My workfolk see me following you about the field and are wondering. O, this is dreadful!" (203) Later, her increased isolation and status as an object on which the collective eye is focused is symbolized by her moment alone in the circus tent when "many eyes were turned upon her." She "make[s] the best of it," (393) however, in a manner that signifies her growing maturity and portends her protectiveness of another person exposed to the social gaze, when she removes her husband's corpse from Boldwood's parlor, unwilling to leave it "neglected for folks to stare at." (439) Thus throughout the novel characters implicitly face the judgments of the community as they explicitly confront its eyes, for "they see" is, as always in the fictive Hardyan world, an inevitable prologue to "they say."

II

There is, of course, along with a felt sense of social and sexual vulnerability, an element of paranoia in this hypersensitivity to being seen. Hardy may have been anticipating (and articulating) some of the linkages between paranoia and the constitution of the ego made by Jacques Lacan decades later, when his formulation of the theory of the *stade du miroir* grew out of his early studies of paranoia, and by Jean-Paul Sartre, who pointed out that "the Other is not only the one whom I see but the one who sees me."[8] Certainly there are some suggestive mirror scenes in *Far from the Madding Crowd* that seem, if not pre-Lacanian, at least evocative of his concept of the self awakening to consciousness in awareness of the alienated non-self, the mirrored Other. When Oak first sees Bathsheba in the opening pages of the novel, she is gazing into a looking-glass where she "survey[s] herself attentively," (4) smiling and then blushing. "Seeing her reflection blush, [she] blushed the more." (5) Oak adjudges her action as motivated by simple vanity arising from narcissism of a sort that also made George Eliot's vain heroines gaze into mirrors, as in *Adam Bede*; but Hardy's narrator reminds us that Oak's assessment may be inadequate, for it is based on "conjecture," and, in fact, "nobody knows" why she smiled. (5)

What is also important is that Bathsheba comes into being as it were, in that mirrored moment, comes alive for herself for Oak, the narrator, and for us. The most vivid female character of Hardy's early fiction springs into existence in the instant she gazes at herself in a looking-glass. In like fashion, one of Hardy's most memorable male characters, William Boldwood, discovers himself, so to speak, as he looks into a mirror. Bathsheba begins the awakening process by sending him the valentine with a red seal that appears "as a blot of blood on the retina of his eye," portending its ultimate passional and murderous effect. (112) Boldwood places it in the frame of a mirror, and in looking at it again also really looks at himself, perhaps for the first time. His "nervous excitability" is disclosed to Boldwood in the form of his "reflected features," (114) and though the excitability will finally have ruinous effects on himself and others, it signifies the inception of his efforts to participate emotionally in the life around him. Boldwood's physical awareness of himself in a glass mirrors his momentous awareness of another person. In both instances, Hardy strikingly presents central characters beginning the complex interaction of self and world that is signalled by the interaction of self and reflected self. Hardy's mirrors are more than symbols of simple vanity; they are tools for intensifying characters' awareness of themselves and heralding the intense way in which they will "live" for us.

Thus in these brief opening scenes, Hardy manages technically and thematically to posit a series of points of station, each subordinate—and psychologically related—to the previous one as he moves from the narrator to Oak to Bathsheba, simultaneously presenting in complex fashion his essential concept of the eye as it functions in the epistemological, sexual, and socio-moral processes. The pages which follow variously reiterate these techniques and concepts in a series of highly visual scenes of great power as we watch the pastoral melodrama being enacted. These characters may in some sense be archetypal figures out of ballad or the French *pastourelle*, but aspects of both their psyches and their situations derive from Hardy's own ongoing preoccupations and from his efforts to explore the problems inevitably faced by individuals who might find themselves at variance with dominant forces in nineteenth-century English society.

The way in which Bathsheba is introduced, admired, and controlled by the male point of view is entirely relevant to her characterization in the largest sense. Her complex struggles with the various male "looks" she confronts are mirrored by her difficulties with the patriarchal society. Her story depicts both the possibilities open to, and the limitations imposed upon, a spirited woman who tries to affirm her individuality in a society unready to accept unconventional behavior, particularly on the part of a woman. From the very outset, Bathsheba reveals her ambivalence about becoming, like most women, a visual and sexual possession; she wishes to live by her own rules and to take charge of her life. She early asserts that she has no sweetheart because "*I hate* to be thought men's property in that way" and that she is interested in "being a bride at a wedding [only] if I could be one without having a husband." (32-33) She possesses articulateness, almost always an emblem of superiority in Hardy's fiction, glibly teasing and criticizing Oak in their early encounters, and she is, says Hardy's narrator, a "novelty among women—one who finished a thought before beginning the sentence which was to convey it." (23)

Not only is she intellectually in charge, she is physically assertive, as in the scenes in which she runs after Oak to clear up a misunderstanding and in which she rescues him from near death, dashing milk on his face, holding him in her lap, and unbuttoning his collar in a tableau that intriguingly suggests both a *pieta* and a seduction scene with Bathsheba as the sexual aggressor. Oak ironically seems far more "female" than she in these early scenes, passively falling asleep like Tess Durbeyfield at crucial moments, struggling with the language he cannot use effectively, and then appearing as a visual "object" at the Casterbridge hiring fair; the role reversal is striking.

Bathsheba soon progresses from emotional and intellectual control to economic control when her uncle leaves her his farm in recognition of her capabilities. The "unpracticed girl" develops into a "supervising and cool woman." (56) When we see her framed in her bedroom window in a visual moment typical of Hardy's heroines, the scene has a crucial difference, for she is there giving orders to her male employees. When she makes the speech announcing her decision to be her own bailiff, thus augmenting her already considerable responsibility, she performs with great confidence, vowing to "do my best" and to "astonish you all." (93) Women farmers were not unknown in Hardy's day—there were quite a few in the Dorset area, most of them widows—but they were certainly uncommon in fiction; strong, unmarried females running their own farming operations would not appear in works by major writers until the creation of Willa Cather's Alexandra Bergson and Ellen Glasgow's Dorinda Oakley in the early twentieth century.

Both Bathsheba's competence and her desire to succeed are impressive, but she soon encounters a series of difficulties that reveal the dangers for a woman of being alone, being different, and being a cynosure. The first of these is criticism from the denizens of the malthouse who serve as a rustic chorus. They call her "proud as a lucifer," a "very vain feymell," (48) denigrate her as a "tomboy" and a "headstrong maid" and doubt that "she can car' on alone." (76, 118) Much of this is petty or jealous, and Oak often attempts to defend her, but even he irrationally blames Bathsheba for the threat posed to the year's crops by the harvest supper debacle, attributing it to "the instability of a woman." (279) Even when the rustics are not being overtly critical, they subtly deprecate with their praise, as when they call her "a handsome body." (70) Despite her strengths, Bathsheba cannot escape the reductive situation of being a "sight," a physical object to the male eyes around her.

Though Bathsheba is more fortunate than many of Hardy's heroines in having confidantes and being an integral member of a closely knit community, she often feels "friendless" and "unprotected," (226, 233) with "nobody in the world to fight my battles for me." (235) She also, in spite of her desire for independence, feels some pressure to accept a worthwhile offer of marriage, because "in every point of view, ranging from politic to passionate, it was desirable that she, a lonely girl, should marry." (148) About a decade before Hardy began work on *Far from the Madding Crowd*, an article in the *National Review* had lamented the "redundancy" of the single women in England, "who, in place of completing, sweetening, and embellishing the existence of others, are compelled to lead an independent and incomplete existence of their own." The writer called women of strength and intelligence "abnormal" and suggested that no woman should hold a responsible job because "the cerebral organization of the female is far more delicate than that of man."[9]

Certainly Bathsheba's behaviour in much of the novel suggests that she is open to arguments such as these, for she seriously entertains proposals from three men who are not of her caliber in some respects, and ends up marrying two of them. While marriage may improve her social status, the first one imperils her economic well-being, because Troy begins to squander her money on betting, after using some of it to purchase his discharge from the military. There is some evidence that Hardy intended this position of the novel to be set after 1870, because that year saw the passage of the Married Women's Protective Act, which no longer made the acquisition of a woman's property by her husband a foregone conclusion; Troy says, "I have [no money] but what my wife gives me." (300) Nevertheless, Bathsheba apparently feels powerless to prevent her husband's improvident use of her modest wealth.

III

While various degrees of community hostility to her independent life and her sensitivity to the social pressure to marry affect Bathsheba to some degree, direct coercion by men who are representative members of the patriarchal society have the most powerful influence on her. Boldwood, with his burning eyes and coercive speeches, is a man of some substance and community standing, so the pressure she receives from him is simultaneously seuxal, linguistic, and socio-economic. Sergeant Troy, whose power over Bathsheba seems almost exclusively sexual and rhetorical is also in certain respects an emblem of the English patriarchy, for his father was a nobleman, his step-father a physician, and he himself is a non-commissioned military officer.

Bathsheba's extreme ambivalence toward what these suitors represent is revealed by her varying responses, many of them originating in her reaction to being seen, like those in her early encounter with Oak mentioned above. Although she has moments of feeling burdened by her femaleness, she also expresses a desire to be "tamed" and a fear of being too "mannish" that make her receptive to visual-sexual advances. Thus she initially seeks to elicit Boldwood's invasive gaze, finding it "depressing that the most dignified and valuable man in the parish should withhold his eyes," (110) and feeling triumphant once his eyes are "following her everywhere" (135); however, she later finds his stares—and him—too intense and is repelled. In her first encounter with Troy, as his emblematic spurs become entangled with the fragile stuff of her gown in a symbolic moment, she feels assailed by his gaze, which is "too strong to be received point-black with her own." (185) Yet because the strength of Troy's ardent eyes is reinforced by his prowess at rhetoric and sword-play, Bathsheba's defenses are rapidly breached; Troy's linguistic and physical adroitness, coupled with his sexual aggressiveness, make him an almost irresistible emblem of male power.

In the famous sword scene, with its highly charged sexual elements on which critics have commented,[10] Troy deftly wields his phallic and dangerous weapon, controlling it with his keen eyes; in the process he reduces Bathsheba to a mass of sexually quivering femininity and captures a fitting trophy, a lock of her hair. Aside from the sword, however, there are other visual and auditory elements of the scene with sexual associations whose presence would, even in the absence of the sword, portend the process taking place. The sun, that recurrent symbol of masculine power often visible in Hardy's fiction at traumatic moments, is here a "bristling ball of gold" with "long, luxuriant rays" sweeping the feathery ferns that in turn caress Bathsheba. (208) In this scene, the sun's bristling signifies its potency, as it did earlier in the novel, where its reflection in the sheepmen's shears is "strong enough to blind a weak-eyed man," (165) and as it appeared in Hardy's personal memorandum of 1973 about the "brazen sun, bristling with a thousand spines, which struck into and tormented my eyes."[11] The sun makes of Troy's sword "a living thing." Bathsheba's arrival has been heralded by her "rustling" amid the ferns, just as her first meeting with Troy was signalled by a "rustle of footsteps" (183); rustling was obviously for Hardy a sexually evocative sound, associated in the *Life* with Julia Martin's silken dresses and often a factor in scenes in his fiction with emotional and erotic overtones.

The confluence of strong sun, redness, and the sound of rustling in the opening paragraphs of the chapter depicting the sword exercise all portend what is to come, even before Troy unsheathes his weapon. In the scene which follows, the point of station is Bathsheba's, as she watches and experiences her "ravishing" by Troy's impressive strength and dexterity. Significantly, his eye is connected to and necessary for his control of the sword; she can see it "always keenly measuring her breadth and outline." (211) The uniting of eye and sword in a dazzling display of masculine power creates in Bathsheba a response that seems virtually orgasmic. She is "enclosed in firmament of light, and of sharp hisses," aroused and overwhelmed, after which "she felt like one who has sinned a great sin." (211-13) Interestingly, Hardy's narrator intervenes at the most intense moment in the scene, generalizing and explaining and thus asserting himself both as a physical presence and as one capable of having the "last word," revealing in the process that he is another of the male forces inhibiting Bathsheba's freedom.

Yet the novel is balanced, and Hardy depicts two other characters whose difficulties parallel or illuminate Bathsheba's—one male, the other female. Boldwood is the male, at the outset much like her in his self-sufficiency and independence, subsequently succumbing with great rapidity, as did she, to the suggestive presence of a sprightly and attractive member of the opposite sex. Both are punished quite severely for their sudden sexual responsiveness; Bathsheba is consigned to will-lessness and bitter disillusionment, Boldwood to mounting frustration that culminates in murderous anger.

Fanny Robin is the female character whose situation both parallels and contrasts with that of Bathsheba. When the novel was first published, reviewers suggested that Hardy had drawn his material from *Adam Bede*; if so, he divided Hetty Sorrel into two characters, both seduced and in some sense abandoned by the dashing soldier, eliminating the Dinah Moris figure. What is also interesting is that Fanny, a servant impregnated by the man she hopes to marry, faces a plight in which Hardy's mother and grandmother found themselves. Yet they married, while Fanny becomes the archetypal fallen woman of Victorian melodrama and visual art, a wandering outcast pictured most often in the dark and snow, like Eppie's mother in *Silas Marner* or the women in painting such as Frederick Walker's *The Last Path,* Richard Redgrave's *The Outcast*, and the last panel of Augustus Egg's *Past and Present.* As so often in Hardy's novels, he uses visuals as indices of a psychological condition; in Fanny's case, her vulnerability is indicated by the depiction of her seen from a distance as "small," a "spot" on the landscape. (97)

Appropriately, since both Fanny and Bathsheba are victims of the predatory Troy, Hardy suggests similarities between the two. In moments when Bathsheba confronts romantic predicaments, she is described as a "robin," (30, 218) and both women are shown in moments of desperation "unfemininely" running after a man in order to clear up a misunderstanding. At the same time, significant differences between the two reveal that, as the narrator points out, "their fates might be supposed to stand in some respects as contrasts to each other." (337) While Fanny is weakened by having no socio-economic power and little self-confidence, Bathsheba has a good deal of both; Fanny often seems hyper-feminine in her helplessness, while Bathsheba frequently stands her ground "manfully." Hardy tacitly underscores the contrasts between the two by showing them in alternating scenes. Bathsheba's confident speech to her workers is followed by the chapter depicting Fanny in the snow outside the barracks, even as the chapter describing Fanny's agonizing trip into Casterbridge is bracketed by two scenes of Bathsheba with her husband, both times in emblems of prosperity, her gig and her house. The women may be "sisters" in their susceptibility to male sexual power, but Bathsheba has other qualities that make survival possible. Some of these could be called masculine, so Hardy may be implying something about the merits of an androgynous model, because he also kills off, by the end of the novel, the highly feminine Fanny and the hyper-masculine Troy, concluding the work with the union of a strong woman and a man who has displayed a number of traits that might be described as "feminine."

At one point Bathsheba expresses her admiration for the goddess Diana, and even in times of great difficulty she exhibits strength and resolution that could identify her with that mythological figure, as in the moments when she staunchly helps Oak in his battle to save the hayricks from the thunderstorm and when she advises Liddy about coping with marriage, "stand your ground, and be cut to pieces." (351) Yet she is more than a female warrior, for she has significant moral strengths, showing remorse for her capricious treatment of Boldwood, revealing a sense of responsibility, on more than one occasion, for the hapless Fanny, and evincing compassion even for the husband who mistreated and then abandoned her. Here, as elsewhere in the novel, the changing nature of her interior situation is indicated in visual ways. She bravely confronts the "worrying perceptions" engendered by her traumatic discoveries of the lock of blond hair in Troy's watch and the corpse of Fanny's baby and reveals a protective and forgiving decency when she cradles Troy's body to rescue it from the stares of onlookers. By the end of the novel, she has grown in moral stature and been rewarded, not only with what promises to be a serene and comradely marriage but also with tributes from those crochety male voices, the rustics and the narrator. The former praise her bravery and honesty and the latter, in a memorable back handed compliment, calls her "the stuff of which great men's mothers are made." (436)

IV

If Bathsheba passes from an early phase marked by stubborn independence to a second one where she exhibits, as the narrator says, "too much womanliness to use her understanding to the best advantage," (214) falling into a state of listless dependency, she emerges finally as an individual capable of meshing both sorts of impulses. Her arrival at this final stage is signalled by her visit to Oak, a courageous and rather aggressive act, during which she coyly cajoles him into acknowledging his feelings for her, even as she has fully acknowledged to herself her emotional dependency on him; she thus evinces a harmonious blend of the masculine and the feminine. Oak, too, arrives at a point where he effectively meshes disparate tendencies. Early in the work he had seemed both to be somewhat "feminine" and to reveal qualities that would later prove problematic for Jude Fawley—a wish to improve his lot in life, a sympathetic concern for animals, and a moment of contemplating suicide by water; Oak's vulnerability is evinced by moments of being, like most of Hardy's women and like Jude, a visual "object" exposed to the investigative and occasionally dismissive stares of others. Yet he has strengths not shown by Jude—persistence and perceptiveness among them—and he also assumes an increasingly "masculine" socio-economic role, when his evident competence is rewarded by jobs as bailiff for Bathsheba and as the manager of Boldwood's property. At the same time, he never loses the tenderness that makes him so responsive to the plights of others and we come to view some of his passivity as an almost aggressive tenacity.

Thus the marriage of Oak and Bathsheba seems highly appropriate as an outgrowth of their separate arrivals at a point where the masculine and feminine in each of them are nicely integrated, for it represents the merging of those balanced individuals in a larger whole. Each has undergone, at differing times, the experiences of being both helpless and in control, of being both seen and seer, object and subject. Their angles of vision, so suggestively presented in the opening pages of the novel, have not only been juxtaposed but have attained a harmonious equilibrium. Hardy celebrates their union with the narrator's disquisition in the penultimate chapter, on the merits of camaraderie between men and women which "is unfortunately seldom superadded to love between the sexes, because men and women associate, not in their labours, but in their pleasures merely." (456) It is a moment, to be sure, calculated to remind us that if the consummate "eye" in the novel is that of the narrator, the dominant "I" is also, but the attainment of an equilibrated state between the male and female protagonists is singular in a Hardy novel.

NOTES

1. Katharine Rogers, "Women in Thomas Hardy," *Centennial Review*, 19 (1975), pp. 249-58.
2. In E.H. Gombrich, *Art and Illusion* (New York: Bollingen, 1965), and Rudolph Arnheim, *Art and Visual Perception* (Berkeley: University of California Press, 1954).
3. See Rosemary Sumner, *Thomas Hardy: Psychological Novelist* (New York: St. Martin's, 1981).
4. *The Standard Edition of the Complete Works of Sigmund Freud*, trans. James Strachey (London: Hogarth, 1953), VII, p. 156.
5. See, for example, Sandor Ferenczi, "On Eye Symbolism," in *First Contributions to Psychoanalysis*, trans. Ernest Jones (London: Hogarth, 1952), pp. 270-76.
6. See Otto Fenichel, *The Psychoanalytic Theory of Neurosis* (New York: Norton 1945), pp. 71-72, 92, 345-49; Otto Fenichel, "The Scoptophilic Instinct and Identification," *Collected Papers*, First Series (New York: Norton, 1953); David W. Allen, *The Fear of Looking* (Charlottesville: University of Virginia Press, 1974).
7. All page references are to the Wessex Edition (London: Macmillan, 1912-31). The spectatorial quality of Hardy's narrator has been commented on by, for example, J. Hillis Miller, *Thomas Hardy: Distance and Desire* (Cambridge: Belknap Press of Harvard University Press, 1970), pp. xii, 7; and David Lodge, "Thomas Hardy and Cinematographic Form," *Novel*, 7 (1974), p. 250.
8. Jacques Lacan, "The Mirror Stage as Formative of the Function of the I as Revealed in Psychoanalytic Experience," *Ecrits*, trans. Alan Sheridan (New York: Norton, 1977), pp. 1-7; Jean-Paul Sartre, *Being and Nothingness*, trans. Hazel Barnes (New York: Washington Square Press, 1966), p. 310.
9. W.R. Greg, "Why Are Women Redundant?" *National Review*, 14 (April 1862), pp. 434-60.
10. See Richard Carpenter, "The Mirror and the Sword: Imagery in *Far from the Madding Crowd*," *Nineteenth Century Fiction*, 18 (1964), pp. 331-45.
11. *The Personal Notebooks of Thomas Hardy*, ed. Richard H. Taylor (London: Macmillan, 1978), p. 14.

Passion and Flood in *Far from the Madding Crowd*

LEWIS HORNE

A reader of *Far from the Madding Crowd* could hardly fail to note how often the events of the novel work against the concept of a peaceful pastoral that the title leads him to expect. The nature of Hardy's world is succinctly given in Ian Gregor's generic description "the realist version of pastoral" and in Corin's speech that Gregor quotes from *As You Like It*: "I know the more one sickens, the worse at ease he is; and that he that wants money, means, and content, is without good friends; that the property of rain is to wet, and fire to burn; that good pasture makes fat sheep; and that a great cause of the night is lack of the sun."[1] The description in the stanza from Gray's "Elegy" that gives the novel its title is less of a way of life for the figures in that world than of an ideal. Peaceful life has to be earned. Sometimes at hard price. From a statement that concludes the novel's penultimate chapter a reader gathers that Gabriel and Bathsheba have succeeded by binding themselves through a particular kind of love:

> Theirs was that substantial affection which arises (if any arises at all) when the two who are thrown together begin first by knowing the rougher sides of each other's character, and not the best till further on, the romance growing up in the interstices of a mass of hard prosaic reality. This good-fellowship—*camaraderie*—usually occurring through similarity of pursuits, is unfortunately seldom superadded to love between the sexes, because men and women associate, not in their labours, but in their pleasures merely.[2]

Ian Gregor has made a further observation about the passage. Though he does not deny the lovers' achievement, he registers qualms about the aptness of the lines as a summary of the story, feeling that "in this speech . . . we can feel the pressure of the form of the novel, exerting itself against the story." A little further, he states: "Complacency, disdain, a dry judicial analysis these are the tones of that speech and they don't reflect back happily on the passionate and exuberant life which so much the novel has revealed."[3] Perhaps not. But Gregor omits the last sentence of the paragraph he quotes: "Where, however, happy circumstance permits its development, the compounded feeling proves itself to be the only love which is strong as death—the love which many waters cannot quench, nor the floods drown beside which the passion usually called by the name is evanescent as steam." (456-57)

This sentence makes a difference. It describes in metaphor the love Bathsheba and Gabriel have found. But in addition, as it draws on the Song of Solomon, it turns us back to the events of the novel and to the manner in which some of those events are presented. The analytical tone fades, and the sense of the natural world returns. We think of storm, stream, snow, of sheep-washing of tears. The imagery of water reminds us of the passions of the novel, turns our glance back to some of those "moments of vision." so characteristically Hardyean that point up something about the world Hardy has created and the individuals who live in it.

What Hardy's use of the passage from the Song of Solomon calls our attention to is a distinction between passion and love. His source speaks of love's strengths, and Hardy adds to it the statement about passion's brevity. When a reader observes Bathsheba's lovers—Oak, Boldwood, and especially Troy—he sees dramatized the activities and effects of passion as well as of love. At the same time, he can note the variety of ways in which Hardy uses the imagery of water to describe the inner storm derived from passion and love, both the extent to which the three men weather the storm and their manner of doing it.[4]

Gabriel's ability to survive the stresses of love—the floods of passion, as it were—is suggested in the early description of his hut on Norcombe Hill as "a small Noah's Ark on a small Ararat allowing the traditionary outlines and general form of the Ark which are followed by toy-makers." (10) A simple resemblance noted in an effort to sketch Gabriel's hut more vividly, the reference to the Ark is not without import, if seen in the context of later events of the story. Granted, this Ark has come to rest. But linking Gabriel with the figure of Noah gives him some power of survival over the element so destructive to the efforts of others. Still another image, frequently noted by readers, suggests likewise Gabriel's ability to assimilate experience of despair, something Boldwood is unable to do. After he loses his sheep,

> Oak raised his head, and wondering what he could do, listlessly surveyed the scene. By the outer margin of the pit was an oval pond, and over it hung the attenuated skeleton of a chrome yellow moon, which had only a few days to last—the morning star dogging her on

> the left hand. The pool glittered like a dead man's eye, and as the world awoke a breeze blew, shaking and elongating the reflection of the moon without breaking it, and turning the image of the star to a phosphoric streak upon the water. All this Oak saw and remembered. (41)

The picture is made striking through its grotesque features—"the attenuated skeleton," the "dogging" star, the "dead man's eye"—while the last sentence seals our impression that we have glimpsed Gabriel's inner world and noted the impact of the calamity upon him. But the way the verb "remembered" suggests that time goes on also shows us what a later passage tells: that in contrast to Boldwood, Gabriel is not so stricken by calamity that he is rendered incapable. Out of the experience, he achieves "a dignified calm he had never before known, and that indifference to fate which, though it often makes a villain of a man, is the basis of his sublimity when it does not. And thus the abasement had been exaltation, and the loss gain." (44)

What these passages show is not only Gabriel's growing stoicism that Bathsheba comes to admire but also his ability to move through the stresses of passion, whether of love or of despair. Events are subsumed into the stream of experience. Not so with Boldwood. This man sees Bathsheba less as the humanly flawed creature that Gabriel does than as an Ideal. If a reader places each man against a hypothetical time-scale, Boldwood's life is not like Gabriel's flowing from the past into the future, but rather it is fixed on some future time when his hope might be realized, his desire fulfilled.

Boldwood's tendency to move to extremes of passion, once aroused, is shown in references to water and its flooding or movement: "If an emotion possessed him at all, it ruled him; a feeling not mastering him was entirely latent. *Stagnant or rapid, it was never slow*. He was always hit mortally, or he was missed." (137) "Though it was possible to form guesses concerning his wild capabilities *from old floodmarks faintly visible, he had never been seen at the high tide which caused them.*" (138) "A man's body is as the shell, or the tablet, of his soul, as he is reserved or ingenuous, *over-flowing* or self-contained." (139) "The insulation of his heart by reserve during these many years, *without a channel of any kind of disposable emotion*, had worked its effect." (139) "This . . . seemed to open *the sluices of feeling* that Boldwood had as yet kept closed." (144, Italics added) But more interesting than these passages—these metaphors which link feeling with natural environment, which carry out the Biblical idea of flooding waters—are the references to a different condition of the element. They describe the cold February morning after Boldwood receives Bathsheba's valentine, a wintry condition in which movement is stilled.

The winter background described in this chapter carries no references to the floods and tides that characterized the momentum of earlier passions. Everything points toward obsession, toward emotions stopped and fixed, and toward dislocation. The valentine affects Boldwood as the potion does Tristan, removing from the farmer much of his control over himself. Significantly the valentine with its "large red seal [that] became as a blot on the retina of his eye" sits upon a time-piece, "surmounted by a spread eagle," the valentine itself resting on the eagle's wings. (112) Flight is stilled: that is, time and its impact from this moment have little of their old meaning for Boldwood. He loses the ability to discipline time and with that the ability to discipline passion.[5] He is driven to live for the future, recognizing "the symmetry of his existence to be slowly getting distorted in the direction of an ideal passion. The disturbance was as the first floating weed to Columbus—the contemptibly little suggesting possibilities of the infinitely great." (112) The sender of the valentine is a "vision," "a misty shape," taking "form" only when Boldwood sleeps and dreams. (113)

Distortion, disturbance—these qualities are reflected in the same chapter in the strange way the light is cast off the snow, a "preternatural inversion of light and shade" (115) that mirrors the dramatic upset in Boldwood's emotions. But important as well is what snow—moisture frozen, stilled—suggests. If flooding water is reflective of passion and its effects, then snow is an apt register of the effects of Boldwood's passion, of the heavy imprint the valentine and its two words "MARRY ME" set upon him. What is frozen does not change. Nor does Boldwood once his passions are seized. Consider the wintry landscape the man looks upon:

> Boldwood was listlessly noting how the frost had hardened and glazed the surface of the snow, till it shone in the red eastern light with the polish of marble; how, in some portions of the slope, withered grass-bents, encased in icicles, bristled through the smooth wan coverlet in the twisted and curved shapes of old Venetian glass; and how the footprints of a few birds, which had hopped over the snow whilst it lay in the state of soft fleece, were now frozen to a short permanency. (115)

The bird's footprints, a detail both striking and characteristic of Hardy in its minuteness and particularity, show the reader Boldwood's emotional state. Though these are "frozen to a short permanency" while Boldwood's set of attitudes is much more enduring, the impact on his soul of the two words on the valentine is made vividly apparent.

With Troy is most of the water imagery associated. As an alien to the community's way of life, having been away from it long enough to become a stranger, his connection with the forces of weather, and of water in particular, tends to be harsh in effect. As the man of greatest romantic flamboyance, the man who "was vulnerable only in the present," whose "outlook upon time was as a transient flash of the eye now and then," (190) who views Bathsheba at their first meeting rather theatrically as "Beauty" (186)—as the man caught like Don Juan by woman, a kind of Ancient Mariner of Sex—Troy is involved in some of the novel's most striking scenes. They entail images and the accoutrements of water in a variety of forms.

Most involve his association with Fanny. When Fanny disappears, many think she has drowned. The gossip in Warren's Malthouse suggests it, and even Boldwood wonders.[6] That Fanny died in part because of a kind of outlaw passion is suggested in the description of the landscape through which her coffin is driven:

> Not a footstep or wheel was audible anywhere around, and the dead silence was broken only by a heavy particle falling from a tree through the evergreens and alighting with a small rap upon the coffin of poor Fanny. The fog had by this time saturated the trees, and this was the first dropping of water from the overbrimming leaves. The hollow echo of its fall reminded the waggoner [Joseph Poorgrass] of the grim Leveller. Then hard by came down another drop, then two or three. Presently there was a continual tapping of these heavy drops upon the dead leaves, the road, and the travellers. The nearer boughs were beaded with the mist to the greyness of aged men, and the rusty-red leaves of the beeches were hung with similar drops, like diamonds on auburn hair. (324)

The idea of saturation, the detail of "the overbrimming leaves," the reminder of "the grim Leveller," the aged greyness of the mist—within the larger framework of flood and flow, these are suggestive of a wearing-out, of the tag-ends of passion, the residue of violent act.

The nature of that act is suggestively revealed in two earlier scenes—the first when Fanny speaks to Troy from outside his barracks and the second when the water from the gargoyle's mouth washes the flowers from her grave. In the first, Fanny stands outside the building, Troy is within, and between them runs the river. The sound of the river echoes what one might consider responses to Fanny's plight:

> The river would have been seen by day to be of that deep smooth sort which races middle and sides with the same gliding precision, any

> irregularities of speed being immediately corrected by a small whirlpool. Nothing was heard in reply to the signal but the gurgle and cluck of one of these invisible wheels together with a few small sounds which a sad man would have called moans, and a happy man laughter—caused by the flapping of the waters against trifling objects in other parts of the stream. (97-98)

The passage recalls a statement Hardy entered in his notebook in 1866: "July 13. A man's grief has a touch of the ludicrous unless it is so keen as to be awful."[7] The stream's sound registers the feelings of individuals on both sides of it—the distress Fanny feels and the pleasantries Troy shares with the soldiers. The pleasantry shows itself as "a low peal of laughter [from inside the building], which was hardly distinguishable from the gurgle of the tiny whirlpools outside." (100) What is interesting is the way a reader begins to sense some other force within or behind the object, that vague and ambiguous universal force that takes a number of names throughout Hardy's work. When Boldwood looks at the birds' footprints embedded in the snow, the reader observes and draws connections set there by the author; the outer world, he gathers, matches Boldwood's inner world. But here Hardy pushes further. In the barracks scene, and more especially in the later churchyard scene, one finds more than the connection between character and surroundings. One senses that the object—stream or gargoyle—is either itself a judgemental force or a tool of some more abstract observer. The noise of the stream might be reminiscent, the narrator suggests, of moans or laughter, depending upon the auditor. A reader is invited to judge. But he is not a participant within that world as is the force that acts and comments finally. In the noise of the stream—moan or laughter—its presence is felt: dimly perhaps. But through the gargoyle in the churchyard scene, the presence acquires stronger impact, is given fuller definition.

Before examining the scene, however, I wish to consider a paragraph describing the landscape outside the barracks, for the description sets the relationship of Fanny and Troy in a perspective that illuminates the gargoyle's activity and Troy's failure because of it. The passage reads as follows:

> This climax of the series [of changes brought by winter] had been reached to-night on the aforesaid moor, and for the first time in the season its irregularities were forms without features; suggestive of anything, proclaiming nothing, and without more character than that of being the limit of something else—the lowest layer of a firmament of snow. From this chaotic skyful of crowding flakes the mead and moor momentarily received additional clothing, only to appear momentarily

> more naked thereby. The vast arch of cloud above was strangely low, and formed as it were the roof of a large dark cavern, gradually sinking in upon its floor; for the instinctive thought was that the snow lining the heavens and that encrusting the earth would soon unite into one mass without any intervening stratum of air at all. (96)

Two items in this description are suggestive. The first is the curious echo of Genesis in the phrase "forms without features," an echo that turns the moor on which Fanny stands into a kind of void like that out of which the world was created—"anything," "nothing"—a part of that firmament, this one "a *firmament* of snow."[8] Chaos awaits the Word. Or as in a second creation myth, recounted by Hesiod, Chaos awaits Love. A reader can hardly be unaware of the sexually suggestive diction—"climax," "clothing," "naked," "unite." The selection of words reminds one of the union of Earth and Heaven, after Earth and Love had themselves created Heaven as an abode for the gods, especially if one notes other imagery in the passage.[9] The low arch of clouds, like the roof of cavern sinking upon its floor, "the snow lining the heavens and that encrusting the earth" merging the heaven and earth "into one mass"—these images imply sexual union.

Both myths, one suggesting chaos, the other creation, point to the relationship between the two lovers. Fanny expects Love and the resolution that a declaration of love might bring, manifesting itself in legal union—hence, order, the bonding of a family. Seeking that union, she has made her journey. And fails to find it. She has also created in Frank Troy a lover, but one who is not what she believes him to be as evidenced by his behaviour, the laughter of the soldiers, the chuckling "gurgle" of the river. He is no human counterpart to the Heaven that will make Earth fertile. When Fanny lies in her grave, his efforts at restitution are mocked.

The narrator finds an "element of absurdity" in Troy's graveside gardening, however carefully the flowers are set out, referring to "the futility of these romantic doings," noting with a kind of awkward pedantry that Troy's "idiosyncrasies" have both English and French qualities in them. (358) There is more to the act than romance and nationality, however. The description of the gargoyle, as Gregor points out, draws upon Ruskin's description of the grotesque, an art form characterized by qualities of both the ludicrous and the terrible.[10] Describing the gargoyle's features with such adjectives as "hideous," "horrible," "wrinkled," mixing attributes of such creatures as dragon and man, animal and fiend, describing the flow of water as being "vomited," Hardy emphasizes the quality of the terrible, the sense of the dreadfulness of the universe that weighs upon the artist of the grotesque. Here some force—numinous and ironic and powerful—seems to work against Troy, the torrent of water "from the gargoyle's jaws" directing "its vengeance into the grave." (362) The leering grin of the gargoyle reminds us of the earlier laughter in the "gurgle" of the stream outside the barracks. Through the water it spills from its mouth, it comments on Troy's passion, on its irresponsible nature, and on its destructiveness.

Troy's flowers are a memorial to Fanny, a register of his sorrow. But for the reader they are more than that. If after union with Heaven, Earth brought forth mountains and streams and, one assumes, the verdure covering them, Troy's planting becomes an effort on his part to do through artifice what was not done through compassionate act. His union with Fanny has not been creative; it has brought forth hardship and death. Troy's are efforts to repair, to make abundant, but he does it alone—and fails. He brings flowers to plant not for the moment, but—untypical of him—for time to come: "There were bundles of snowdrop, hyacinth and crocus bulbs, violets and double daisies, *which were to bloom in early spring*, and of carnations, pinks, picotees, lilies of the valley, forget-me-not, summer's farewell, meadow-saffron and others, *for the later season of the year*." (358, Italics added) He has tried to beautify the earth. But when Troy returns to the graveyard the following morning to find the flowers "washed clean out of the ground," lying "roots upwards," (363) the reader recognizes how this man of the present has been denied the lost future to which he tried to pay respect. In addition to this manifestation of "the wreck the stream had made" (363) is another: "The pool upon the grave had soaked away into the ground, and in its place was hollow." (363) The image is of barrenness, not just of the grave, but also, by implication, of the womb, of posterity, for Fanny's dead child is buried with her. Troy has not simply been denied any possibility of mitigating or eluding grief. Providence has not simply "jeered." (365) It has mocked him with its image of the consequences of passion.

Troy's love, like Boldwood's, has been quenched or drowned by the irrational qualities of passion; it is a kind of love that in both cases not only fails to survive but also causes death, disrupting what might be the projected calm of a "cool, sequester'd vale." The love that "many waters cannot quench, nor the floods drown" is the love that both Gabriel and Bathsheba attain. The calm that can be achieved "far from the madding crowd" knows many disruptions. Yet the two lovers in the end achieve its refuge—from stress caused by unruly emotions, from incidents struck by human vagaries.

By associating water in its various forms with passion—in qualities, its effects—Hardy not only strengthens the traditional tie between region and inhabitants but he also registers the complexities and intermingling of nature and the world of the emotions. He idealizes neither. He shows error and calamity. But he also shows strength. And in Gabriel Oak and that character's "realist" devotion to Bathsheba, and in Bathsheba's growth in her awareness of his good qualities, Hardy has shown "the substantial affection" that can be developed into a "love which is strong as death."

NOTES

1. *The Great Web: The Form of Hardy's Major Fiction* (Totowa, New Jersey: Roman and Littlefield, 1974), p. 59. Other critics have used different terms. For example, in Chapter 6 of *The Pastoral Novel* (Charlottesville: University Press of Virginia, 1974), Michael Squires finds in the novel "a modified version of traditional pastoral in which the manner and the underlying attitudes of pastroal are present but in which real details of rural life form the substance of the work" (125); in "*Far from the Madding Crowd* and *The Woodlanders*: Hardy's Grotesque Pastorals," *English Literature in Transition*, 17 (1974), pp. 147-58, Charles E. May argues that the novel is a "distortion" of pastoral, creating a "totally estranged world of the absurd and the grotesque." (p. 155)
2. Thomas Hardy, *Far from the Madding Crowd* (London: Macmillan, 1962), p. 456. Further citations within the text are to this edition.
3. Gregor, p. 74.
4. Howard Babb, "Setting and Theme in *Far from the Madding Crowd,*" *ELH*, 39 (1969), pp. 147-61, discusses ways in which Hardy relates "his characters to setting," (p. 150) commenting among others on the barracks scene and the scene describing Boldwood with Bathsheba's valentine. My focus, however, is on water imagery. This concern derives less from exact parallels in the novel with the Biblical passages—waters quenching, floods drowning—than from the general association of love and passion with water that the passage seems to invite.
5. I draw on comments about Tristan and later Don Juan from W.H. Auden, *The Dyer's Head* (1962; rpt. New York: Vintage-Knopf, 1968), especially from the sections "Balaam and His Ass" and "The Prince's Dog."
6. According to Jacob Smallbury: "I met Farmer Boldwood, . . . and I went with him and two of his men, and dragged Newmill Pond, but we found nothing." (p. 87)
7. Florence Emily Hardy, *The Life of Thomas Hardy 1840-1928* (London: Macmillan, 1962), p. 55.
8. Note Ruskin's description of the term in Part V, "Of Mountain Beauty," in *Modern Painters*, IV, Vol. VI of *The Works of John Ruskin*, ed. E.T. Cook and Alexander Wedderburn (London: George Allen, 1904), pp. 112-13.
9. I cannot point to any direct borrowing in translation. C.A. Elton's translation, *Hesiod* (London: George Routledge, n.d.), reads:

Earth first produced the Heaven; whose starry cope
Like to herself immense, might compass her
On every side, and be to blessed gods
A mansion unremoved for aye. (p. 102)

The later passage where she lies with Heaven so her sons can avenge her is more explicitly sexual:

Vast Heaven came down from high,
And with him brought the gloominess of night
On all beneath: desiring Earth's embrace,
He lean'd above her, and lay now diffused
In his immensity. (pp. 104-5)

Other translations like the prose translation of A.W. Mair and the recent one of Richmond Lattimore echo the same sense of union one finds in Hardy's paragraph.
I am indebted to Miss Sharon Werbicki for first calling my attention to this parallel with myth.

10. *The Stones of Venice, III,* Vol. XI of *The Works of John Ruskin*, p. 166. Gregor's reference appears on p. 61, though it points to Ruskin's discussion in *Modern Painters*.

'Misreadings'[1] of Self: Eustacia Vye in *The Return of the Native*

ARTI MATHUR

Rereading *Jane Eyre*, critic Maurianne Adams underscored the experience of women reading when she referred to the "inevitability" of being led to certain feminist issues. These issues predominantly focus on the status and economics of "female dependence in marriage," the "limited options" available to Jane for her education and energies, her needs and impulses, and her aspirations. The perspective from which the character of Jane is viewed sensitizes the reader to the limitations of the social world circumscribing her. Eustacia Vye's sense of entrapment on Egdon heath in *The Return of the Native*[2] borne out of frustrated aspirations requires a similar contextualization in order to understand the deep discontent that afflicts her life. Her isolated state on the heath provides Eustacia with long, uninterrupted, introspective moments which precipitate raging conflicts alternating with bitterness and depression of life's "injustices" in her heart. Lawrence formulates her turmoils in a series of questions: "What does she want? She does not know, but it is evidently some form of self-realization; she wants to be herself, to attain herself. But she does not know how, by what means."[3] The kind of fulfilment that Eustacia seeks is provided to her by convention, namely, love and marriage. Acceptance of these as the norms of her life initiates the process of 'misreading' in Eustacia. She fluctuates between Wildeve and Clym in her attempt to seek fulfilment, but it constantly eludes her. Convention prevents her from fully understanding the complexity of the social and ideological repressions to which she is subjected. Yet, she remains a figure of rebellion against convention, too.

Eustacia thinks that it is the heath which is preventing her from being happy. If she finds the right man, and is placed in an environment of her choice, she feels that she will be content. Her hatred of Egdon is expressed vehemently by her restless wanderings on the heath, irrespective of the time. For, had it been "possible for the earth and mankind to be entirely in her grasp for a while—few in the world would have noticed a change" (89) everything would have endured as before except her own confinement on the heath. She spurns the heath primarily due to her brief experience of a dazzling life led in Budmouth. She had "romantic recollections of sunny afternoons on an esplanade, with military bands, officers, and gallants around, which stood like gilded letters upon the dark tablet of surrounding Egdon. Every bizarre effect that could result from the random intertwining of a watering place glitter with the grand solemnity of a heath "was to be found in her seeing nothing of human life now, she imagined all the more of what she had seen." (91) The charms of Budmouth, the little sea-side resort, multiply in her contemplations regarding Paris. The brilliant people she wants to associate with live in Paris. Consequently, Eustacia's visions contrast despairingly with her actual existence on the heath. Yet her turmoils, restlessness and discontent prevent her from falling into passivity or stagnation on the heath. The narrative emphasizes that Eustacia's sighs at her condition make it evident that "she had been existing in a suppressed state, and not in one of languor or stagnation." (79)

In the course of the narrative, Eustacia gains tremendous vitality through the frequent allusions to her "hot little bosom" and "quivering lips" which according to Hardy, made one "suspect" that even her "soul is flame-like." Eustacia's sexuality is perceived as a powerful invigorating force in the novel. The element of unconventionality in the celebration of Eustacia's sexuality defies accepted Victorian notions of immoral women. Hardy's portrayal of Eustacia, instead, problematises stereotypical criticism of Victorian womanhood. Thus, in the novel Hardy abstains consistently from condemning Eustacia's grand passions. He comments that "she had the passions and instincts which make a model goddess, that is, those which make not quite a model woman," (89) whereby, the satire is levelled at society's conventional picture of a desirable woman, and not at Eustacia.

One may broadly divide Victorian heroines into stereotypical images of desirable and undesirable women with only a few exceptions to this categorization. The desirable woman is the "angel in the house" figure whose "helpless and dependent status, submissive and cultivated lady-like manners, and quiet air of patient suffering"[4] make her a delightful creature to men. In the novel the model woman is easily identifiable in the person of Thomasin who "exhibits submissiveness not imperiousness, docility not fervour, amiability not anger, demureness not passion."[5] Eustacia is of course everything that Thomasin is not. And yet her life is hardly that of an immoral hussy who deserves a final downfall. There are enough instances of Eustacia's unconventionality in the text, apart from the celebration of her sexuality, to concede that she is beyond the desirable/undesirable, or moral/immoral categories. That she prefers the Philistines to the pious, wonders whether Pilate was handsome, are only a few indications of her thought process. Her one great desire is "to be loved to madness" for "love was to her the one cordial which could drive away the eating loneliness of her day. And she seemed to long for the abstraction called passionate love more than any particular lover." (92) With Wildeve as her lover, Eustacia largely remains in a state of expectancy, since his promises of taking her away from the heath consolidate with the exciting reciprocation of passion she experiences with him in their sexual encounters. As the owner of the 'Quiet Woman' with the meaningless 'Engineer' attached to his name, Wildeve presents himself as a viable choice to a woman with strong class notions. Moreover, his frequent desertions, before his marriage to Thomasin, considerably excite her since they bring about a more passionate renewal of their love each time. In actual terms Eustacia experiences the thrill of power in being able to recall him back to her each time. Paradoxically, his frequent absences also provide her with desired objectivity, by which she contemplates that "I think when I become calm after your woundings . . . do I embrace a cloud of common fog after all?" (87) This qualitative resemblance to a detritus-like form accurately fits Wildeve's fickleness which prevents him from acting justly towards either Thomasin or Eustacia.

Eustacia rejects him the moment a much better prospect in the figure Clym Yeobright enters the scene. Yet, a qualitative difference between Eustacia's wavering of affections, and that of Wildeve's fickleness remains because Eustacia's desperation to escape the heath, and her idealism regarding love which prods her into seeking unrealizable passions, in a sense explicate her motives. Wildeve's lust, on the other hand, is mere seizing of opportunity under false pretences, since he does not really intend fulfilling any of his promises to Eustacia.

What makes Clym desirable to Eustacia is his identification with Paris, but undoubtedly her heart too is engaged this time. Hence, she confesses to Clym that "to be your wife and live in Paris would be heaven for me." (189) The active social life of Paris holds the prospect of "freedom" to her. Radically, the "freedom" she refers to is not merely the "splendid life" she has envisioned but also a space where she need not fear a decline of their mutual passions. Her candid confessions to Clym, whereby, she unashamedly admits her experience in matters of love, reveal her deep insight into the flux of life. Thus, she forlornly tells Clym even before they are married that "we shall not love like this always." (212)

Even though Clym leaves her in no doubt regarding his intentions of never returning to Paris, Eustacia persists with the illusion and clings to its evocative descriptions as a lifeline. Clym, in turn, persists in his fantasy of moulding Eustacia into a model wife who with fervour matching his own would abandon all hopes of leaving the heath and help him in "educating" the rustics. Clym's mediocrity, especially in relation to Eustacia, debunks his claims to rationality, since he completely remains a victim of convention. For instance, he assumes that the heath folk could be educated to share his disgust of materialism and would thank him for saving them from its corrupting clutches. Thus, his grand plan of elevating the rustics, existing at the very edge of poverty, into an intellectual and rational mode of existence without subjecting them to the evils of material prosperity reveal a certain lack of insight into their circumstances. There is enough satire levelled by the author at Clym's intended project to conclude that Clym's fame among the heath folk most certainly exceeds what he actually merits.

In a sense, Clym is instrumental in problematizing the concept of 'rationality' and hence, by contrast the 'irrationality' associated with Eustacia and renders the terms ambiguous. Nevertheless, Clym's dominating gender position and social status allow him to pursue his ambitions, however misconceived, and in the process create space for the roles he assumes in society as he wills. Though Eustacia shares the same status and subjects herself to a far more rigorous process of introspection than Clym, she has no power to create a space in society for herself, according to her will. Clym's process of regression, whereby he crawls into demeaning roles is a truly embittering process for Eustacia as a spectator. For her, it is a display of exertion of will which day by day sinks Clym deeper into a meaningless mire. Her dependence on such a will as Clym's which ultimately achieves nothing spurs her into taking the desperate decision of escaping with Wildeve. She fervently wishes to cut herself off all the humiliation associated with Clym. In the light of her predicament it is reductive to view her powerful struggle against her circumstances as capricious waverings of an immoral woman.

"Consequently, in the course of the narrative, we discover that what Eustacia resents most is her lack of freedom. Her very placement upon the heath is her grandfather's decision, rather than 'fate.' In fact, everything she considers 'fate' is predominantly decisions of men around her. Rosemarie Morgan in her essay on *The Return* writes that "the world of freedom and action Hardy's greater heroines would shape for themselves disintegrates as rapidly as the man-made world superimposes upon them its own curbing shape. With the advent of adulthood and a fully awakened sexual consciousness, every exploratory move towards self-discovery, self-realization and sexual understanding meets with obstruction in a male-dominated world intent upon highranking the docile woman over the daring, the meek over the assertive, the compliant over the self-determining, the submissive over the dynamic. There is no area of exploration, whether occupational, sexual or merely developmental, that does not eventually conflict with the dominant male will to dispossess woman of autonomy, identity, purpose and power."[6] The continuous tension between her and what to her appears as fate lends validity to her rebellion. In the characteristic manner of Hardy, fate itself becomes a complex interplay of larger uncontrollable forces, and the decisions of human beings.

At the same time, her grandfather's lenient and unquestioning nature gives her a taste of freedom on the heath which creates within her an intense desire to live and control her own life. She resents decisions which take no account of her wishes. Her limited taste of power over Wildeve only intensifies her desire to assume control over her circumstances, which has been denied to her even regarding her own life. For instance, she considers herself "banished" from Budmouth, an indication of her own unwillingness in the matter. Eustacia here seems to be at the point of realizing that "gender is not only a question of difference, which assumes that the sexes are separate and equal; but of power, since in looking at the history of gender relations, we find sexual asymmetry, inequality, and male dominance."[7] Even while attaining sexual liberation, Eustacia is bound by gender, a "complex social, cultural, and psychological determinant"[8] imposed upon a biological identity. Her struggle against this determinacy declares Eustacia as non-conforming to her gender position in society. But Eustacia's uncritical placing of faith in the kind of active life illustrated by Budmouth of Paris as the ultimate prospects of self-fulfillment, takes away her means of completely grasping gender based exploitation in society.

Eustacia is unable to comprehend that her shifting, unstable, but vibrantly alive, restless passions indicate a discontent which has the larger implications of a protest against gender based injustices of society which render women passive. Instead, Eustacia thinks that it is the heath which is preventing her from being happy. Hence Wildeve, Clym, Paris become goals for her. By accepting certain conventions as norms of her life, Eustacia is unable to recognize the constructive nature of society, which conditions men, women and all discourse to maintain women as "willing slaves." Society "assigns different roles to the two sexes, surrounds them from birth with an expectation of different behaviour, plays out the whole drama of courtship, marriage, and parenthood in terms of types of behaviour believed to be innate and therefore appropriate for one sex or for the other."[9] This gives birth to cultural stereotypes which practised over a period of time become the provenance of convention. Conventions are maintained obviously when there is a certain group which benefits from them. And to these we refer as the socially given and hence unalterable notions which in actual terms are ideological or social constructs. The nature of her discontent is such that the men in her life, as well as the places she uncritically craves for can only be preoccupational. Her rebellion is against the circumscribed, repressed, and completely closed existence 'destined' for women. *The Return*, then, lends itself as a site for these ideological debates challenging the conventionally ascribed sphere for women, primarily through the portrayal of Eustacia.

Feminist approaches to literature, such as indicated by the contextualization of Jane by the critic Maurianne Adams provide useful methodology to deconstruct ideologies governing gender conditioning. Thus, as gender studies they reveal that "nature" of women is an "artificial" thing. The stereotypical image of Victorian womanhood as passive, self-sacrificing and content with a purely domestic role was progressively challenged by scores of activist women in the nineteenth century who campaigned together for suffrage and education. They raised public opinion in order to reform the institution of marriage, to provide wider vocational opportunities, and in the process protested vociferously against Victorian patriarchy. Gender studies base themselves upon such active tools to expose the hypocrisies and injustices inflicted on women under the guise of convention.

Eustacia's indulgent and carpe-dium existence, thus, is an expression of her rebellion against conventional gender expectations. Eustacia's conception is perhaps the most radical force in the novel which explores the problem of lack of space for a confrontational woman in society. Eustacia's rebellion itself is partial, for she never does succeed in "attaining" herself. For the success of her rebellion implies a kind of upheaval that would uproot the patriarchal structures of society—a chaos hinted as "confusion" in the first image of Eustacia on the Rain barrow: "the form was so much like an organic part of the entire motionless structure that to see it move would have impressed the mind as a strange phenomenon. Immobility being the chief characteristic of that whole which the person formed portion of, the discontinuance of immobility in any quarter suggested confusion." (41) But the valid aspect of her rebellion lies precisely in her non-conforming attitude till her death, which remains a challenge, a question, to preconceived ideas about woman's destiny. Even in her death, she remains unreconciled to the heath. Though Eustacia does not have the necessary experience or tools by which to analyse her dilemma, she initiates questioning of fundamental issues of individual and society, and more specifically, of women and society relationships.

NOTES

1. The term 'misreads' is used for Eustacia by A.J. Guerard in "The Women of the Novels," *Hardy: A Collection of Critical Essays*, ed. A.J. Guerard (New Jersey, Englewood Cliffs: Prentice Hall, 1963).
2. Thomas Hardy, *The Return of the Native* (London: Macmillan, 1979).
3. D.H. Lawrence, "Study of Thomas Hardy," *Phoenix—The Posthumous Papers of D.H. Lawrence*, ed. E.D. McDonald (London, 1936), p. 414 .

4. Carol Dyhouse, "The role of women: from self-sacrifice to self-awareness," *The Context of English Literature: The Victorians,* ed. Laurence Lerner (London: Methuen, 1978), pp. 174-75.
5. Rosemarie Morgan, *Women and Sexuality in the Novels of Thomas Hardy* (London and New York: Routledge, 1988), p. 62.
6. *Ibid.*, p. 58.
7. Elaine Showalter, ed., *Speaking of Gender* (New York and London: Routledge, 1989), p. 4.
8. *Ibid.*, p. 2.
9. Margaret Mead, "Sex and Temperament," *The Feminist Papers: From Adams to de Beauvoir*, ed. Alice Rossi (New York and London: Columbia University Press, 1973), p. 659.

The Role of the Heath in *The Return of the Native*

V.P. SHARMA

The discussion of *The Return of the Native* has often been influenced by Hardy's classification of the novel as a novel of character and environment. And therefore the heath has become the governing deity of the novel—those who conform to its code enjoy happiness—at least finally; those who do not are destroyed. According to Davidson, you have two sets of characters in Hardy—the changeless and the changeful and "tragedy does not arrive until changeless and changeful are engaged in bitter conflict—They [the rustics] are . . . the basic pattern [i.e. the changeless ones] to which other characters conform or from which they differ. . . . Eustacia and Clym have passed over the line, though not beyond the possibility of redemption. They are changeful characters strongly touched by Promethean influences—as Wildeve, in a vulgar way is also touched."[1] This analysis of the novel is further reinforced by Hardy's consciously giving *The Return of the Native* the structure of a Greek tragedy. The heath is not only the setting of the novel in which the characters live out their little lives, it has also been imbued with enormous power and becomes Hardy's timeless symbol of nature. The fate of the main characters Clym, Eustacia and Wildeve is linked to their relationship with the heath; the rustics play the part of chorus.

In an interesting analysis, David Lodge suggests that Hardy uses the filmic technique of close-up to emphasize the symbolic properties of the heath.[2] It becomes a synecdoche of the nineteenth century pessimism. Indeed, Hardy provides a panoramic view of the heath in the finest chapter—to the exclusion of any human characters—in order to stress its dominance over its residents. As the novel develops it looks like a struggle between the heath and Eustacia Vye, and an unequal struggle it is. She hates it and would do anything to escape it.

Hardy, like Lawrence, had watched with dismay the decline of the rural order. The heath is therefore the symbol of this order whose 'vitality' is greater than that of modernity. Eustacia and Wildeve, and at first Clym too, are alienated from it: indeed this very alienation lies behind their ostensible successes. . . . But because of the alienation the successes are ill-placed and precarious, they are the successes of those who have lost the soundness, the inner strength, the power to choose and to achieve wisely which belongs to men whose life is "in harmony with their world. . . . By the end, Egdon has triumphed, even if on its own stern terms. The renegades have been destroyed or won over."[3] The brooding presence of the heath is emphasized in Hardy's characterization of it as 'a near relation of the night':

> The spot was, indeed, a near relation of the night, and when night showed itself an apparent tendency to gravitate together would be perceived in its shades and scenes. The sombre stretch of rounds and hollows seemed to rise and meet the evening gloom in pure sympathy, the heath exhaling darkness as rapidly as the heavens precipitated it.

In fact darkness presides over important events: Clym working as furze-cutter in semi-darkness, the game of dice between Wildeve and Diggory Venn in pitch dark, and the death of Wildeve and Eustacia. Like the heath itself Eustacia too is introduced to us against the background of darkening sky. The dark mysterious movements of Diggory Venn keep reminding us of the awesome presence of the heath in the lives of the chief protagonists. The heath is obviously not seen as a mere passive bystander: "The place became full of a watchful intentness now; for when other things sank brooding to sleep the heath appeared slowly to awake and listen." (Book 1, Chap. 1) Does the novel live upto its description of the awesome mysterious heath capable of "tragic possibilities"?

There is no doubt that the heath is an ever-present reality in the lives of its denizens and lends poignancy to their tale. It is witness to deaths of Mrs. Yeobright, Eustacia and Wildeve, to the moonlight dance that rediscovers the lost passion of Eustacia, to the fateful game of dice by the light of glow-worms between Diggory Venn and Wildeve. But to raise the heath to a divine status is to exaggerate its role. It has been seen to have elements of Lear's heath[4] and as Dante's Limbo suggesting 'the lightless world of ancients.'[5] As Wing suggests the heath has been overdone in its tragic possibilities.[6] In its divine incarnation it assumes the power to punish and reward. The simplistic equation between Egdon Heath and its dwellers explains the death of the two non-conformists, Eustacia and Wildeve, the suffering of Clym and the ultimate happiness of Diggory Venn and Thomasin. But it does not account for the death of Mrs. Yeobright or the unhappiness of Susan Nunsuch and her son Johnny who is always falling ill. And things would have been more complicated if Hardy had stuck to his original design of the story with Diggory Venn quietly disappearing at the end as he had always done. In fact Hardy adds to the mysterious influence of the heath by avoiding neat equations: Eustacia 'rises' and 'falls' here, Wildeve is destroyed here before he can destroy others, Clym's purgatory is the heath and Mrs. Yeobright's sufferings end here. The heath is like a living canvas whose colours change to harmonize with the brush strokes. It seems to understand the turmoil in the heart of the protagonists. The darkness of the night and the boiling cauldron are not merely on the heath, they are there in the heart of Eustacia herself.

As Butler suggests the question "whether the action of *The Return of the Native* is worthy of or appropriate to the heath on which it takes place,"[7] is not really applicable. The action is inseparable from its environment.

The roots of the tragedy lie in the nature of Clym-Eustacia—Mrs. Yeobright relationship. They form what one might call a triangle of 'incomprehension'—the inability and unwillingness to understand one another. As Rehdar observes: "The difficulty of communication is at the centre of his satires and the breakdown of communication frequently leads to tragedy. . . . It is the communication of feeling that is specially difficult. Characters are often isolated by their emotions, emotions that they can neither express nor explain even to themselves. Clym and Eustacia, Angel and Tess, are only briefly in touch with each other."[8] Like Paul Morel in Lawrence's *Sons and Lovers*, Clym too is caught between two women, his mother and his wife. But if the tragedy arises in *Sons and Lovers* because the two women understand each other's motives and emotion much too well, the tragedy in *The Return of the Native* arises from their inability to understand each other. And as in *Sons and Lovers* the central characters here, too, are prisoners of their gender. Even during their courtship Clym and Eustacia are emotionally isolated from each other.

> 'I have come to clear away those cobwebs,' said Yeobright.
>
> 'Would you like to help me by high class teaching? We might benefit them much.'
>
> 'I don't feel quite anxious to. I have not much love for my fellow-creatures. Sometimes I quite hate them.'
>
> 'Still I think if you were to hear my scheme you might take an interest in it. There is no use in hating people—if you hate anything, you should hate what produced them.'
>
> 'Do you mean Nature? I hate that already. . . . I cannot endure the heath, except in its purple season. The heath is a cruel taskmaster to me.'
>
> 'Can you say so?' he asked. 'To my mind it is most exhilarating, and strengthening, and soothing. . . .'

With this kind of contradictions their marriage is foredoomed. Pinion calls the conflict between Clym and Eustacia as one between altruistic zeal and hedonistic selfishness.[9] But paradoxically, Clym's altruism is insensitive as much as Eustacia's hedonism is selfish. He is confident that Eustacia will become his accessory in the noble task of reforming and educating the rustics. But Eustacia has never concealed her purpose in marrying him which is to escape the heath and join the gay world of Paris. She cares little for his noble ideals and believes he will outlive his infatuation for the oppressive simplicity of the heath and go back to Paris—and she with him. She is confident of luring him away to Paris. Marriage between the two individuals who refuse to shed their cocoons can only lead to disaster. His relations with his mother again show that his altruism does not embrace those nearest him. Mrs. Yeobright—a curate's daughter who had married below her position—had hoped to achieve her ambitions of a better life than her marriage had afforded, through her son. Clym's decision not to return to Paris obviously had disappointed her because it meant the end of her hopes. But she had resigned herself to it. It was, however, difficult for her to approve of his choice of Eustacia Vye for a wife. But if she cannot really understand her son's desires and aspirations, the son too makes little effort to gauge the depth of her anguish. And by the time he will do it, it will be too late.

Clym peremptorily decides to leave home and get married. *Her* pride and *his* sense of self-righteousness mean that Mrs. Yeobright does not attend her son's wedding. The same kind of self-righteousness marks his decision to become a furze cutter when his eyes go bad. Clym considers it perfectly natural to take his own decision without regard to the sensitivities of his wife, or even telling her about his plans. If Clym's hopes of starting a school now fade, so do Eustacia's hopes of ever escaping the heath. She who had always hated the heath could find nothing more galling than to share life with a man who now identifies himself more strongly than ever with the heath. Neither of them tries to understand the other's predicament. Furze cutting offers adequate recompense to Clym for the loss of hope of becoming a teacher; for Eustacia it is the end of the road. But the reader is expected to give his sympathy wholly to Clym not only because of the 'nobility' of his frustrated hopes but also because Eustacia, as a woman and his wife is part of *his* universe; she must empathize with him and not the other way round. Much of our understanding of Eustacia-Clym relationship after this is conditioned by this approach. The emotional communication between Clym and Eustacia has at the best of times been very fragile; it is quite gone now. They only breathe under one roof. As Eustacia is to admit, their honeymoon has lasted a bare two months.

When Clym announces that he is going to be a turf and furze cutter,

Eustacia is shocked. Her grandfather, she says, is willing to assist them. But Clym is firm.

> 'We don't require it. If I go furze cutting we shall be fairly well off.'
>
> 'In comparison with slaves, and the Israelites in Egypt, and such people!' A bitter tear rolled down Eustacia's face, which he did not see. There had been *nonchalance* in his tone, showing her that he felt no absolute grief at a consummation which to her was a positive horror.

Eustacia can be accused of being insensitive to Clym's need for sympathy and understanding in his hour of distress. But his eye ailment had thwarted her plans to escape the heath. The heath was winning again. When he becomes a furze cutter her despair reaches its zenith. When Clym sings to lighten his distress, Eustacia remarks bitterly: "Even had you felt careless about your own affliction, you might have refrained from singing out of sheer pity for mine. God! if I were a man in such a position I would curse rather than sing."

The heath has come into her life with a vengeance. There is bitter irony in the fact that Clym whom she has hoped to make her agent of deliverance from bondage to the heath has now become the heath's agent to torment her. Eustacia has never been able to gauge the depth of Clym's commitment to his idea. But Clym too—perhaps blinded by his idealism—had been ignorant of the intensity of Eustacia's fascination for the world beyond the heath. Rustics like Sam seem to know her mind better than Clym.

Clym and Eustacia are at the crossroads when she meets Wildeve again at the fair. The moonlight dance is a cathartic effort to release her frustration but it only leads to the awakening of her old passion. Yet it must be noted that she is no longer the old temptress; the initiative comes entirely from Wildeve.

The inherent hostility in the Eustacia-Mrs. Yeobright relationship precludes all possibility of their ever trying to understand each other. There has never been any cordiality between the Vyes and the Yeobrights though the reasons for the mutual antipathy are not very clear. When Eustacia asks her grandfather why the two families were not friendly, the old man merely says that he once accidentally offended the lady and had never seen her since. She, therefore, does not want her son Clym to take interest in Eustacia. She even accepts his idea of becoming a school master. Her acceptance, she hopes would let her influence him to give up his 'new crotchets.' Her antipathy changes into hostility after Clym marries Eustacia and leaves home, for, she thinks that Eustacia has bewitched her son. Ironically, Clym's meeting with Eustacia in which she "bewitches" him comes immediately after we learn about Susan's having pricked Eustacia's arm with a long needle because she believed Eustacia had bewitched her child Johny.

There is one brief and bitter confrontation between the two women, Mrs. Yeobright and Eustacia, beside the pool on the heath and whatever possibility we ever thought there was of a rapprochement is snuffed out. The doors to any further communication between them are closed for ever—figuratively now, and later, literally. Neither woman tries to understand the other. Mrs. Yeobright has come to find out if Eustacia has received a gift of money from Wildeve, thanks to the imbroglio created by Diggory Venn, but the subject is only a springboard for mutual recriminations. It is referred to only tangentially except at the beginning. The older woman does not hide her dislike of the younger one and the latter declares that she had 'condescended' to marry him only because she wanted to escape the heath. She holds Clym's mother responsible for pouring poison in their married life. They depart in hostility, unable or unwilling to come to terms with the present but their confrontation echoes through the rest of the novel. Mrs. Yeobright dies of a broken heart when she is not admitted to her son's house but the struggle between the two women goes on in Clym's heart. Only Eustacia's own death ends it.

II

The second aspect of the tragedy is the heath and Eustacia's and Clym's relationship with it. As we noted earlier, the action of the novel is inseparable from its environment. Most of the criticism of *The Return of the Native* has tended to judge the characters and events in terms of a code ordained by the heath. And this code requires its dwellers, as we noted earlier, to conform to it or pay the price of defiance. It has been ascribed human qualities and has been considered a character in itself.

Our first glimpse of Eustacia underscores her supreme isolation. Her figure rises above the barrow like Aphrodite above the sea waves. She is not part of the rustic community that gathers there to celebrate Guy Fawkes Day. This image of Eustacia trying to thwart the heath's dominance is to be the motif of the novel. But there is a striking similarity—and contrast too—between the imagery Hardy uses to invest the heath with awe and mystery and the imagery he uses to cast Eustacia in the mould of an enduring rebellious Greek goddess. "Every night its [the heath's] Titanic form seemed to await something, but it had waited thus unmoved, during so many centuries, through the crises of so many things, that it could only be imagined to await one last crisis—the final overthrow." (Book 1, Chap. 1)

The 'final overthrow' is a terrifying reminder of man's ultimate and inevitable surrender to Nature. And again,

> Then Egdon was aroused to reciprocity: for the storm was its lover, and the wind its friend. Then it became the home of strange phantoms; and it was found to be the hitherto unrecognized original of those wild regions of obscurity which are vaguely felt to be compassing us about in midnight dreams of flight and disaster, and are never thought of after the dream till revived by scenes like this. (Book 1, Chap. 1)

Likewise, Hardy begins by calling Eustacia 'the raw material of divinity . . . she had the passions and instincts which make a model goddess,' that is, 'those which make not quite a woman.' But she is also a Titaness in her rebelliousness and a Cleopatra in her pride and passions and, to some, a witch too. If the heath became full of a watchful intentness when night fell, her Pagan eyes too were, full of "nocturnal mysteries." If at twilight "darkness had to a great extent arrived here on [the heath], while day stood distinct in the sky," Eustacia, in contrast, is 'a creature of light surrounded by an area of darkness.' She is of the heath, yet not of it.

As if to emphasize the titanic struggle between Eustacia and the heath, Hardy calls her the 'Queen of the night' and perhaps in a mock-ironic tone suggests that 'On Olympus she would have done well with a little preparation.' She roams over the heath, unafraid, at night but she hates it: 'Egdon was her Hades and since coming there she had imbibed much of what was dark in its tone, though inwardly and eternally unreconciled thereto.' Tragedy, then, is inevitable.

In contrast, Clym is the native who has come back to the heath disillusioned after a brief experience of the 'other' world: 'Clym's interpenetration with the heath' reminds us of one of the conditions for 'integrated existence in Hardy—the condition of knowledge, awareness, consciousness. . . . This intelligent young man is not an unthinking part of the Egdon landscape; there would be no drama in that. He must *know* his heath: 'He gazed upon the wide prospect as he walked, and was glad. . . . Nature, in some sense, becomes a touchstone for humanity to live by and make judgements by.'[10] But even Clym is not in the same category of 'changeless' characters as the rustics and Diggory Venn who identify themselves completely with the heath. If Eustacia has always refused to merge her identity in it and felt only contempt for the wildness and 'swarthy monotony' of the heath, Clym deserts it for the glitter of Paris though he comes back to it realizing the value of its stability and vitality. And yet he does not accept it as it is. He thinks he can humanize it. In a sense, therefore, both are changeful characters and suffer for it.[11] This would suggest that the conflict between Clym and Eustacia is secondary to the main conflict between the heath on one side and Clym and Eustacia on the other.

In this approach and other similar approaches, the environment, that is the heath as representing the old changeless order is the reference point for assessing characters. Tragedy arises out of the tension between the character and his environment. Eustacia invites her destruction by refusing to accept the established order. But the implications of Eustacia's desire to escape the drabness of the heath are much wider than a mere refusal of the values implied in a life on the heath.

Paterson looks at it as more than an individual's revolt against his environment. (109 ff) He considers the opposition between the Christian and pre-Christian values vital to the novel's total effect. The contrast is not between Eustacia's fatal attraction for modernism and Clym's revulsion to it but, on the contrary, between the diminished consciousness of modern times in Clym and the heroic consciousness of Eustacia: 'Identified with a world not yet touched by the spectral hand of Christianity, Eustacia Vye reincarnated on the withered parish of Egdon Heath the larger and braver vision of the ancient Greeks.' In her suffering and death she dramatizes the tragic humiliation, in a diminished world, of the heroic pre-Christian understanding of things. . . . Eustacia stands in this in opposition to her husband, whose allegedly advanced views only thinly disguise the Christian champion.'[12]

The Christian-anti-Christian opposition gives a greater dignity to the novel's theme but it aligns Eustacia with Egdon's community of indifferent Christians and makes her isolation look like a mere idiosyncrasy rather than a symbol of her challenge to accepted order.

A true understanding of Eustacia's actions and motivations is possible only if we judge her outside the socio-cultural code which she is expected to subscribe to but which she transgresses. Her prototype is Marlowe's Faustus not Prometheus. If Faustus tried to be more than a man, Eustacia tried to be more than a woman and suffered the fate of her prototype. She struggles against predestination in a universe ruled by male prejudices against her sex.

It has often been argued that neither Clym nor Eustacia, and especially the latter, lives upto the expectation aroused in the beginning. Deen comments that Hardy makes her more impressive than she has a right to be, considering her age and sex and the apparently frivolous nature of her desires.[13] She does little to demonstrate or to justify the dazzling array of qualities ascribed to her. The apparently frivolous nature of her desires has to be seen in the background of the limitations of her existence. Her desire to escape the heath is, in fact, symbolic of her refusal to accept the limitations imposed on her by her environment—the kind of limitations that confronted a woman in the nineteenth century. And if she cannot live up to her divine image, it only points to her pathetic realization, and our awareness, that she lives in an oppressive universe which does not allow her sex to give full play to instincts and emotions. Clym can leave Egdon to see the glitter of Paris and then come back disillusioned but Eustacia is expected not to thirst for it because Clym knows it is only a false glitter. In the mumming scene, Eustacia consciously crosses the limits of female respectability. In stepping out of her sex she is not expressing a desire to 'change sex' but is questioning the traditionally passive role assigned to women in society. Deen observes: "Eustacia in the mumming scene assumes the heroic masculine role to which she is always aspiring. She wants to alter her essential human condition, to change her sex. A dissatisfaction so thoroughgoing amounts to a denial of life itself, which is begging the question." (122-23)

The conflict between Clym and Eustacia arises from a conflict between the male ego of the former which gives him the confidence that he will be able to get Eustacia around to assist in *his* project—which, ironically, is concerned with altering human condition, too—and Eustacia's ambition to get out of a woman's socially acceptable role in life.

When Thomasin is taken to the altar and then spurned by Wildeve she follows the rulebook of conventional morality and waits for him to come back. He takes his own time because he can afford to make her wait. That is the male prerogative. And after marriage Thomasin is content to be the unprotesting wife of a reluctant husband. As against this, Eustacia never really accepts her marriage, especially after she learns that Clym will never get her to Paris. And she has no hesitation in saying that it was a 'condescension' in her to be his wife.

Guerard puts Hardy's heroines into several categories in terms of their dominant characteristics. (65 ff) Eustacia, by that classification, is 'a hedonist tending to neurosis' in contrast to the 'altruistic' Clym, and 'highly sexed' but possessing masculine intellect in contrast to the rather unintelligent 'sweet ingenue' Thomasin. Women like Thomasin prosper, but those like Eustacia are bound to destroy themselves. Eustacia knows how to use her charms to deadly effect. She conquers Wildeve with them but once she is convinced that he is unworthy of her, she turns away from him. She conquers Clym with equal ease. But this is her 'necromancy' which she hopes will help her rise above her situation. When Clym comes on the scene, she sees her Mephistophilis in him. She knows that "Clym's aims are inconsistent with her own, and that his personality fails to satisfy her dreams of the heroic, yet she succeeds, at different times, in altering both Clym and Wildeve to something sufficiently like the image of her desire."[14] But the charm does not last. Her frustration after marriage stems mainly from her realization of her limitations as a woman: Clym was not going back to Paris and she could not go alone. Deen thinks that Eustacia acquiesces in illusion: "Her life is primarily nocturnal, a moonlight existence." (125) In fact Eustacia's illusion of a heroic life is only matched by Clym's idealism. Clym comes back to try and set up a Christian Republic on the heath that is not pre-Christian but primeval in its mode of existence. It is not without significance that if our first glimpse of Eustacia is of a 'goddess' rising above the barrow on the heath which she is trying to escape, our last glimpse of Clym is of a preacher at the same place trying to enlighten a congregation that is curious and attentive but rather unbelieving.

When Clym's eyes go bad, Eustacia-Clym relationship reaches a dead end. Eustacia's Mephistophilis has failed her. Unaware of the seething cauldron of frustration in her heart or, perhaps, unmindful of it, he adopts a course that is most hateful to her. Furze-cutting symbolizes Clym's further integration with the communal life on the heath, the very heath whose authority Eustacia had never accepted. But she now understands the despair of a woman's situation. Years later, another character in fiction, Lady Chatterley was to kick up a big storm by refusing to accept denial of fulfilment in her relationship with an invalid husband. At this stage Eustacia is, indeed, like a trapped bird 'at once our tragic goddess and a trapped bird' as Butler puts it. (46) But she was even earlier a prisoner on the heath. To the passionate Eustacia, love was 'the one cordial that could drive away the eating loneliness of her days' but she found none matching her passion. However, unlike in the case of Lady Chatterley, it is not passion alone that now drives her to Wildeve, although that is what she has been accused of. In fact, her attitude to him is rather ambivalent. The freeze in her relationship with Clym draws her to Wildeve but she also sees in him her last hope of flying away from her cage. This is no display of the imbalance in the overwhelming of her reason by her passion as Deen suggests here. (125) She has wanted to break free of her bondage for a long time now. Clym's self-centredness is largely responsible for the tragedy. If Clym sought his emancipation in escape from Paris, she seeks hers in escape from the heath. But being a woman makes it doubly difficult for her. The self-destructiveness, which she shares with other heroines of Hardy, arises from her challenge to an environment that was hostile to a woman's desire to seek her own destiny.

The incident of 'Closed Door' holds her guilty of infidelity and mother-in-law's murder. In fact, she is guilty of neither. It is difficult to imagine how else she could have behaved with a woman who had been so hostile to her especially when she had thought Clym was there to receive her. Later, when Clym confronts her with the 'truth,' she displays remarkable restraint and dignity and blunts his male assertiveness. But the violent confrontation has knocked out whatever little remained of their relationship. Reconciliation is alien to her nature. She finds it hard to harmonize the outer world with her inner world'[15]; the only option left to her is to escape from her prison through death or through flight. Wildeve is her last hope. But as she stands besides the seething waters of the weir she realizes that she could not trust another Mephistophilis to give her freedom from her bondage. She seeks her own release by jumping into the hell below.

NOTES

1. Donald Davidson, "The Traditional Basis of Thomas Hardy's Fiction," in *Twentieth Century Views on Hardy*, ed. Albert J. Guerard (Englewood Cliffs, N.J. : Prentice Hall, 1963), pp. 21-22.
2. David Lodge, "Thomas Hardy as a Cinematic Novelist," *Thomas Hardy after Fifty Years*, ed. Lance S.J. Butler (London: Macmillan, 1977), pp. 78 ff.
3. John Holloway, "Hardy's Major Fiction," *Twentieth Century Views on Hardy*, pp. 53-54.
4. Lance S.J Bulter, *Thomas Hardy* (Cambridge University Press, 1978).
5. John Paterson, "An Attempt at Grand Tragedy," in *Thomas Hardy: The Tragic Novels*, ed. R.P. Draper (Hampshire: Macmillan, 1975).
6. George Wing, *Hardy* (Edinburgh: Oliver and Boyd, 1963).
7. *Thomas Hardy*, p. 40.
8. R.M. Rehdar, "The Form of Hardy's Novels," *Thomas Hardy after Fifty Years*, pp. 19-20.
9. F.B. Pinion, "The Ranging Vision," *Thomas Hardy after Fifty Years.*
10. *Thomas Hardy*, pp. 50-51.
11. Cf. Davidson, pp. 21 ff.
12. Paterson, p. 116.
13. Leonard W. Deen, "Heroism and Pathos in *The Return of the Native*," *Thomas Hardy: The Tragic Novels*, p. 120.
14. *Ibid*, p. 125.
15. *Ibid*, p. 130.

Sale and Sacrament: The Wife Auction in *The Mayor of Casterbridge*

LEONORA EPSTEIN

The remarkable wife sale that opens *The Mayor of Casterbridge* is one of those scenes that varies in interpretation, not only from reader to reader but from reading to reading. The episode has invited a variety of critical responses—historical, humanist, feminist, Marxist, even moralistic—and yet, no one, to my knowledge, has detected the submerged allusions to the Anglican wedding ceremony embedded within the text. Henchard's dramatic gesture—violating as it does our most cherished sanctions—is so powerful that readers are apt to overlook its logical corollary: the sale that severs the alliance between Mr. and Mrs. Michael Henchard is also a wedding that creates a union between Mr. and Mrs. Richard Newson. Hardy's discreet reference to the more orthodox ceremony is more than just sly irony; for by simultaneously allowing readers to perceive two opposing images, the wedding/ sale dramatically recreates the central dialectic in a work devoted to exploring the uneasy tensions between the primitive and the civilized.

The fair where Henchard sells Susan seems initially to rise out of the monochromatic countryside like a fever dream. Traditionally, carnivals and fairs represent emblematic landscapes restricted to the liberation of weekday restraints; and indeed, Henchard's sense of conjugal frustration steadily mounts until it finds drunken release at the furmity tent. This carnival, however, is more than just a saturnalian sojourn, but an extension of the society it seemingly opposes. With its "peep-shows, toy-stands, waxworks, inspired monsters, disinterested medical men, . . . thimble-riggers, nick-nack vendors, and Readers of Fate,"[1] the fair, ironically, is a thriving pocket of commercialism, and its seemingly bizarre inhabitants, a paradigm of bourgeois society. In fact, the fair *is* Casterbridge, pushed to an absurd—and yet logical extreme. So, too, the auction: to the extent that the carnival mirrors normative society, the act it generates, the drunken sale, parallels modern marriage. The main point of connection between the two events is, of course, the cash nexus. The verbal and stylistic echoes of the wedding ceremony, as well as the corresponding visual image, press the similarities between culture and carnival to their most uncomfortable conclusions:

> "Five guineas," said the auctioneer, "or she'll be withdrawn. Do anybody give it?" [who gives this woman?]
>
> "Yes," said a loud voice from the doorway. [And here we are to imagine the sailor as groom striding down an aisle from the back of the tent to the front where he takes his place beside Susan and Henchard as they wait for a prospective buyer.]
>
> "You say you do?" asked the husband, staring at him. [The patriarchal Henchard is the self-authorized preacher.]
>
> "I say so," replied the sailor. (43-44, additions mine)

Perhaps most convincing, however, is the inevitable coda to this ritual, for after the transaction is complete, Newson, the new husband, turns to his bride and asks, "'That you swear?' 'I do,' said she." (44) With these final and irrevocable words, Susan Henchard Newson, like countless brides before her, seals her fate.

Susan's compliance is crucial, for without it, Henchard's act is merely cruel. Her willingness to accept the sailor, as well as her implicit faith in the legality of the transition, points to Hardy's analogy with marriage. A voluntary sale: how else to describe bourgeois marriage? For Hardy, most modern middle class weddings are sales disguised as sacraments; Susan's alliance with the sailor is a marriage disguised as a sale. And, surprisingly once we have disengaged ourselves from inherited notions of love and sacrament, it is easy to see that the bargain is profitable for all: Susan receives a more genial companion; Elizabeth-Jane, a more loving father; and Henchard, relieved of the clogs of marriage, rises to mayor of a thriving city. If wife selling is a crime, then marriage is as well.

Thus in unleashing his aboriginal self Henchard also sheds the defenses of his culture and reveals its primitive underside. The fair suggests the underlying atavism upon which society rests, while the auction reflects marriage stripped of its sacramental and romantic varnish. Hardy's characteristic tendency to probe beneath inherited sanctions reflects the theories beginning to be set forth by Darwinian social anthropologists. The exchange of a marriageable female for money or goods is the primitive antecedent of modern marriage; Henchard's act is merely a throwback to the earlier custom from which middle-class matrimony evolved. The anthropologist, Edward Westermarck, in his compendious *The History of Human Marriage* (1891) (and the qualifier "human" should not pass unnoticed), devoted several chapters to "marriage by purchase" and its relevance to contemporary marital practices throughout the world. Westermarck notes: "Purchase by wives may, with even more reason than marriage by capture, be said to form a general stage in the history of man. The more recent character of marriage by purchase appears clearly from the fact that marriage by capture very frequently occurs as a symbol where marriage by purchase occurs as a reality."[2] Sir John Lubbock, in the *Origin of Civilization* (1871), points out that marriage, far from being a divinely appointed imperative, is, in fact, a pragmatic social custom designed to insure legitimacy and protect property.[3] The consequences of Henchard's sale, his inability to distinguish his offspring from a stranger's, points to marriage's original function.[4] Hardy does not wholly reject the necessity for some sort of social bond: what he indicts here is marriage's inauthenticity, its pretensions to being something other than what it is, and society's complicity in concealing and denying its origins. Throughout *The Mayor* Hardy imaginatively recreates what social anthropologists were just acknowledging: that the primitive and the sacred are not isolated poles of experience, but cut from the same elemental fabric.

Such assumptions are also at work behind Henchard's supposed redemption, his remarriage. The Christian meaning of redemption reverts to its original financial significance, "the buying back," as Henchard literally "buys back" his former wife: before negotiating their second union, he sends his prospective bride five guineas, her original price. Because the nature of the sale casts the sanctity of marriage itself into doubt, this second alliance can never simply be the reenactment of the earlier ceremony. Instead, the sacrament is a reversion of the earlier perversion, thus forming a part of the wrong it seeks to right. Quite simply, marriage is the wife auction in reverse.

And yet, one could also argue that marriage is a perversion of the earlier custom, and that both acts are in fact mirror images of one another. Is the sale a distorted image of the marriage ceremony or is the ceremony a perversion of the sale? The striking resemblances between church wedding and carnival sale suggest that both events partake of the same impulse, and that each, despite the disparity of their settings and contexts, is morally neutral. The cluster of associations and meanings commonly ascribed to carnival and sale, marriage and religion, interpenetrate and ultimately exchange meanings, as each takes on qualities more properly belonging to the other. The spontaneous auction appears ritualistic and formalized, the codified ceremony moves into a carnival atmosphere.

It is interesting to note that readers, denied access into the church, and instead treated to Henchard's wedding through the distorted eyes of the Casterbridge "freaks," Nance Mockridge, Christopher Coney, and Mother Cuxsom, who assemble outside to watch the bridal couple depart before going off to the local pub. The carnival ambience is further enhanced by their allusions to the mayor as "bluebeardy" and Susan as the "skellinton"—as well as to such local wonders as Toad-skin—epithets which suggest that the burgher and his wife would feel more at home in a wax museum than the mayor's mansion.

These Casterbridge citizens are also not exempt from viewing marriage as a business transaction, as each in turn speculates what each party stands to profit by the bargain. Such an antiromantic view is apparently endorsed by the narrator who notes that Henchard conducts his courtship with "business-like determination" (111) and a "dogged, unflinching spirit which did credit to his conscientiousness." (112) Ironically, although the sale as sale is pragmatic, the sale as wedding has strong ties to the romance. Newson's spontaneous acceptance of his bride (love at first sight?), his almost magical appearance in her hour of need, and his gallant rescue suggest the scene's ironic affinities with the chivalric romance.

Conversely, while Henchard's wedding descends into comic grotesquerie, his sale modulates into high seriousness. At first, the spectators in the furmity tent regard the affair as a drunken caprice of a frustrated man, but with the appearance of money, the joke quickly becomes earnest, and the whole tenor of the scene undergoes a profound alteration: "A lurid colour seemed to fill the tent, and change the aspect of all therein. The mirth-wrinkles left the listeners' faces, and they waited with parting lips." (43) No longer funny, the jest has moved into another more solemn, almost transcendent realm, characteristic of the sacred, as a new note of hushed formality is introduced.

The sudden shift in tone and atmosphere is further highlighted when, Henchard, cursorily summarizing his deed, evokes nothing less than the full weight of biblical authority: "'Tis simple as Scripture history." This *ad hoc* referential meaning imparts an aura of legitimacy, making Henchard's deed seem less self-authorized and arbitrary. (And, of course, unknown to Henchard and his spectators, the sale does indeed possess an ancient history—one far more ancient than the Bible.) Moreover, the antiphonal questioning between the three participants suggests the prescribed responses of a liturgical drama.

The ritualistic nature of the scene closely aligns it with theatre, and it is worth noting that Hardy carefully applies a dramatic metaphor to both auction and wedding.[5] The eyes of the spectators in the furmity tent "became riveted upon the faces of the chief actors, and then upon the notes." (43) "The Scotchman, who assisted as groomsman, was of course the only one present, beyond the chief actors, who knew the true situation of the contracting parties." (113) When isolated from their respective contexts, both passages read as if they were describing the same event, and it is difficult to distinguish which is sale, which is wedding.

The spectators, no less than the "chief actors," enjoy a participatory role in these dramas. At the sight of Newson's cash, all the diverse voices of the spectators resolve into a uniform response. Cash is the tangible evidence which elicits the audience's faith in the sale as a "real" event and not just a hypothetical whim. At this point, they became a community of believers. Henchard's private desire to rid himself of an annoying wife has now become a collective event. How crucial this element is may be illustrated by imagining how different the scene would read if Henchard had peddled Susan on a street corner or offered her to a passing stranger. The difference between public auction and solitary sale roughly corresponds to the difference between ritualized gestures and private acts. As in religious ritual, Henchard's deed transforms the disparate observers into a makeshift fellowship, and they, in turn, socialize the sale, embedding it within a public context.

The gesture that opens the novel is just as morally ambiguous as the world its characters inhabit. Such ambiguity ultimately checks the traditional reading of the novel as tragedy. If Henchard's sale is not a crime, but a logical extension of the bourgeois view of marriage; if marriage, rather than representing a fixed and absolute ideal, is, in fact, a pragmatic social custom, one which, like wife selling, is doomed to extinction; and if sin and salvation form part of the same impulse, then the novel cannot be considered tragedy. By imposing a formal structure on what should be multifarious, such generic distinctions flatten Hardy's novel and deny its very meaning. Elizabeth-Jane's life, the narrator tells us in the much cited phrase, is a "general drama of pain" with occasional episodes of happiness. Drama of pain does not make for tragedy any more than occasional happiness makes for comedy. The novel's concluding statement, like its opening scene, is an expression of life's multiplicity and its resistance to any uniform interpretation.[6]

Thus despite its heavy handed plotting, *The Mayor of Casterbridge* is a novel of shifting impressions. As an anatomy of character, it offers a close examination of the unstable boundary that separates the interior self from the public persona. At what point, Hardy seems to ask, does the barbaric and the fetishistic veer into the civilized and the pious? Henchard's unforgettable act, like the man himself, integrates such oppositions. The hybrid gesture that opens the novel is not the manifestation of its hero's tragic flaw, but a carefully orchestrated proem that introduces the novel's primary focus: the problematic life and death of a "man of character," the drunken fetishist, the Mayor of Casterbridge.

NOTES

1. Thomas Hardy *The Mayor of Casterbridge*, ed. Ian Gregor (New Wessex Edition; London, 1974), p. 38.
2. Edward Westermarck, *The History of Human Marriage* (London, 1881; 1901*)*, pp. 399-400.
3. Sir John Lubbock, *The Origin of Civilization and the Primitive Condition of Man* (London, 1871; seventh ed. 1912). See Chapter IV, "The Origin of Marriage."
4. Elaine Showalter, in her illuminating essay, "The Unmanning of the Mayor of Casterbridge," observes that "paternity is the central subject of the book, far more important than conjugal love." Showalter points out what should be obvious, and yet it is surprising how few critics have drawn attention to this crucial detail: in addition to his wife, Henchard also sells his infant daughter. Showalter adds, "Perhaps one reason why the sale of the child has been consistently ignored is that the child is a female." Printed in *Critical Approaches to the Fiction of Thomas Hardy*, ed. Dale Kramer (London, 1979), p. 103.
5. And, of course, the second most crucial scene in the novel, Henchard's reunion with Susan, takes place in the Roman amphitheatre, the arena for yet another ancient ritual, now extinct.
6. See Ian Gregor's superb study of the novel, and especially this passage, in *The Great Web: The Form of Hardy's Major Fiction* (London, 1974), p. 128.

Hardy's Concept of Tragedy as Reflected in *The Mayor of Casterbridge*

SUMAN BALA and SUBHASH CHANDRA

According to Hardy "a tragedy exhibits a state of things in the life of an individual which unavoidably causes some natural aim or desire of his to end in a catastrophe."[1] And he goes on to aver that "The best tragedy—highest tragedy in short—is that of the WORTHY encompassed by the INEVITABLE. The tragedies of immoral and worthless people are not of the best."[2] Hardy was taken up with "mankind's predicament in the universe," which he found to be "a tragic theme."[3]

Hardy acquired a gloomy perspective on life because of the world he grew in. It was the world of agricultural labourers, whose life was full of tragedy. The vagaries of weather and oppressive social system made them helpless victims of forces beyond their control.

Hardy was a tender-hearted boy, extremely sensitive to pain and suffering around him. Such simple things like chopping of boughs off the trees or the death of a bird caused him anguish. His being witness to the two public hangings bruised his tender psyche lastingly. Since the world the young Hardy was exposed to was full of pain and disappointment, he came to regard these as the dominant features of man's life. He himself had begun to be haunted by a fear of insecurity and failure. He imagined "that a figure stood in his van, with arm uplifted, to knock him back from any pleasant prospect he indulged in as probable."[4]

Industrial revolution, eighteenth-century rationalism (which united with the new romantic spirit of rebellion against convention), criticism of the Bible and, above all, the Darwinian theory of evolution led to an atmosphere of fear and doubt towards the middle of the century. Like Matthew Arnold, Scott Fitzgerald, Thompson and other writers of the age, Hardy's greatest grief was that the old world was passing away with all its old beliefs, traditions, manners and customs. He eventually lost his faith at the age of twenty seven. But having lost his faith, he realized that he had nothing to fall back upon except for his own innate resources. He also felt that the new scientific interpretation of life resulted in a general loss of happiness.

The contention of the present paper is that Hardy's world view which subsumes man's nearly inevitable unhappiness in life, his undeserved suffering and the inscrutability of the forces which inflict misery on man is largely similar to the world view of the Greek tragic writers, with the mere difference that in Greek tragedy it is the divine agency of gods as against Hardy's unseen, abstract (even absurd) force called Fate, which brings unhappiness to human beings.

Hardy's writings reflect his tragic philosophy. The universe for him became a gigantic, "impersonal mechanism," functioning in accordance with some mysterious principle which he called the Immanent Will. This unknown, inscrutable principle operated in complete disregard of the feelings of human beings. Not only that, Hardy visualized man struggling with an omnipotent and indifferent Fate in the course of his existence. More often than not, man fought a losing battle with Fate which assumed different guises: nature, chance, social machinery, love or the inner inexplicable but mastering compulsions of a protagonist which forced him to act in a certain way and brought about his destruction. Elizabeth-Jane, for instance, perceives that many were treated cruelly by Fate and that "happiness was but an occasional episode in a general drama of pain."[5]

It has been almost unanimously agreed that "Hardy's works are tragedies of Fate rather than tragedies of character,"[6] though Guerard does not consider Hardy's "fatalism" as "philosophical commitment."[7] F. Manning, however, denies that Hardy's novels are tragedies because, he argues, that unlike the great art of Sophocles or of Shakespeare, Hardy's writings are didactic. Manning goes on to discuss the case of *Tess of the d'Urbervilles* and points out that Hardy shifts "the responsibility for the catastrophe on God, or Nature, or Fate, or Chance," which "is a fault in art."[8] Manning refers to the entirely passive character of Tess. "She interests us, not by what she does or says, but entirely by what she feels, entirely by her capacity for suffering."[9] Undoubtedly, Tess is much more a victim of circumstances than any other protagonist of Hardy is, but what Manning conveniently ignores is that Tess has "a certain d'Urberville strain that shows itself in occasional heedlessness and impulsive outbreaks."[10] Not only that, several actions are taken by Tess consciously which prove that she has a will of her own. She tries to stay at home after she has been raped, persistenly refuses to believe Alec's declarations that her husband, Angel, would not come back, murders Alec and enjoys five days of intense fulfilling love with Angel. More importantly, she is ready for her punishment without any trace of fear. Thus, she hits back at the circumstances, and she defies Fate by accepting it with dignity, courage and pride. In the manner of her death, she rises above her Fate. These are the essentials of tragedy. It is for this reason that J.I.M. Stewart does not find *Tess* to be a "depressing book."[11] Like all great tragedies, the novel graphically portrays the suffering of the protagonist, but it cheers the reader, at the same time, by establishing the superiority of the indomitable spirit, the Sisyphus-like quality which enables humans to spurn Fate.

Tragedy results for other protagonists also largely because they insist on living life on their own terms. They feel suffocated and restless in the walled security and imprisonment of the established conventions. Therefore, they escape into the wilderness to be able to act freely and in the process they meet their tragic death. Lawrence vehemently asserts, and rightly so, that Hardy's protagonists inhabiting Wessex "are always shooting out of a tight convention, a tight, hide-bound cabbage state into something quite madly personal. . . . And from such an outburst the tragedy usually develops."[12] Virginia Woolf also believes that Hardy's characters "live as individuals and they differ as individuals" and because they suffer through their "conflict with fate [they] enlist our sterner sympathies."[13]

Let us, for example, take the case of Eustacia Vye in *The Return of the Native*. She is powerful, grandly heroic and rebellious. A tragic chorus of country folk (differentiated from the actors in the drama) emphasizes her heroic isolation. Eustacia Vye is a young woman with romantic dreams of love and social brilliance. She marries under the illusion that her husband, Clym Yeobright, will fulfil her dreams, and help her to get away from her remote and constricted life on Egdon Heath. She attempts a desperate elopement with a former lover because of her disillusionment, conflict with her mother-in-law and a violent quarrel with her husband. While trying to escape to Paris, she is drowned and Wildeve also gets drowned in the process of rescuing her. Her passion, her pride and her pursuit of the illusory dream which she came to regard, though mistakenly, as the only way to fulfil herself, become her undoing. "Egdon Heath had been her 'cross' and, like Mrs. Yeobright, she was its victim."[14] Egdon Heath, in fact, serves as an evocative symbol and a powerful reminder of man's unchangeable place in nature. Simultaneously, the Heath measures each character's acceptance of his earthly fate. Clym, the native, for example, returns to the Heath as a humble furze-cutter and lives there as a blind suffering preacher. The Heath seems to effectively convey that human involvement in the grinding round of existence is unavoidable and that all visions of freedom or paradise are unfounded. Death is the only escape. J.I.M. Stewart rightly observes that Hardy "tended to equate tragedy with the play of Aeschylus and Sophocles."[15]

Jude the Obscure may have been trenchantly criticized for its excessive contrivance, but it remains a great tragic novel. Jude is continually torn between the flesh and the spirit. He has a keen ambition for higher education, but simultaneously he is gripped by an overpowering impulse for a sexually fulfilling relationship. His ambition for higher education is thwarted by the conservative deans of colleges, the conventions of the society and his sexual and self-degrading impulses. Jude's succumbing to the sensual charm of ignorant and crude Arabella because of his irrepressible sexual passion and his marriage to her have a touch of fatality about them. His desire for a vibrant, satisfying relationship with Sue is crushed by the society, religion and the tragic split in Sue's personality. When Sue decides to leave Jude, for him the whole "creation groans" with pain. Charity and compassion are snuffed out by the society and the church. Jude is not only buffeted around by his women, he is also ill-treated by life at large. He seems to be one who has been born to "accumulate bitter disasters about him."

The novel is as much a tragedy of Jude as it is of Sue. The contraries in her nature become responsible for her suffering. The tragic action of the novel is precipitated by her continual reversals. She continues to alternate between warmth and aloofness, commitment and withdrawal, propriety and unconventionality, her desire to project herself as sexually attractive and powerful, and yet remain sexually unavailable. She is an inveterate coquette, not by design, but by nature. The tragic split that creates the coquette becomes instrumental in bringing about Jude's as well as her own ruin.

More than any other novel, *The Mayor of Casterbridge* reflects the Greek vision of tragedy. It is "a Sophoclean-type drama played out in mid-nineteenth-century Dorchester."[16] Chance and the hero's temperamental characteristics combine to bring about his ruin. The first crucial act of Henchard is the sale of his wife, Susan, and this act is like the slaying of Laius by Oedipus as in both cases serious consequences ensue. Hardy deftly builds up the scene of the sale to culminate into the tragic action. Henchard, having entered the tent of the furmity woman, starts drinking furmity, with rum in it. "At the end of the first basin the man had risen to serenity; at the second he was jovial; at the third, argumentative; at the fourth, the qualities signified by the shape of his face, the occasional clench of his mouth, and the fiery spark of his dark eye, began to tell in his conduct; he was overbearing—even brilliantly quarrelsome." (6) In this intoxicated state, he gets into a conversation about the sale of wives and offers his own wife for sale. It is undeniable that both choice and chance play their role in the sale of Susan Henchard. Henchard's state of drunkenness cannot be attributed to chance. He accepts the rum of his own free choice, and he does so in order to induce in himself a frame of mind in which he may uninhibitedly express his accumulated frustrations. But the fact that the furmity woman is offering rum on the sly is a chance. Therefore, Henchard is not himself when he indulges in the act of bravado of offering Susan for sale. And above all, the appearance of Newson at that very moment like a spectre is a matter of pure chance. But for them, the sale would not have taken place. Likewise, Oedipus is no doubt a hot-tempered person, but he does not know the identity of the person whom he confronts and slays. Had he known who Laius was, the crucial act would not have taken place. However, between the two, Henchard remains relatively more culpable of his (mis)deed.

After this brief introductory account of Henchard's economic downfall and moral transgression at Weydon Priors and his resolution to make a start in a "new direction," Hardy suddenly bridges the gap of eighteen years and shows the outcome of the vow Henchard had made. Henchard is presented as a completely changed person who is rich and enjoys social standing. Not only that, events now seem to point to his further financial and social success. He gets the support and companionship of Farfrae, makes amends to his wronged wife and daughter and seems on the verge of finding a solution to the awkward situation created by his relationship with Lucetta. But just as Fate was lurking in the background all the time in *Oedipus the King* (Thebes was stricken by plague when Oediups was at the height of his glory), it registers its presence in the form of grown-corn (the result of a quirk of weather) at a time when Henchard is at the height of success.

Henchard's success and his personal goodness coincide. Even though Henchard's goodness is fitful, Hardy seems to emphasise at this stage the relation between the two. Henchard's frankness and affection for Farfrae, his anxiety for Lucetta, his efforts to atone his ill-treatment of Susan and Elizabeth Jane, his resolve to suffer the pangs which "these restitutory acts brought in their train," sum up Henchard's character in the initial few chapters.

Then start Henchard's worries and disappointments. His fortunes suffer a marked reverse. The games he arranges end up in a fiasco. He parts company with Farfrae who becomes his adversary. Not only that Farfrae's fortunes rise as a tradesman. At this time, the action is so organised that it again seems to have a connection with Henchard's moral decline, manifested in his frustrated fits of rage inflicted on persons who do not appear to deserve them and who in the process suffer intensely. This makes Henchard morally culpable. Hardy seems to suggest that Farfrae prospers because he is blameless and Henchard suffers decline as he is blameworthy. Then a coincidental degradation of the city, over which Henchard rules, takes place. A brutalized populace become witness to the moral degeneration of a society that has turned callous towards crime. The inhabitants of the Mixen Lane exhibit their despair of a society whose magistrates (having themselves offended against justice) have lost their moral authority. It is noteworthy that the furmity woman, "commits her low offence against the Church wall." This is very much reminiscent of the bad times in Thebes "where Sphinx is rampant."

As Henchard becomes vindictive and harsher, his fortunes register a perceptible decline. The "tussle . . . at fair buying and selling" had begun as a result of Henchard's impulsive nature, but it grows into a calculatedly vicious and desperately savage attempt to engineer Farfrae's financial ruin. Henchard becomes increasingly vengeful and determined to make Farfrae lick the dust and "to starve him out." Henchard's ire against Farfrae is followed by his visible coldness towards Elizabeth Jane. She becomes an innocent victim of Henchard's rage as he, by chance, discovers that she is not his but Newson's daughter. And, finally, Henchard makes his last bitter effort to score over Farfrae. He adopts the still more vicious method of extracting a promise of marriage from Lucetta against her will. This he does by cruelly threatening her that he would expose their former affair and defame her. Thus, Lucetta is calculatedly blackmailed into making the promise of marriage. The furmity woman is reintroduced at this stage by Hardy. She publicly exposes Henchard's past misdeed of selling his wife and becomes instrumental in bringing about Henchard's ruin.

But this relation between moral goodness and prosperity and happiness on the one hand and moral decline and failure and grief on the other is made inoperative by Hardy intentionally towards the end of the novel. Henchard tries his utmost to redeem himself. He takes several steps in this direction: he attempts to get pardon for his insane attack on Farfrae, makes efforts to save Lucetta's life, vows not to interfere with Farfrae's courtship of Elizabeth Jane, knowing fully well that he would lose her for ever. All these serve as incontrovertible proofs of the genuineness of Henchard's desire to do right. But his life does not register a corresponding happy change. On the contrary, he finds himself divested of all that he possessed. He leaves Casterbridge as an abandoned, lonely, self-condemned outcast. Hardy here emphatically underlines the idea that there is no connection between Henchard's moral stature and the factors which blindly nullify and negate his repentance.

It is, therefore, in the fitness of things that *The Mayor of Casterbridge* should conclude with the ruminations of Elizabeth Jane. She finally comes to the realization that one has to make the most of the limited opportunities life affords. She reflects on the inexplicable "persistence of the unforeseen" in the lives of men and comes to the conclusion that "neither she nor any human being deserved less than was given" while "there were others receiving less who had deserved much more." Hardy's intention in the novel is to show that there is no morally ordered universe, and that there is no connection between the moral stature of the protagonist and what he receives in life. Hardy achieves his end by underscoring the idea that it is a matter of pure coincidence that when a man is morally blameworthy, his fortunes decline and when he is morally good, he happens to prosper. It is nothing but Chance or Fate which according to the novelist, regulated men's lives and more often malignantly, with a view to depriving people of what they rightfully deserve and queering their quests for happiness.

Hardy's comments on Elizabeth's mental state towards the end of the novel, after Henchard has died, leaving his will (which is of a piece with Henchard's character, tending to swing between extremes of passion) reflect his philosophy about human existence: "Her experience had been of a kind to teach her, rightly or wrongly, that the doubtful honour of brief transit through a sorry world hardly called for effusiveness, even when the path was suddenly irradiated at some half-way point by daybeams rich as hers."[18]

The sub-title of the novel, "A Story of a Man of Character," has prompted some critics to explicate the novel in terms of the relationship of Henchard's character to his fate. Two discussions of *The Mayor of Casterbridge* reflect the almost polar extremes to which this divergence can tend: according to the interpretation of the novel offered by John Paterson, Henchard is a man guilty of having violated a moral order in the world and thus brings upon himself a retribution for his crime. On the other hand, Frederick Karl maintains a radically different view of the hero of the novel as he believes Henchard to be an "essentially good man who is destroyed by the chance forces of a morally indifferent world upon which he has obsessively attempted to impose his will."[17] But the critics have a tendency to go off the mark, in their desire to peel off the layers of meanings which they stoutly believe are covering a work of art. And that is what has happened in this case. All Hardy wanted to ensure by giving the sub-title was that the reader should not be misguided by the inconsistencies in Henchard's character and secondly to emphasize the tragic stature of his protagonist.

The novel remains, as discussed above, an explication of man's place in a Darwinian world, but simultaneously it affirms the transcendent worth of the human person, whose dignity is arrived at by test, denial, humiliation, disillusion, and defeat—by every possible accident of fate, ironic mischance, and the apparently hostile action of nature.

One could conclude that the tragic characters of Hardy, in spite of the buffetings they get at the hands of Fate, manage to retain the essence of human worth and dignity and survive, Greek-like, their havoc of ruin and defeat.

NOTES

1. Florence Emily Hardy, *The Life of Thomas Hardy, 1840-1928* (London: Macmillan, 1962), p. 76.

2. *Ibid.*, p. 251.
3. David Cecil, *Hardy: the Novelist* (Ludhiana: Lyall, 1987), p. 19.
4. Qtd. by David Cecil, p. 20.
5. Thomas Hardy, *The Mayor of Casterbridge* (London: Macmillan 1952), p. 330.
6. F.R. Southerington, *Hardy's Vision of Man* (London: Chatto and Windus, 1971), p. 34.
7. Albert J. Guerard, ed., *Hardy: A Collection of Critical Essays* (Englewood Cliffs, N.J.: Prentice-Hail, 1963), p. 5.
8. F. Manning, "Novels of Character and Environment," in R.P. Draper, ed., *Hardy: The Tragic Novels* (London: Macmillan, 1975), p. 61.
9. *Loc. cit.*
10. F.B. Pinion, *A Hardy Companion* (London: Macmillan, 1968), p. 47.
11. J.I.M. Stewart, *Thomas Hardy: A Critical Biography* (Thetford, Norfolk: Longman, 1971), p. 168.
12. D.H. Lawrence, "The Real Tragedy," in R.P. Draper, p. 64.
13. Virginia Woolf, "The Novels of Thomas Hardy," in R.P. Draper, pp. 73-74.
14. F.B. Pinion, p. 34.
15. J.I.M. Stewart, p. 93.
16. Martin Seymour-Smith, Introduction to *The Mayor of Casterbridge* (Harmondsworth, Middlesex: Penguin, 1978), p. 22.
17. Qtd. Robert C. Schweik, "Character and Fate in *The Mayor of Casterbridge*," in R.P. Draper, p. 133.

Nature and Paganism in *Tess of the d'Urbervilles*

CHARLOTTE BONICA

In May 1877, Thomas Hardy observed of himself, "I sometimes look upon all things in inanimate Nature as pensive mutes." And, nearly twenty years later, he confessed, "In spite of myself I cannot help noticing countenances and tempers in objects of scenery."[1] The same tendency to imbue nature with human qualities characterizes a well-known description of an August dawn in *Tess of the d'Urbervilles*:

> The sun, on account of the mist, had a curious sentient, personal look, demanding the masculine pronoun for its adequate expression. His present aspect, coupled with the lack of all human forms in the scene, explained the old-time heliolatries in a moment. One could feel that a saner religion had never prevailed under the sky. The luminary was a golden-haired, beaming, mild-eyed, God-like creature, gazing down in the vigour and intentness of youth upon an earth that was brimming with interest for him.[2]

The impulse that Hardy perceived in himself and that characterizes this passage—the tendency to perceive sentience in an inanimate environment, and particularly in nature—arises, in Hardy's view, from an innate and inescapable human need to make sense of the universe in humanly understandable terms, a need that ran counter to Hardy's own intellectual understanding of things. Hardy invests his characters, particularly those in his later novels, with the same inexorable need to discover in the universe a moral significance and a system of value capable of replacing the traditional orthodoxies that no longer satisfy them. Angel Clare, having rejected the "untenable redemptive theolatry" of his parents' faith, (153) arrives at Talbothays Dairy suffering from what Hardy calls "the ache of modernism," what David DeLaura has described as "the distress and rootlessness of those whose intellectual honesty forces them to live without a sense of Providence."[3] At Talbothays Angel seems to find a satisfying alternative to

Christianity in the "pagan" existence of the "summer-steeped heathens in the Var Vale" (197-98):

> Latterly he had seen only Life, felt only the great passionate pulse of existence, unwarped, uncontorted, untrammelled by those creeds which futilely attempt to check what wisdom would be content to regulate. (199)

Life at Talbothays seems to Angel more closely attuned to the natural world, and hence, more nearly suited to human desire than the life he has known before. More important, it seems to bear out his notion "that it might have resulted far better for mankind if Greece had been the source of the religion of modern civilization, and not Palestine." (199)

At the heart of the country people's paganism is the tendency to see congruence between events and situations in their own lives, and phenomena in the natural world: the dairy workers account for the failure of the butter to come by surmising the presence of lovers in the dairy (172); they interpret the cock's crow on the afternoon of Tess's wedding as a bad omen. (257-58) Tess herself, in spite of her Christian training, peoples the natural world with projections of her own imagination and emotions.

Angel, of course, never subscribes to the country superstitions, never deliberately adopts the rural consciousness that animates nature with human forms and human qualities. Yet he does begin to make:

> close acquaintance with phenomena which he had before known but darkly—the seasons in their moods, morning and evening, night and noon, winds in their different tempers, trees, waters and mists, shades and silence, and the voices of inanimate things. (157)

This passage immediately follows the statement that at Talbothays Angel has become "wonderfully free from the chronic melancholy which is taking hold of the civilized races with the decline of belief in a beneficent Power." (156) The implication is that, in the pagan attitude toward the natural world, Angel begins to discover a new source of value and a replacement for the exhausted creed of his parents' faith—a new way of making sense of a universe bereft of Providence.

Hardy's sympathy for Angel is clear: it is the sympathy of one whose own intellectual conclusions prevented him from belief in any sort of Providence, but who, late in life, described himself as "churchy; not in an intellectual sense, but insofar as instincts and emotions ruled." (*Life*, 376) Hardy understood the impulse to seek meanings and Providential designs in existence. He also understood the uneasiness and pain of "advanced" individuals who could no longer find such meanings in traditional orthodoxies. Yet Hardy shows that Angel's solution, a kind of vague and unexamined neopaganism, proves not only illusory, but dangerous. In enshrining Tess in his pagan pantheon as "a fresh and virginal daughter of Nature," (158) Angel turns her into a symbol of a way of life and a system of values, and ultimately plays an important role in her destruction.

In comparison to Hardy's harsh treatment of Angel's neopaganism, his treatment of the rural pagans is sympathetic. Indeed, the fact that many of their superstitions, like the two cited above, prove correct suggests that for them paganism is, in Hardy's view, an appropriate way of comprehending existence. But because their culture is circumscribed by the encroachment of civilization, their paganism is powerless. Like the genteel evangelicalism of the elder Clares, whom he also renders in a sympathetic light, their creed is dying. Though Stonehenge remains as a reminder of its past brutality, paganism is no longer powerful enough, except in the hands of a neopagan like Angel, to effect real harm. Indeed, Hardy portrays the country pagans, including Tess herself, with such sympathy that critics have argued that his intention in *Tess* is to suggest that the pagan relationship with nature offers modern individuals a useful replacement for Christianity.

Those who do so fail to see that in *Tess* every ascription of human qualities to natural objects, every perception of moral meaning in natural phenomena, is qualified and rendered unauthoritative. Most such passages describe not nature itself, but the response to nature of some character or implied observer. For example, the atmosphere in the Talbothays garden during Tess's first encounter with Angel is "in such delicate equilibrium and so transmissive that inanimate objects *seemed* endowed with two or three senses, if not five." (161) And later the hot weather of July "*seemed* an effort on the part of Nature to match the state of hearts at Talbothays Dairy." (189; emphasis added in both quotations)

Bruce Johnson has recently argued that, though Hardy discounts the validity of Angel's neopaganism, the rural paganism that Tess, unconsciously espouses represents a positive standard in the novel. "Hardy seems to associate the ability to be in touch with primeval pagan meanings with the ability to be in touch with the emotional, primitive sources of one's own being."[4] Using the "heliolatry" passage cited above as a basis for his argument, Johnson claims,

> Hardy implies that Christianity's capacity for creating guilt is unfortunate and that the old heliolatry had no such intent—that it must have been in this regard an unusually sane religion. Unlike Hardy's

> usual conception of deities, the sun-god finds earth "brimming with interest for him."[5]

Johnson overlooks the fact that the sun appears a beneficent deity because of the presence of the mist, a distorting medium that functions throughout *Tess* as a signal of moral or intellectual confusion. (Tess is seduced on a misty night; the morning mist encourages Angel's dangerous illusions about her.) Furthermore, Johnson fails to see as significant the phrase "one could see that," which implies the presence of an interpreting observer. What Hardy is saying here is that the appearance of the sun—distorted by the mist—makes it possible to understand the pagan impulse to perceive it in an anthropomorphic and beneficent deity. The old "heliolatries" may seem saner, may even seem to have a more understandable basis in the appearance of things. Hardy may even be implying that, in comparison with Christianity, paganism may represent an ethic more nearly suited to human desire. But for all that, paganism, in whatever form, is nevertheless based on the impossible premise that the natural world can function as a source of human value.

Moreover, the pagan perception of nature as alive with meaning to humans can be a double-edged sword. Although at times nature seems to reinforce human joy, it can also intensify human sorrow. If Tess can feel on her way to Talbothays that

> her hopes mingled with the sunshine in an ideal photosphere which surrounded her as she bounded along against the soft south wind. She heard a pleasant voice in every breeze, and in every bird's note seemed to lurk joy. (140)

She can also feel, after hearing the story of Jack Dollop, who refused to marry the woman he had seduced, that

> the evening sun was now ugly to her, like a great inflamed wound in the sky. Only a solitary cracked-voiced reed-sparrow greeted her from the bushes by the river, in a sad, machine-made tone, resembling that of a past friend whose friendship she had outworn. (174-75)

And later, oppressed by the conflict between her wish to accept Angel's proposal of marriage and her scruples against doing so, she sees in the setting sun

> a great forge in the heavens, and presently a monstrous pumpkin-like

> moon arose on the other hand. The pollard willows, tortured out of their natural shape by incessant choppings, became spiny-haired monsters as they stood up against it. (219)

Hence, although the sun may sometimes seem a beneficent deity, it can sometimes seem also to heighten human experience of suffering and sorrow. Worse, the natural world seems at times to be animated with a consciousness antipathetic to Tess's situation. After her liaison with Alec, during her evening walks,

> her whimsical fancy would intensify natural processes around her till they seemed a part of her own story. Rather they became part of it, for the world is a psychological phenomenon, and what they seemed they were. . . . A wet day was the expression of irremediable grief at her weakness in the mind of some vague ethical being whom she could not class definitely as the God of her childhood, and could not comprehend as any other. (120)

Although Tess's sense of guilt and her conception of a disapproving deity may be derived from conventional morality and traditional Christianity, her ascription of a disapproving consciousness to the natural world is entirely pagan. In short, she is a victim as much of her paganism as of her Christian training. And Hardy is quick to dismiss her sense of guilt as based on illusion:

> She looked upon herself as a figure of Guilt intruding into the haunts of Innocence. But all the while she was making a distinction where there was no difference. Feeling herself in antagonism, she was quite in accord. She had been made to break an accepted social law, but no law known to the environment in which she fancied herself such an anomaly. (121)

Citing this passage in support of his argument that in *Tess* pagan attitudes toward nature represent a valid model for human values, Johnson argues,

> Tess animates Nature with an attitude or mood that is antipathetic to it: she feels she is "guilty" and that nature is "innocent." But, says Hardy, both she and Nature are innocent. . . . Although she creates the world of Nature as a psychological phenomenon, the passage suggests that there is a more "real" Nature that her psychological perceptions cannot touch, a Nature not susceptible to judgments of guilt that must be called innocent.[6]

The truth is that when Hardy says that Tess is "in accord" with nature, he is merely saying that her sexuality, rather than separating her from the natural world, actually represents her connection to it. Her mistake consists not in her perception of a moral distinction between herself and the natural world, but in her ascription to nature, in the first place, of any morality at all.

The point is that human notions of innocence and guilt are entirely irrelevant in nature. When Tess feels guilty in comparison with nature, she is wrong, not because she, like nature, is actually innocent, but because in the natural world innocence and guilt are not at issue. Judging Tess and nature according to Christian values renders both guilty. Judging Tess and nature according to pagan values renders them both innocent. But Hardy's point is that both value systems are simply irrelevant in the natural world. Contrary to Johnson's conclusion, nature is neither innocent nor guilty, except insofar as it functions as a "psychological phenomenon" animated by the pagan impulse to perceive meaning in it. In itself, nature is devoid of moral significance.

For Hardy, nature operates according to laws that are not only independent of but at times at odds with human desire and the human sense of order. Its indifference to human suffering is clear in the episode in which Tess and her brother transport the bees to Casterbridge. It is Tess who ascribes a kind of moral order to the stars, imagining some as "blighted" and some as "sound." The stars themselves shine "amid the black hollows above, in serene dissociation from these two wisps of human life." (59) Nature is clearly indifferent to human notions of worldly distinction. At Talbothays, the sun casts against the barn wall the

> shadows of these obscure and homely figures [the dairy workers] every evening with as much care over each contour as if it had been the profile of a court beauty on a palace wall; copied them as diligently as it had copied Olympian shades on marble *facades* long ago, or the outline of Alexander, Caesar, and the Pharaohs. (142)

More important, the sun beats indifferently upon individuals without regard for moral distinctions. Even the country pagan Tess wonders "why the sun do shine on the just and the unjust alike." (165)

In fact, an essential quality of the natural world is the absolute absence from it of any moral value. It comprises myriad dynamic and urgent forces, indifferent not only to human life, but indeed to its own individual components:

> The season developed and matured. Another year's instalment of

> flowers, leaves, nightingales, thrushes, finches, and such ephemeral creatures, took up their positions where only a year ago others had stood in their place when these were nothing more than germs and inorganic particles. (168)

There is in Hardy criticism a long tradition that argues that the *summum bonum* in Hardy's universe is the life lived "in tune" with nature. Gabriel Oak and Diggory Venn are often cited as examples of individuals who live such lives successfully and, for the most part contentedly. Characters like Bathsheba, Farmer Boldwood, Eustacia, and Clym make the mistake, in this view, of failing to acknowledge the supremacy of nature; consequently, they remain unhappy until and unless they learn to do so. John Holloway, the most distinguished and persuasive proponent of this position, says, "The single abstraction which does most to summarize Hardy's view is simple enough: *it is right to live naturally*. . . . To live naturally is to live in continuity with one's whole biological environment."[7]

Holloway bases his argument in large part on Hardy's use of metaphor—his tendency to describe humans in terms from the natural world, and to see in the natural world human qualities. He cites, for example, a passage from *The Woodlanders* that "contains no less than ten metaphors. All of them do something to reinforce the impression that Nature has a quasi-human life."[8] He lists a number of comparisons of humans to animals, stating that among other things these metaphors "suggest a continuity between man and Nature."[9] Holloway concludes, "the ultimate effect of deliberately confusing human and natural in this way is to make them seem in essence, one and the same."[10] Similarly, John Paterson has more recently argued that Hardy's use of such metaphors makes people in novels . . . functions of wholly natural values and conditions . . . participants in some larger nonhuman drama."[11] In each case the critic has drawn a moral conclusion from what is, for Hardy, an essentially aesthetic technique.

One of Holloway's statements echoes a passage from Hardy's notebooks—an observation prompted by Edward Clodd's answer to Hardy's query about the similarities between the superstitions of "a remote Asiatic and a Dorset labourer":

> "The attitude of man," he says, "at corresponding levels of culture, before like phenomena, is pretty much the same, your Dorset peasants representing the persistence of the barbaric idea that confuses persons and things, and founds wide generalizations on the slenderest analogies."
>
> (This "barbaric idea which confuses persons and things" is, by the

way, also common to the highest imaginative genius—that of the poet.) (*Life*, 230)

Hardy's ironically amused observation—which is dated December 1890, shortly after he has completed the adaptation of *Tess* for serial publication—suggests that his use of metaphors that "confuse" the human and the natural is a function of his artistic, not moral, vision.

In an earlier notebook entry, Hardy pondered the question of the portrayal of nature in art:

> So then, if Nature's defects must be looked in the face and transcribed, whence arises the *art* in poetry and novel-writing which must certainly show art, or it becomes merely mechanical reporting. I think the art lies in making these defects the basis of a hitherto unperceived beauty, by irradiating them with "the light that never was" on their surface, but is seen to be latent in them by the spiritual eye. (*Life*, 114)

That Hardy is here thinking of "defects" that are moral rather than aesthetic is suggested by his use of a phrase from Wordsworth's "Elegiac Stanzas." In the poem the poet ponders the question, raised by his brother's death at sea, of nature's cruelty. Before that event, the poet would have cast upon an imagined seascape "the gleam./ The light that never was on sea or land,/ The consecration and the Poet's dream."[12]

Hardy's decision to make "Nature's defect . . . the basis of a hitherto unperceived beauty" represents a decision to portray nature not in terms of humanly conceived notions of moral value, but in purely aesthetic terms, by seeing them not with the eye of the moralist, but with that of the poet.

In 1890, Hardy wrote in his journal,

> Art is the changing of the actual proportions and order of things, so as to bring out more forcibly than might otherwise be done that feature in them which appeals most strongly to the idiosyncrasy of the artist. (*Life*, 228)

Hardy's own self-confessed "idiosyncrasy," as the passages quoted at the beginning of this paper suggest, was to emphasize the apparent likenesses he perceived between human life and the natural world. His metaphors, therefore, may "confuse" human and natural for aesthetic reasons, but they are not intended to suggest a moral connection between man and nature.

Paterson's awed response to Hardy's use of metaphors from nature blinds him to the larger moral issue of *Tess*. His claim that "to Hardy, Nature . . . was what his Angel Clare would call 'actualized poetry'" ignores the unconscious irony in Angel's worlds—Angel sees Tess not as she is, but as a figure in a Romantic poem celebrating rural simplicity. Paterson celebrates the "transfigurations" of the country folk on their walk home from the Chaseborough dance, without taking into account the larger implications of the situation—the country folk, immersed in an alcoholic dream of "at oneness" with nature, are soon to begin the fracas from which Tess is forced to escape into Alec's arms. Paterson fails to see that the mist that settles on Tess's hair like seed pearls serves to reinforce Angel's tendency to see Tess not as she is, but as a goddess.[13]

In short, by failing to notice "how Hardy's nature similes function fictionally,"[14] Paterson begs important questions raised in *Tess*. By claiming that Hardy makes his characters not "functions of their merely social values and conditions[,] . . . participants in a merely human drama," but instead "functions of wholly natural values and conditions[,] . . . participants in some larger nonhuman drama," Paterson ignores, first, that Hardy's characters, and Tess in particular, are indeed participants in a concrete social system; second, that there are no such things in Hardy's universe as "wholly natural values," because there are no values in nature, except those imagined by humans; and third, that, though nature itself may be a "larger nonhuman drama," the introduction of humans into it must necessarily introduce "social values and conditions."

The interpretation offered by both critics—explicitly by Holloway, implicitly by Paterson—is that since the natural world is grander than human life, since in a sense it supersedes human life, man ought to seek lessons in how to live from nature, lessons that in effect are moral. It is true that in Hardy's universe nature supersedes human life in a purely biological sense, but nature can never entirely satisfy the human need to find value and moral meaning in existence. It is, in fact, man's moral nature that distinguishes him from the natural world and that unfits him to find satisfaction in a universe devoid of humanly understandable notions of justice, morality, and value. Hence, Hardy's often-quoted lament, recorded in his notebooks during his work on *Tess*:

> A woeful fact—that the human race is too extremely developed for its corporeal conditions, the nerves being evolved to an activity abnormal in such an environment. . . . It may be questioned if Nature, or what we call Nature, so far back as when she crossed the line from invertebrates to vertebrates, did not exceed her mission. This planet does not supply the materials for happiness to higher existences. (*Life*, 218)

In a letter that appeared in the May 17, 1902, issue of *The Academy and Literature* and was reprinted in the *Life*, Hardy responded to a published review of Maeterlinck's *Apology for Nature*. Hardy takes exception to the reviewer's "approval [of Maeterlinck's] vindication of Nature's ways, which is (as I understand it) to the effect that, though she does not appear to be just from our point of view, she may practise a scheme of morality unknown to us in which she is just." Hardy goes on to expose the "sophistry" in Maeterlinck's argument:

> Pain has been, and pain is: no new sort of morals in Nature can remove pain from the past and make it pleasure for those who are its infallible estimators, the bearers thereof. And no injustice however slight, can be atoned for by her future generosity, however ample, so long as we consider Nature to be, or to stand for unlimited power.

Hardy agrees with Maeterlinck only in his conclusion, "that to model our conduct on Nature's apparent conduct . . . . can only bring disaster to humanity." (*Life*, 314-15)

The "continuity" that Holloway sees, the human participation in "some larger nonhuman drama" that Paterson sees, do exist in a limited way; but the continuity is not moral. Human values, human desires, human distinctions between good and evil are, as Tess sometimes notices, entirely irrelevant in nature. To argue that the natural world could, in any sense, provide man with any principle of moral order is to ignore the profound moral *dis*continuity between man and nature.

The one particularly exigent connection between man and nature is that of sexuality. Like other natural forces, the sexual impulse is essentially amoral; it influences human destiny without regard for human notions of appropriateness. In *Tess* especially, Hardy dramatizes its effect on human life:

> Amid the oozing fatness and warm ferments of the Froom Vale, at a season when the rush of juices could almost be heard below the hiss of fertilization, it was impossible that the most fanciful love should not grow passionate. The ready bosoms existing there were impregnated by their surroundings. (189)

It is quite significant that the metaphor in the last sentence is clearly sexual. The only real "continuity" between man and nature consists in nature's "impregnation" of the sexual impulse into human life.

Holloway's often sound discussion of nature itself in Hardy's fiction does not take into account the pervasiveness, especially in the later novels, of sexuality throughout nature. Thus, he fails to notice that a number of the metaphors he sees as reinforcing the idea of "continuity" between man and nature occur in situations charged with sexuality. He points out, for example, a passage from *The Woodlanders* that describes the affection between Grace and Fitzpiers as growing "as imperceptibly as the twigs budded on the trees." He notices in *Tess* the notion that Tess and Angel are "converging, under an irresistible law, as surely as two streams in one vale." He cites the garden scene in which Tess listens to Angel's harp "like a fascinated bird." But he fails to notice that the natural metaphors in these passages are particularly significant in view of Hardy's conviction that natural forces and human life converge only in the human sexual impulse.[15]

Holloway's formula, "It is right to live naturally," though perhaps appropriate to Hardy's earlier novels, is no longer sufficient in the universe of *Tess* precisely because "to live in continuity with one's whole biological . . . environment" would mean to surrender to the force of sexuality. Apart from moral objections to such a way of life, the issue is complicated by human choice in such matters, by human emotions, and by human notions of value. Indeed, Holloway undermines his own argument with the statement,

> The people whom Hardy presents in an altogether sympathetic light are like Gabriel Oak, Diggory Venn and Giles Winterbourne—all solid sterling characters completely satisfied with their position in life and at one with it. Their only misfortunes are in love.[16]

Love, a wholly human emotion, is precisely what bars these characters from living out Holloway's dictum. And Hardy's point is that human emotions and human values make it impossible to "live naturally," By the time of *Tess*, he shows that such a way of life is impossible not only for the modern individual like Angel, but indeed for Tess herself, easily the most "natural" character, by Holloway's definition, in Hardy's fiction. Even the dairymaids, whom Holloway describes as "resigned to disappointments[,] . . . taking it for granted that Angel will not marry one of them,"[17] suffer acutely from the intransigence of their sexual impulses:

> The air of the sleeping-chamber seemed to palpitate with the hopeless passion of the girls. They writhed feverishly under the oppressiveness of an emotion thrust upon them by cruel Nature's law—an emotion which they had neither expected nor desired. . . . The differences which distinguished them as individuals were abstracted by this passion, and each was but portion of one organism called sex. (187)

To live as these women do in the midst of natural processes means to feel acutely the inescapable influence of the sexual force, which operates without regard for human feelings. In their case, it means also to suffer acutely the thwarting of their sexual impulses by the restraints imposed not only by conventional morality, but also by the realities of human emotions. That is, even without conventional moral restraints, these women would suffer because they prefer above other men Angel Clare, who himself prefers Tess above them. In his notebook Hardy says, "Emotions have no place in a world of defect," (149) and in *Tess* he dramatizes the statement vividly with the plight of the dairymaids.

Holloway seems to forget that after Angel marries Tess, Betty attempts suicide, Marion seeks another sort of oblivion in alcohol and Izz sinks into a deep depression. The point is that far from providing human life with moral significance, the natural world, particularly through its inexorable sexual force, displays cruelty and injustice.

The idea that nature in Hardy's fiction is fraught with moral meaning is common. As I have suggested, this view springs from the failure to take into account a shift in Hardy's attitudes. The earlier novels reveal a pastoralism that, though qualified, seems to illustrate the superiority of the simplicities of the rural state of mind over the complexities of the modern consciousness. Even *Tess of the d'Urbervilles* reveals a deep regret over the passing of the rural culture. Yet however nostalgic Hardy feels about the death of country life, he does not suggest that its central, though unconscious, attitudes toward nature—its paganism—can realistically provide a balm for "the ache of modernism."

Angel Clare's freedom from this "ache" is brief. As soon as he realizes that Tess is not the goddess he has imagined her to be, the fragile construct of his neopaganism collapses. Hardy invites his reader to condemn Angel's cruelty to Tess, but he also reveals an acute understanding of Angel's need to find values that can make sense of existence. Indeed, the self-conscious, almost sheepish, tone of the second of the two notebook entries cited at the opening of this paper suggests Hardy's awareness of the persistence, after twenty years, of the impulse in himself to imbue with meaning a morally vacuous universe.

NOTES

1. Florence Emily Hardy, *The Life of Thomas Hardy, 1840-1928* (1928, 1930; rpt. London: Macmillan, 1962), pp. 114, 285 (second quotation, 10 Feb. 1897).
2. *Tess of the d'Urbervilles* (1891; rpt. London: Macmillan, The New Wessex Edition 1974), p. 122.

3. "'The Ache of Modernism' in Hardy's Later Novels," *ELH*, 34 (1967), pp. 380-99.
4. "'The Perfection of Species' and Hardy's Tess" in *Nature and the Victorian Imagination*, ed. U.C. Knoepflmacher and G.B. Tennyson (Berkeley: Univ. of California Press, 1977), pp. 259-77.
5. Johnson, p. 262.
6. *Ibid.*, pp. 261-62.
7. "Hardy," *The Victorian Sage: Studies in Argument* (1953; rpt. New York, 1965), pp. 245-89.
8. Holloway, p. 257.
9. *Ibid.*, p. 270.
10. *Ibid.*, p. 267.
11. "Lawrence's Vital Source: Nature and Character in Hardy" in *Nature and the Victorian Imagination*, pp. 455-69.
12. *Wordsworth: Poetical Works*, ed. Thomas Hutchinson, rev. Ernest de Selincourt (London: Oxford Univ. Press, 1969), pp. 452-53, ll. 15-16.
13. Paterson, pp. 456, 465.
14. David J. DeLaura, "Nature Naturing: Literary Natural History," *Victorian Studies*, 22 (Winter 1979).
15. Holloway, p. 269.
16. *Ibid.*, p. 282.
17. *Ibid.*, p. 283.

Jude the Obscure: Reading and the Spirit of the Law

RAMON SALDIVAR

The letter killeth, but the spirit giveth life.

II Corinthians

Concern for the nature and response of an author's audience is, in some respects, one of the original tasks of literary criticism. Over the past decade, however, attempts to incorporate rhetorical, linguistic, and cognitive theories into literary criticism have led to the development of a hefty bibliography on the nature of the reader's role in the communication network of author, text, and reader. These reader-oriented studies stress, from their various perspectives, that the reader, as much as any character, contributes to the shaping of the novel's fictive world through his interpretive actions.[1]

The value of the recent emphasis on the reader's role in fiction and of "reception history" in general could very well be tested by a text such as the author's "Postscript" to *Jude the Obscure*. There, the reading pubic is accused of "curing"[2] the novelist of all desire to write prose fiction. In this case Hardy would seem to have us question the reader's role in the *destruction* of texts, for in no uncertain terms, it is the reader, in his incapacity to read, who is the problem. Since we cannot read his meaning properly even where there has been no "mincing of words" in its enunciation, complains Hardy, he will spare himself and the reader by simply ceasing to write novels.[3]

Yet readers often find this and Hardy's later comment that he expected *Jude the Obscure* to be read as "a moral work" (ix) somewhat disingenuous. We can hardly imagine, after the reception of *Tess* and after his attempt to cancel his contract with Harper & Brothers for *Jude*, that Hardy would not have anticipated the "shocked criticisms" (ix) that the publication of the novel evoked. In fact, when Hardy announces in the "Preface to the First Edition" that the novel will "deal unaffectedly with the fret and fever, derision and disaster, that may press in the wake of the strongest passion known to humanity," (vii) and then denies that "there is anything in the handling to which exception can be taken," (viii) he raises the very real possibility that the novel will be misread.

And it was misread. Angry reviewers and a solemn bishop saw in it, among other things, a cynical attack on the sacrament and institution of marriage. In a letter of November 1895 to Edmund Gosse, Hardy continued to express his concern for the proper reading of his novel by indicating that *Jude* was not merely "a manifesto on 'the marriage question' (although, of course, it involves it)," but was more the story of the tragic result of two marriages because of "a doom or curse of hereditary temperament peculiar to the family of the parties."[4] The fact is, of course, as critics have convincingly argued, that the novel is concerned with the marriage laws in more than just a casual way.[5] And Hardy himself points out that the plot of *Jude* is "geometrically constructed"[6] around the marital realignments of the four principal characters. They repeatedly change their relationship through their alternately prospective and retrospective visions of one another and of the options society and nature allow them.

Poised between a desire for natural freedom and the need for a stabilizing social order, Hardy's characters try to act within their "geometrically constructed" system of marital and symbolic associations to accommodate their desires and needs. Hardy is clear about this. He tells us that *Jude the Obscure* dramatizes the sociological effect of the Victorian failure to reconcile the antithetical realms of culture and nature: "The marriage laws [are] used . . . to show that, in Diderot's words, the civil law should be only the enunciation of the law of nature." ("Postscript," x) But the difficulty of reading *Jude* properly may well stem from the fact that the novel is more than a realistic analysis of the historical condition of marriage in late Victorian England. I would like to suggest that the ambiguous status of the act of reading in the author's prefatory statements is only an indicator of a more radical investigation concerning reading and interpretation. By considering the interplay between "natural" and "civil" law, and by examining the nature of Hardy's "geometrically constructed" plot, we will be able to reflect on the possible relation of these issues to the apparent ease with which, according to Hardy, the novel can be misread. A reading of *Jude* that attempts to account for this cluster of formal and thematic elements can, I think, provide a new perspective on Hardy's conception of the realistic novel.

A first difficulty in understanding the novel is thematic and stems from the portrayal in the text itself of numerous cases of misreading. From the beginning, for instance, Jude sees in Christminster and its university the image of an attainable ideal world. His desire for this ideal vision involves a rejection of reality. For his own sporadically controlled, partially understood world, he substitutes the image of a unified, stable, and understandable one. Beguiled by his desire for order, the young Jude thus turns initially to language study both as a means of entering university life and as a possible course of stability. The narrator tells us:

> Ever since his first ecstasy or vision of Christminster and its possibilities, Jude had meditated much and curiously on the probable sort of process that was involved in turning the expressions of one language into those of another. He concluded that a grammar of the required tongue would contain, primarily, a rule, prescription, or clue of the nature of a secret cipher which, once known, would enable him, by merely applying it, to change at will all words of his own speech into those of the foreign one. . . . Thus he assumed that the words of the required language were always to be found somewhere latent in the words of the given language by those who had the art to uncover them, such art being furnished by the books aforesaid. (I. iv.30-31)

Jude feels betrayed, consequently, when in his attempt to learn Latin he finds that "there was no law of transmutation, as in his innocence he had supposed." (31) Jude's desired "law of transmutation," the "secret cipher" to a system of translation, could exist only if a prior permanent code existed to allow a free substitution of signifiers for one autonomous signified. The metaphor of translation at this early point in the novel is doubly interesting. It both reveals Jude's desire for a serenely immobile text whose content might be transported without harm into the element of another language, and alludes to the relation Hardy establishes in the "Postscript" of 1912 between civil and natural law, making one the "enunciation" (x) of the other. These will continue to be decisive issues throughout the novel. At this point, Jude has no doubt that the voice of nature can, indeed, be read and translated, for when he "address[es] the breeze caressingly," it seems to respond: "Suddenly there came along this wind something towards him—a message . . . calling to him. 'We are happy here!'" (I.iii.22) By imposing single terms on the disparate variety of experience, we come to know and control our environment. Early on, however, Jude intuits that language is not a fixed system through which meaning can be "transmuted" from one system to another. Yet this is precisely the insight that Jude refuses to apply to his other readings of the world around him.

As he proceeds into the countryside, where the markings that hint at the limitations already imposed on his life stand to be deciphered, Jude's readings continue: "The only marks on the uniformity of the scene were a rick of last year's produce . . . and the path . . . by which he had come. . . . [To] every clod and stone there really attached associations enough and to spare—echoes of songs . . . of spoken words, and of sturdy deeds." (I.ii.10) History, echoing across the generations, seems to focus on Jude at the bottom of "this vast concave" field, (I.ii.9) but he does not yet understand its voice. The substance of this discourse latent in the countryside is the essential dimension of the tradition into which he has been born. These "marks" and "associations" in the landscape of Wessex are "signs" inscribed by the force motivating all events, which Hardy was in *The Dynasts* to name the "Immanent Will." Thus, long before his birth, long before the story of his family has been inscribed, this tradition has already traced the pattern of behaviour within which are ordered the possible changes and exchanges that will occur in Jude's short life. Each crucial event in Jude's life seems to invite the reader to interpret Jude's actions as an attempted reading of the role ascribed to him in some determining book of fate.

Initially, the young orphan Jude seems to see the schoolmaster, Phillotson, as an embodiment of his controlling "dreams," (I.iii.20) and as a symbolic substitute for the absent "real" father.[7] Accordingly, when Phillotson leaves Marygreen, Jude replaces him with an ideal representation. Jude reads that ideal presence into the natural landscape of Wessex as Christminster "that ecclesiastical romance in stone" (I.v.36):

> Through the solid barrier of cold cretaceous upland to the northwards he was always beholding a gorgeous city—the fancied place he likened to the new Jerusalem. . . . And the city acquired a tangibility, a permanence, a hold on his life, mainly from the one nucleus of fact that the man for whose knowledge and purposes he had so much reverence was actually living there. (I.iii.20)

In this ecstatic vision, Christminster, whose mark is "a halo or glow-fog," (I.iii.21) seems to send that "message" (I.iii.22) I mentioned earlier, but it is a message that must be translated from natural to human terms with all the inherent errors of language and its "figures." (I.iii.25) In a moment of revelation, George Eliot's narrator in *Adam Bede* comments that "Nature has her language, and she is not unveracious; but we don't know all the intricacies of her syntax just yet, and in a hasty reading we may happen to extract the very opposite of her real meaning."[8] Now, as Jude attempts to learn the "syntax" of nature's "message," Christminster, through Phillotson, becomes the organizing center of his life: "It had been the yearning of his heart to find something to anchor on, to cling to—for some place which he could call admirable. Should he find that place in this city if he could get there?" (I.iii.24) The phrasing of his question in the rhetorical mode produces a grammatical structure that implies the existence of freedom of choice, when in fact, the pattern of choices has already been established for Jude by his own propensity for misreading. As he answers the questions posed in indirect discourse, beguiled by the transformation his mind has imposed on the scene through figurative language, Jude takes literally his own metaphors of the "new Jerusalem." "the city of light," and "the castle, manned by scholarship and religion." (I.iii.24-25)

Sue Bridehead is also presented in the metaphoric language that names Christminster. Jude has seen, for example, "the photograph of [her] pretty girlish face, in a broad hat, with radiating folds under the brim like the rays of a halo." (II.i.90) In fact, the metaphoric process by which Sue will later replace Christminster and Phillotson in Jude's dreams has been facilitated by the nature of Jude's language long before he is even conscious of Sue: earlier, he had become "so romantically attached to Christminster that, like a young lover alluding to his mistress, he felt bashful at mentioning its name." (I.iii.22) The transfer from Phillotson to Christminster, and finally to Sue as metaphors of that sustaining vision is thus a simple, determined step. Jude's false reading of Sue at a chapel in Christminster as being "ensphered by the same harmonies as those which floated into his ears" leads him to conclude that he has "at last found anchorage for his thoughts." (II.iii.107) When Jude finally meets Sue, he approaches her cautiously and speaks to her as he has spoken of Christminster, "with the bashfulness of a lover." (II.iv.117) At each step in the evolution of his story, his controlling dream is a fiction that he imposes on wayward circumstances.[9]

From the beginning then, the object of desire is not "real" in any sense, but is a "phantasmal" (II.ii.97) creation of Jude's own mind, as are the "ghosts" that hunt Christminster. For Jude, however, the ghosts of his desires disappearing into the "obscure alleys" of Christminster are as real as Arabella's "disappearance into space." (II.i.92) Constituting himself as a whole subject by an identification with another who repeatedly disappears, "A hungry soul in pursuit of a full soul," (III.x.233) Jude is accordingly threatened by the possibility of disappearing too: "Jude began to be impressed with the isolation of his own personality, as with a self-spectre . . . seeming thus almost his own ghost." (II.i.92) Phillotson, Christminster, Arabella, and most strikingly, Sue, thus become the figures of an ideal paradise, which is fundamentally inaccessible, insofar as it is one more metaphor in a structuring system of substitutions and exchange of phantasmal dreams. The displacement of desire among the various characters points out the existence of a symbolic order, which creates the idea of autonomy when, in fact, the characters exist determined by their propensity for interpretive error.

As an exegetic scholar, "divining rather than beholding the spirit" of his texts, (I.v.34) Jude can never resist the temptation to read deep meanings, the "assemblage of concurring and converging probabilities" of "truths," into a scene. (II.i.95) Yet it is less "absolute certitude" (II.i.95) that lies hidden beneath the manifest content of human experience in the novel than it is a mystified, but nonetheless threatening, organization of that content. When Jude thereafter looks into Sue's "untranslatable eyes" (II.ii.104) and immediately begins to interpret her character, he is only repeating the established pattern of error. Despite the difference in the agency that produces it, Jude manifests again the desire for that earlier "law of transmutation." Here, Sue's eyes reveal a text to be translated, but, as with the Greek and Latin grammars, no master code exists to guarantee the authority of Jude's translation. The rules governing the metonymic transfer, the figure Latin rhetoric calls *transmutio*, belong to the same illusion of a metaphysics of presence in the word, and to the same hallucination of a language determined on the basis of a verbal representation.[10] Just as language is constituted through repetition, so too does Jude's life acquire a narratable consistency. But the symbolic "inscription" of Jude's desires upon the surface of Wessex as he travels its roads from Christminster to Shaston, to Aldbrickham and back again, constitutes only the provisional creation of meaning through a process of deferment. As Jude's dreams are transmuted from Arabella to Christminster, and to Sue, the fantasy of stability creates an apparently meaningful and readable text. It is always only in retrospect, however, that Jude's perception of those illusions of totality and stability can be organized and lived as an aesthetically coherent meaning.

But it is more the inner tensions produced by the characters' shifting relations that shape the action than haphazard or indifferent circumstance. And it is not entirely coincidental that the act of reading surfaces again to indicate these changes in connection with the constant letters that reaffirm the importance of writings, signs, inscription, and marks in the lives of these characters.[11] Altogether there are at least thirty-two letters indicated or implied in the novel, ranging from one-line suicide notes (*"Done because we are too menny"*) to full-sized "carefully considered epistle[s]," (VI.iv.433) directly or indirecly narrated, delivered or not delivered. The numerous instances of inscriptions and carvings reinforce the importance of the "letter" in the text as the emblem for the force of illusion.

The first of these letters between Jude and Sue had simply called for their initial meeting, but it was "one of those documents which, simple and commonplace in themselves, are seen retrospectively to have been pregnant with impassioned consequences." (II.iv.115-16) By the time Sue is engaged to Phillotson, Jude is receiving sudden "passionate" letters (III.i.153) from her that seem to close the psychic distance between them in a way that they can never quite imitate in person. "It is very odd—" Jude says at one point.

"That you are often not so nice in your real presence as you are in your letters!" "Does it really seem so to you?" asks Sue, who then replies, "Well, that's strange; but I feel just the same about you, Jude." (III.vi.197) A letter is a medium that effectively separates the writer from the effects of the message, while the message received is often one created by the reader himself. Even in their coldest tones, Sue's letters, while banishing Jude, nevertheless constantly summon him to her by the very fact that they establish a link of communication between them. Similarly, Phillotson's letter relinquishing Sue paradoxically begins re-establishing his hold on her; for the "shadowy third," (IV.v.288) like the substantial couple, is always primarily constituted by this act of communication.

Moreover, when Sue writes a letter, she simultaneously removes and retains her absence and distance. The simultaneity of absence and presence is primarily an outcome of written discourse and is indicative of Jude's more general mystification concerning the existence of a stabilizing meaning. Sue is an eminently desirable woman, but she also becomes a sign in Jude's mind for an absent source of meaning. Accordingly, the act of writing becomes a bolster for the illusion of presence and wholeness within a discourse that appears innocent and transparent. Sue's letter can never replace her, but, conversely, her "real presence" is never identical with the original self promised in the letter. The written word does not allow access to the thing in itself, but always creates a copy, a simulacrum of it that sometimes moves the reader of the word more strongly than can the actual presence of the represented thing. Thus, the curious result is that the graphic sign, rather than the actual presence, of the desired becomes the cause of emotive energy. For Jude, the desire for this originary "anchoring point" becomes an indispensable illusion situated in the syntax of a dream without origin.

The intersubjective complex that structures the novel *Jude the Obscure* offers us some version of the following schema:

(1) dreams that fail—Jude, Phillotson, Sue;
(2) marriages that fail—Jude and Arabella; Sue and Phillotson; Jude and Sue; Arabella and Cartlett; both sets of parents; the legendary ancestor (mentioned in V.iv.340);
(3) returns to original failures—Jude and Arabella at Christminster; Sue and Phillotson at Marygreen.

We began, remember, with Jude and Arabella at Marygreen, and with Sue and Phillotson at Christminster. The intervening movements in the plot that lead to the present renewal of the characters' former relations thus trace the pattern that characterizes the narrative structure. It is a *chiasmus*, the cross-shaped substitution of properties: the original couples are reunited, but in reverse locales. Hardy had referred to this structure more obliquely as the "geometric construction" behind his novel. Elsewhere he calls it the "quadrille" that puts in motion the opposing qualities of the four main characters. But it turns out that the very process of "construction" that the characters' actions enact is really one more reversal of earlier misguided "constructions." Would it not follow then that this new turn should restore the characters to their "proper" places? That is, if Jude and Sue have been improperly associated at Christminster, might we not recover a measure of truth by simply restoring her to Phillotson at Marygreen? Since this structure of reversal is not only at work on the thematic level of the story, within the marital relationships among the characters, but also animates the greater structure of the narrative, the plot itself, the deconstruction of its pattern has significant implications for the novel's concept of a readable, constructive, integrating process in general.

Jude's idea of synthetic "anchoring point" of semantic stability originates as the effect of a prior requirement, namely, the requirement that the elements of that synthesis can themselves be permanently fixed in relation to stable qualities. Failing to integrate the ideal and the real with Sue, Jude is no more likely to do so with Arabella. Sue's situation with Phillotson and Jude is even more complex, for the two are versions of the same in different registers. Further reversals, consequently, promise only continued instability. And, I would say, it makes little difference in this novel whether one calls the trope governing the structure of the narrative metaphor, metonymy, chiasmus, or simply a "geometric construction," for from the first, the characters' roles have been inscribed in the determining contextual system defined by the marriage laws.

In the Victorian novel marriage is preeminently the foundation of social stability. As a quasi-contractual agreement, it sets up the participants as a center for other integrating relationships. These relationships are not simply necessary for society; they constitute it. And that larger social and historical life, the world of symbolic relationships, forms in dialectical turn the structure that orders individual behaviour in Hardy's novels. In a moment of pure poetic insight Sue comments on the nature of those relations:

> I have been thinking . . . that the social moulds civilization fits us into have no more relation to our actual shapes than the conventional shapes of the constellations have to the real star-patterns. I am called Mrs. Richard Phillotson, living a calm wedded life with my counterpart of that name. But I am not really Mrs. Richard Phillotson, but a woman tossed about, all alone, with aberrant passions, and unaccountable antipathies. (IV.i.246-47)

With remarkable clarity Sue recognizes that the social woman is a representation, transposed and supplemented by desire, of her real self. But the relation between her natural and social selves is like the relation between "real star-patterns" and traditional interpretations of the "conventional" constellation shapes, like that between a referent and its linguistic sign—that is, *aesthetic* and hence *arbitrary*. The concept of the self is the product of an aberrant substitution of rhetorical properties. Sue here clearly understands that this rhetorical operation is at best a metaphorical, interpretive act—one that is necessarily open to a variety of figural misreadings.

We have seen that the law that regulates marriage ties in this novel superimposes the kingdom of *culture* on that of *nature*.[12] Following its dictates, Jude artificially imposes a vision of organic totality (figured at different times by Phillotson, Christminster, Sue, etc.) onto nature and accords it a moral and epistemological privilege. In contrast, the narrator's ironic comments show Jude's substitutions and realignments within the marriage system and within the pattern of metaphors for his vision of an "anchoring point" to be purely formal, analogous only by contingency, and hence without privilege. When the value of those associations is questioned, when the notion of Sue as the representation of Jude's dreams is made problematic, the possibility of a simple relation between signified and signifier is also questioned.

That formerly unquestioned assumption is the original moment of illusion that the narrative demystifies. The narrator reveals to us that Jude's and Sue's notion of a privileged system of law is an hypothesis, or a fictional construct (*a doxa*), that makes the orderly conduct of human affairs possible. It is not a "true" and irrefutable axiom based on knowledge (*an episteme*).[13] Their tendency, as revealed by the metaphorical rhetoric of their desires, is always to abide by the lawful order of "natural" logic and unity: "It is," Sue says at one point, "none of the natural tragedies of love that's love's usual tragedy in civilized life, but a tragedy artificially manufactured for people who in natural state would find relief in parting!" (IV.ii.258) But if the order of "natural" law is itself a hypothetical construct rather than a "natural" occurrence in the world, then there is no necessary reason to suppose that it can, in fact, provide "relief." And it is Sue once again, who, after the tragic deaths of their children, perceives that possibility when she says to Jude:

> We said . . . that we would make a virtue of joy, I said it was Nature's intention, Nature's law and *raison d'etre* that we should be joyful in what instincts she afforded us—instincts which civilization had taken upon itself to thwart. . . . And now Fate has given us this stab in the back for being such fools as to take Nature at her word! (VI.ii.408-9)

Jude, who likes to think of himself "as an order-loving man" of an "unbiased nature," (IV.ii.252) can only stand by helplessly as he hears Sue destroy the basis of their "natural" marriage.[14]

Hardy's novel situates itself explicitly within the context of the marriage laws that establish Victorian society. It portrays, as Hardy tells us, the attempted translation of the law of nature into civil terms. The characters, however, cannot legitimately perform this translation without confusing the names of two such divergent semantic fields as those covered by "natural law" and "civil law." Confusion arises because the terms designate contextual properties, patterns of integration and disintegration, and not absolute concepts. In Hardy's Wessex, the "law of nature" designates a state of relational integration that precedes in degree the stage of "civil law" since civil law only "enunciates" what is already present in nature to be read. The undoing of a system of relations codified in "civil law" will always reveal, consequently, a more fragmented stage that can be called "natural." This prior stage does not possess moral or epistemological priority over the system that is being undone.[15] But Jude always does assign it priority.

Remembering that "his first aspiration—towards academical proficiency—had been checked by a woman, and that his second aspiration—toward apostleship—had also been checked by a woman," Jude asks himself ungallantly: "Is it . . . that the women are to blame; or is it the artificial system of things, under which the normal sex-impulses are turned into devilish domestic gins and springs to noose and hold back those who want to progress?" (IV.iii.261) The weight of the second clause of the question makes it simply rhetorical: the women are of course not to blame. Although the "natural" pattern that Jude and Sue attempt to substitute for the accepted "civil" one is itself one system of relations among others, they see it as the sole and true order of things and not as an artifice like civil structure. But once the fragmentation of the apparently stable structure of civil law is initiated, endless other versions of "natural law" might be engendered in a repeating pattern of regression.

The decisive term characterizing Jude's and Sue's relationship, "natural law," thus presents itself to be read as a chiastic pattern also. Natural law deconstructs civil law; but natural law is then itself open to the process of its own analysis. Far from denoting a stable point of homogeneity, where they might enact the mythic integration of their "one person split in two," (IV.iv.276) the "natural law" of Hardy's Wessex connotes the impossibility of integration and stability. Any of Hardy's texts that put such polarities as natural and civil law, desire and satisfaction, repetition and stability into play will have to set up the fiction of a synthetic process that will function both as the deconstructive instrument and as the outcome of that deconstruction. For Hardy, dualisms are never absolute. Deconstruction, however, is the process that both reveals the deluded basis of the desire for the synthesis of dualism, and also creates the elements necessary for a new and equally deluded desire for integration. *Jude the Obscure* thus both denies the validity of the metaphor that unites "natural" and "civil" law, and elaborates a new metaphor to fulfill the totalizing function of the original binary terms. This new metaphor of life as an organic and orderly process now allows the narrative to continue by providing a myth of a future moment when, as Phillotson's friend Gillingham says, Jude and Sue might make "their union legal . . . and all would be well, and decent, and in order." (Vi.iv.433) This mythic moment, however, never comes.

It is crucial, then, that the basic conflicts of the novel occur within the "give and take" of marriage, for it situates the issue directly in the referential contexts of ethics and legality. Civil law, in fact, can be conceived as the emblem of referentiality *par excellence* since its purpose is to codify the rules for proper social intercourse. But to abide by the law, we must be able to read its text; ignorance is after all, in English common law, no excuse. Attempting to read it, Jude concludes that "we are acting by the letter; and 'the letter killeth'!" (VI.viii.469) Jude thus interprets the Pauline dictum, "The letter killeth but the spirit giveth life," as an injunction against a *literal* reading of the codes governing ethical action. Yet his *figural* reading leads to no spiritual truth either. On the contrary, Jude's illusions result from a figurative language taken literally, as with Sue he takes "Nature at her word." For Jude and Sue, then, there is no text present anywhere that is yet to be transmuted, yet to be translated from natural to civil terms. There is no *natural* truth written anywhere that might be read without being somehow altered in the process. The text of associations Jude fabricates around him is already woven of interpretations and differences in which the meaning of dreams and the desire for illusions are unnaturally coupled. Everything in Wessex "begins" with repetition, with secondary images of a meaning that was never present but whose *signified* presence is reconstituted by the supplementary and belated world of Jude's desires.[16]

I am saying, of course, that the narrative of *Jude the Obscure*, while telling the story of Jude's and Sue's unhappy marriages, also dispels the illusion of a readable truth, that the novel gains its narrative consistency by the repeated undoing of the metaphor of life as organic unity. But the story that tells why figurative denomination is an illusion is itself *readable* and *referential* to the negative truth that Jude never perceives, and the story thus relapses into the very figure it deconstructs. The structure of the narrative as chiasmus, the cross-shaped substitution of properties, also tells, therefore, another story in the form of allegory about the divergence between the literal and figural dimensions of language. That the text reverts to doing what it has claimed to be impossible is not a sign of Hardy's weakness as a novelist, for the error is not with the text, nor with the reader who attempts to understand it. Rather, I would say that with Jude we find that language itself, to the extent that it attempts to be truthful, necessarily misleads us about its own ability to take us outside its own structures in search of meaning.

The myth of a stabilizing natural or civil law, then, is actually the representation of our will to make society seem a unified and understandable organism. But Hardy's novel persists in showing society's laws as open to subversion by the actions of the individuals who make up society. In everyday life, there is an ever possible discontinuity between the word of the law, its spirit, and the practice, the letter, of the law. And the necessary failure of the law to enforce its monologic interpretations of the infinite variety of human behaviour can lead to the subversion of the entire relational system. This explains why Jude, by his actions, constantly and unintentionally subverts the Word that he figures in Sue and in his dreams of a university career.

In applying the accepted social law to themselves, Jude and Sue constitute a version of the law, but in applying the general law to their particular situation, they instantaneously alter it. Rather than serving as a source of universal order from which social relations might be stabilized and unified within a social totality, the accepted social law exhibits its inability to constrain the heterogeneity of social relations. The law, then, is always shown to be grammatically structured, since it always engenders only a contingent, contextual meaning. Jude's revolutionary attempt to establish a ground for authentic meaning thus produces an anarchy of mutually exclusive readings of the one piece of language, "The letter killeth." This discontinuity between the "letter" and the "spirit" of the law, between a literal and a figural reading of its sign, is what constitutes Hardy's break with referentiality. Although the law indicates that "The letter killeth," Jude finds it impossible to decide what is the *letter* and what the *spirit* of the law. In each reading, whether within a "natural" or a "civil" system, the law is transposed, altered, and led to produce the conditions for its own undoing. Like Sue's ambiguous letters, the law is consequently only a promise (which cannot be kept) of a future stability and is never adequate to deal with the instability of the present moment.

The repetitions in the novel put at stake not only the relation between Jude's present actions and his family's history, but also the very readability of the initial text of that history. Everywhere about him, history calls out to be read, but Jude consistently fails to do so properly. Because he cannot read it, his actions are never simply a representation of that past, but are an interpretation that has gone awry. Since the novel is itself a kind of history, it too is open to all the errors of interpretation of which it speaks. Hardy's "Postscript," which calls attention to the decisive issues of reading and interpretation, must thus be seen in retrospect as an ironic repetition of the situation dramatized in *Jude* concerning the impossibility of authoritative readings, for it accuses the reader of partaking in Jude's error. We cannot read the novel as Jude reads the motto of his life, that is, with the expectation of encountering an ideally sanctioned stable truth.

But how are we to read it then? If the notion of representation is to be at all meaningful, we must presuppose the stability of subjects with stable names who are to be represented, and a rapport between the sign and the referent in the language of the representation. Yet both conditions are absent from this text (notoriously so in the allegorical figure of little Father Time). We can, of course, discern similarities among the characters' various actions. And as we read, attempting, in Hardy's words, "to give shape and coherence to this series of seemings," (viii) we too must rely on Jude's example in constructing an interpretive model. But we cannot accept his model of metaphoric synthesis as an absolute.[17] Jude's model of metaphor (governing the patterns of idealization and substitution) is erroneous because it believes in its own referential meaning—it believes that the inwardly desired "anchoring point" can be concretely encountered in the external world as Phillotson, as Christminster, as Arabella, or as Sue. It assumes a world in which literal and figural properties can be isolated, exchanged, and substituted. For the reader and the narrator, metaphoric synthesis persists within the interpretive act, but not as the ground of ultimate reconciliations. Jude himself, however, remains caught in the error of metaphor. But it is an error without which reading could not take place.

We thus find that Hardy's narrative puts the assurance of the truth of the referent into question. But in making this situation thematic, it does allow a meaning, the text, to exist. We are not dealing simply with an *absence* of meaning, for if we were, then that very absence would itself constitute a referent. Instead, as an allegory of the breakdown of the referential system, *Jude the Obscure* continues to refer, to its own chiastic operations. This new referentiality is one bounded strictly by the margins of textuality. In our courses on the nineteenth-century novel we find it convenient to use *Jude* as a "transitional" text; it is either the last of the Victorians or the first of the Moderns.[18] Morton Zabel has written, for instance, that Hardy was "a realist developing toward allegory . . . who brought the nineteenth century novel out of its slavery to fact."[19] This seems to me fine, as far as it goes. But I would add that this allegorical pattern manifests itself in *Jude* primarily through the subversive power of the dialogic word, which refuses to be reduced to the single "anchoring point" of a transcendent and determining

Will, Immanent or otherwise.

As Hardy came to see early on, the function of realistic fiction was to show that "*nothing* is as it appears."[20] It is no wonder, then, that Hardy's last novel was misread. The suggestive and poetic force of *Jude* arises less from its positive attempt to represent appearance than from its rejection of any vision pretending to convey the totality and complexity of life. Accordingly, in *Jude* Hardy repudiates the notion that fiction can ever be Truth, that it can ever "reproduc[e] in its entirety the phantasmagoria of experience with infinite and atomic truth, without shadow, relevancy, or subordination."[21] He dramatizes, instead, the recognition that in narrative "Nothing but the illusion of truth can permanently please, and when the old illusions begin to be penetrated, a more natural magic has to be supplied."[22] To be realistic, the text must proceed as if its representing systems correspond to those in the world; it must create a new illusion of reference to replace the old of representation.

But this transmutation of illusion modifies the original considerably. Like Sue's "real presence," perpetually deviating from the ideal figure of Jude's dreams, the letter of the text, "*translat[ing]* the qualities that are already there" in the world,[23] contains after all only the inadequate ciphers of the spirit of meaning, not the "thing" itself. The deconstruction of the metaphorical model of substitution and translation (operating in Jude's various desires for Christminster, Sue, natural law, etc.) is performed by the rhetorical structure of chiasmus, whose own figural logic both asserts and denies referential authority. From the reader's point of view, the results of each of the figural movements can then be termed "meanings," but only by forgetting that the resulting sociological, ethical, legal, or thematic categories are undone by the very process that creates them.

It may well be, therefore, that Hardy's final novel does not "mean"; but it does signify to a redoubtable degree. It signifies the laws of language over which neither Hardy nor his readers can exercise complete control. To read those laws is to undermine their intent. This is why Hardy, like Jude who adds to the textual allegory of Wessex and generates its history while making its closure, is bound to allegorical narratives: he creates the fiction of an ideal reader while he constructs a narrative about the illusion of privileged readings. On this level of rhetorical self-consciousness, prose fiction is on the verge of becoming poetry.

NOTES

1. See, as a sampling, the following studies that stress the need to recognize

the reader's role and the process of reading as crucial aspects of the development of meaning in literature: Wayne Booth's *The Rhetoric of Fiction* (Chicago: Univ. of Chicago Press, 1961) is still the most widely influential of these studies. After Booth, the topic develops in several directions. Cf. Martin Price, "The Fictional Contract," in *Literary Theory and Structure* (New Haven: Yale Univ. Press, 1973); Richard Ohmann, "Speech, Literature and the Space Between," *New Literary History*, 5 (1974), pp. 37-63; Georges Poulet, "Phenomenology of Reading," *New Literary History*, 1 (1969-70), pp. 58-68; Roland Barthes, *S/Z* (Paris: Seuil, 1970) and *Le Plaisir du texte* (Paris: Seuil, 1973); Wolfgang Iser, *The Implied Reader* (Baltimore: Johns Hopkins Univ. Press, 1974), "Indeterminacy and the Reader's Response in Prose Fiction," in *Aspects of Narrative*, ed. J. Hillis Miller (New York: Columbia Univ. Press, 1971), "The Reading Process: A Phenomenological Approach," *New Literary History*, 3 (1972), pp. 279-99, and most recently, *The Act of Reading* (Baltimore: Johns Hopkins Univ. Press, 1978). See also Hans Robert Jauss, "Levels of Identification of Hero and Audience," *New Literary History*, 5 (1973-74), pp. 283-317 on the "aesthetics of reception." And see the current efforts of language philosophers to apply speech act theory to literary discourse: John R. Searle, "The Logical Status of Fictional Discourse," *New Literary History*, 4 (1972), pp. 319-32; and Mary Louise Pratt, *Toward a Speech Act Theory of Literary Discourse* (Bloomington: Indiana Univ. Press, 1977). The most recent and engaging contribution is Paul de Man's "Reading (Proust)," in *Allegories of Reading* (New Haven: Yale Univ. Press, 1980), pp. 57-78.

2. Thomas Hardy, "Postscript" (added April 1912) to *Jude the Obscure* in *The Writings of Thomas Hardy in Prose and Verse* (The Anniversary Edition, New York: Harper, 1920), 3, p. ix. All references are to this, the American issue of the standard Wessex Edition, and will hereafter be identified by part, chapter, and page number in parentheses following the quotation.

3. Hardy, "Preface to the First Edition" of *Jude the Obscure* (August 1895), p. viii. For a more detailed summary of the reception of Hardy's novel, see R.C. Cox, ed., *Thomas Hardy: The Critical Heritage* (London: Routledge & Kegan Paul, New York: Barnes & Noble, 1970), pp. 249-315, and especially, for its difference from the prevailing response, the review by Edmund Gosse in *Cosmopolis* (January 1896), i, pp. 60-69. Cf. Lawrence Lerner and John Holmstrom, ed., *Thomas Hardy and His Readers* (New York: Barnes & Noble, 1968), pp. 103-52. See also the pertinent discussions in Albert Guerard, ed., *Thomas Hardy* (New York: New Directions, 1964); Ian Gregor, *The Great Web* (London: Faber and Faber, 1974); Michael Millgate, *Thomas Hardy: His Career as a Novelist* (New York: Random House, 1971), pp. 317-35; and J. Hillis Miller. *Thomas Hardy: Distance and Desire* (Cambridge, Ma.: Belknap Press, 1970). See also Florence Emily Hardy, *The Life of Thomas Hardy 1840-1928* (1928 and 1930, rpt., New York: St. Martin's Press, 1962), pp. 262-75, which

discusses Hardy's reactions to the negative reception of his novel.

4. Letter to Gosse, cited in Florence Emily Hardy, *The Life of Thomas Hardy*, p. 271. Hardy writes Gosse to thank him for his favorable review of *Jude.*
5. William R. Rutland, *Thomas Hardy: A Study of His Writings and Their Background* (Oxford: Blackwell, 1938), pp. 250-57.
6. Letter to Gosse, cited in Florence Emily Hardy, *The Life*, p. 271. Hardy goes on to say: "I ought not to say *constructed*, for beyond a certain point, the characters necessitated it, and I simply let it come." In a subsequent letter of January 1896, also to Gosse, Hardy elaborates: "The rectangular lines of the story were not premeditated, but came by chance: except of course, that the involutions of four lives must necessarily be a sort of quadrille." (p. 273)
7. I use the term in the sense that Jacques Lacan assigns to it in "The Function of Language in Psychoanalysis," trans. Anthony Wilden in *The Language of the Self* (Baltimore: Johns Hopkins Univ. Press, 1968), and in "D'une question préliminaire à tout traitement possible de la psychose," *Ecrits II* (Paris: Seuil, 1970), pp. 43-102. Lacan speaks of the symbolic substitution of a father figure for an absent real procreator. This symbolic construct need not have a procreative function at all; it is sufficient that the symbolic figure stand for a guarantee of social order with which the child might identify. Although Jude's idealization of Phillotson is shattered at an early stage in the novel, the system of social formulas set up in relation to Phillotson retains its affective force, even after Jude discovers the illusory basis of his beliefs. The process of "idealization" is constant throughout the novel and even characterizes Jude's relations with Arabella: "His *idea* of her was the thing of most consequence, not Arabella herself, [Jude] sometimes said laconically." (I.ix.65)
8. George Eliot, *Adam Bede* (New York: Holt, Rinehart and Winston, 1948), chapter XV, p. 155. In *A Pair of Blue Eyes*, Hardy's narrator makes a similar observation: "Nature seems to have moods in other than a poetical sense. . . . She is read as a person with a curious temper. . . . In her unfriendly moments there seems a feline fun in her tricks, begotten by a foretaste of her pleasure in swallowing the victim." (chapter xxii, p. 243) See also Charles May ("*Far from the Madding Crowd* and *The Woodlanders*: Hardy's Grotesque Pastorals," *English Literature in Transition*, 17 (1974), pp. 147-58), who notes that "Hardy's central vision springs from the tension between his longing for a ground of meaning and value inherent in the natural world and his hard recognition that no such value or meaning exists there." (p. 150)
9. The problem of interpretation is complicated by the formal pattern of the narrative itself, which often ascribes speeches to Jude through the mode of indirect discourse. The *diegetic* instance, the narrative mode that Plato so deplores in book III of *The Republic*, forces the reader to shift attention from the question of the meaning of the characters' linguistic confusions to that of deciding which voice is the cause of ambiguity. In the passages discussed above, for example, some can be readily ascribed to Jude:

I.iii.20; I.iii.24-25; IV.v.243. Other passages, however, seem to be the narrator's interpretations of Jude's interpretations. This layering of interpreting minds dramatizes the difficulty in *Jude* of establishing absolute linguistic reference. Cf. John Sutherland, "A Note on the Teasing Narrator in *Jude the Obscure*," *English Literature in Transition,* 17 (1974), pp. 159-62.

10. See Jacques Derrida, "Freud et la scéne de l'écriture," in *L'Ecriture et la différence* (Paris: Seuil, 1967), p. 316.
11. It is of course appropriate that Jude reads St. Paul at several points in the novel since the Pauline text is itself concerned with the issue of a proper reading. Referring to the relationship of the Old Testament to the New, Paul in fact applies the linguistic metaphor of Christ as the Spirit inseparable from the letter of the Bible where it is expressed. As John Freccero pointed out in a seminar on Dante at Yale University in the Fall of 1975, Paul later suggests that the word of God interprets the hearts of men, turning to stone the hearts of unbelievers, while the Spirit writes upon the fleshy tablets of the faithful. Hardy thus directs our attention to the nature of Jude's spiritual, but apocryphal, word. See also R.P.C. Hanson, *II Corinthians* (London: SCM, 1954), p. 39, commenting on II Corinthians 3 and 4, from which, of course, derives the epigraph to *Jude the Obscure*.
12. See Anthony Wilden's discussion of the relationship between social and linguistic systems in *The Language of the Self*, pp. 253-54.
13. Cf. Friedrich Nietzsche, "On Truth and Falsehood in an Extra-Moral Sense," *The Complete Works,* 2, trans. Maximilian A. Mugge (London: T.N. Foulis, 1911), pp. 173-92. See also Hardy's journal entry of August 5, 1890, cited by Florence Emily Hardy in *The Life*, where he indicates that "Art is a changing of the actual proportions and order of things. . . . Art is a disproportioning—(i.e., distorting, throwing out of proportion)—of realities, to show more clearly the features that matter in these realities, which, if merely copied or reported inventorially, might possibly be observed, but would more probably be overlooked. Hence 'realism' is not Art" (pp. 228-29), and compare with Nietzsche's statements in essay III, section 24 of *On the Genealogy of Morals*, concerning the nature of the interpretive act.
14. See also, among numerous and often contradictory allusions to "natural" and "civil" systems of law in Hardy's novel, the following passages: I.xi.80; III.ii.165; III.vii.206; IV.ii.258; V.viii.384; Vi.i.396; VI.ii.408-9; and VI.iii.418; in addition to "Postscript," x and the epigraphs to Part First from the Book of Esdras and Part Fourth from Milton's *The Doctrine of Divorce*.
15. Paul de Man, in the chapter "Promises (Social Contract)" of *Allegories of Reading*, points out the relation between textual and legal systems: "In the description of the structure of political society, the 'definition' of a text as the contradictory interference of the grammatical with the figural field emerges in its most systematic form." (p. 270)

16. I use the word "supplementary" in Derrida's sense in *Of Grammatology*: "But the supplement . . . adds only to replace. It intervenes or insinuates itself *in-the-place-of*; if it fills, it is as if one fills a void. If it represents and makes an image, it is by the anterior default of a presence" (trans. Gayatri Chakravorty Spivak [Baltimore: Johns Hopkins Univ. Press, 1976], p. 145).
17. See Gérard Genette, "La rhétorique restrainte," and Métonymie chez Proust," *Figures III* (Paris: Seuil, 1972), pp. 21-40 and 41-66, respectively, for instances of the kinds of interpretations that use such a totalizing metaphorical model.
18. Irving Howe, *Thomas Hardy* (New York: Macmillan; London: Collier, 1967), argues for a similar reading when he notes that if "modernist" literature works "on the premise that there is no secure meaning in the portrayed action, or that while the action can hold our attention and rouse our feelings, we cannot be certain, indeed must remain uncertain, as to the possibilities of meaning," then *Jude the Obscure* "does not go nearly as far along the path of modernism" as do Kafka's, Joyce's, or Faulkner's novels (144). In my reading, Hardy's refusal to posit the absolute *absence* of meaning, but only its unverifiability, is, in some respects, a more profoundly "modern" act than would be the simple negation of "meaning." See also Lawrence O. Jones. "Imitation and Expression in Thomas Hardy's Theory of Fiction," *Studies in the Novel*, 7 (1975), pp. 507-25; and J. Hillis Miller, "Fiction and Repetition: *Tess of the d'Urbervilles,*" in *Forms of Modern British Fiction*, ed. Alan Warren Friedman (Austin: Univ. of Texas Press, 1975), pp. 43-71; and also the discussion by Edward Said in *Beginnings* (New York: Basic Books, 1975), pp. 137-39.
19. "Hardy in Defense of His Art: The Aesthetics of Incongruity," *Thomas Hardy*, ed. Albert Guerard, p. 43.
20. Florence Emily Hardy, *The Life*, Journal entry for December 21, 1885, p. 176.
21. Hardy, "The Science of Fiction" (1891), *Thomas Hardy's Personal Writings*, ed. Harold Orel (Lawrence: Univ. of Kansas Press, 1966), p. 135.
22. *Loc.cit.*
23. Florence Emily Hardy, *The Life*, Journal entry for January 1887, p. 185.

Hardy's Poetry of Transcendence

GEOFFREY HARVEY

As the growing list of Hardy criticism testifies, his poetic achievement is at last being given the degree of attention which has so long been accorded almost exclusively to his novels. Donald Davie's *Thomas Hardy and Modern British Poetry* (1973) recognizes Hardy as a major influence on modern English verse and more recently we have had Paul Zietlow's *Moments of Vision: The Poetry of Thomas Hardy* (1974) and Tom Paulin's *Thomas Hardy: The Poetry of Perception* (1975). Together these studies mark the beginning of a revaluation of Hardy's poetic art which is long overdue, and in their concern with the nature of Hardy's poetic imagination and their emphasis on the qualities of compassion and hope in his poetry, Zietlow and Paulin go a long way to redress the balance in Hardy criticism. J. Hillis Miller, for instance, in *Thomas Hardy: Distance and Desire* (1970) regarded Hardy primarily as a passive poet trapped in a mechanistic universe; while Geoffrey Thurley in *The Ironic Harvest: English Poetry in the Twentieth Century* (1974) marshalled an apparently strong case against Hardy. For him, because the existentialist's search for meaning can result only in total self-effacement, Hardy "annihilates . . . metaphysics, mythology, transcendence, rhetoric."[1] Thus, in Thurley's view, Hardy marks the degeneration of English verse from the Romantics' pursuit of transcendence and its accompanying rhetoric of the egotistical sublime and what has been lost in Hardy and subsequent poets, he concludes, is "the *sense of meaningfulness* associated with poetic rhetoric."[2]

Both Tom Paulin and Paul Zietlow take a more positive view. Although Paulin regards Hardy's imagination as "imprisoned in a Humean universe of sense-data" he also recognizes that Hardy is "somewhere between a utilitarian empiricism and a romantic idealism" and that "he would prefer [his imagination] to have a transcending freedom though he knows this is impossible."[3] And Paul Zietlow affirms that Hardy's idealistic impulse leads him to place his faith in human compassion.[4] However, both these views of Hardy are limiting. For these critics, too, Hardy's poetry does not achieve transcendence and his optimism is restricted to fighting a rearguard action against human suffering and misery. And as far as the majority of Hardy's poetic output is concerned they are right. But in my view there is a relatively small group of poems, which includes some of Hardy's finest verse, in which his imagination does indeed achieve a transcending freedom, a liberation of the spirit and an abundant "sense of meaningfulness." In them Hardy strives to establish an authentic mode of being predicated on existence itself and on his own capacity to transcend it; but the paradox of his art, at least in those poems which I would argue lie close to the centre of his poetic genius, is that he achieves the finest articulation of his existential statement within the content of the Romantic tradition.

Hardy's achievement, unique I think in modern English poetry, is his attainment of a synthesis of profound disillusion with a vitality and joy that is almost Wordsworthian. It has often been noted that Hardy's poetry shares some features with Wordsworth; he writes in the tradition of Wordsworth's ruralism, displaying the same deep feeling for rustic society and for landscape and, indeed, his suffering, stoical peasantry, wresting significance from their narrow lives are direct descendants of Wordsworth's Michael. But the affinity between the two poets is, in my view, deeper than this. The major concern of both poets is the relation between the human imagination and the natural world, Hardy's belief that poetry should deal with "*the other side* of common emotions"[5] echoes Wordsworth's concern in his Preface to *Lyrical Ballads* with the intensity of emotional experience and with what he called "the fluxes and refluxes of the mind."[6] More significantly, Hardy's intention to make nature's defects the basis of his art by irradiating them with "'the light that never was' on their surface, but is seen to be latent in them by the spiritual eye"[7] recalls Wordsworth's description of the visionary process in "Tintern Abbey," where the mystical experience is what eye and ear perceive and also what they "half-create." And Hardy amplifies his insistence on the transfiguring power of the imagination:

> The "simply natural" is interesting no longer. . . . The exact truth as to material fact ceases to be of importance in art—it is a student's style—the style of a period when the mind is serene and unawakened to the tragical mysteries of life; when it does not bring anything to the object that coalesces with and translates the qualities that are already there,—half hidden, it may be—and the two united are depicted as the All.[8]

What Hardy strove for, the co-operation between the dead world of fact and the imagination is, indeed, what Coleridge laments the loss of in his "Dejection Ode" when he states that if we wish to know something beyond the inanimate cold world then, "Ah, from the Soul itself must issue forth/ A light, a glory, a fair luminous cloud."

Hardy frequently refers to Wordsworth and Coleridge in his prefaces to his poetry and in his personal writings and it is clear that their poetry and poetic theories were of particular significance to him, especially Coleridge's concern with the transfiguring power of the imagination. But the difference between Hardy's poetic experience and that of Coleridge is as important as the parallels. Whereas in Coleridgean terms the imagination, operating under the gentle control of the will, co-operates in a reciprocal way with an active universe in order to create a living relationship between mind and objects, for Hardy the imagination works in a somewhat different way and fulfills an inevitably different function. Unlike Coleridge and Wordsworth, Hardy's imagination is not intuitive because, quite simply, for him there was nothing "out there" in the universe to be intuited. Moreover, in his art the function of the imagination is not, as Coleridge suggests, to bring "the whole soul of man into activity"[9] but rather to bring it into being. Nor can it achieve the vision of some immanent ideal, but strives instead to gain some fundamental sense of meaning grasped and articulated. This is why J. Hillis Miller's suggestion that Hardy regarded the mind as little more than a puppet of the Universal Will is, in my view, too large a generalization.[10] Although in the poem, "He Wonders about Himself," Hardy admits that "Part is mine of the general Will," like Schopenhauer, his favourite philosopher, Hardy felt that there are moments when the imagination gains its freedom, "actuated by the modicum of free will conjecturally possessed by organic life when the mighty necessitating forces—unconscious or other—that have 'the balancings of the clouds,' happen to be in equilibrium, which may or may not be often."[11] This statement goes a long way to explain the comparative rarity of visionary poems in Hardy's large output of verse, for it is only in this state that the poet is able to create a clearer vision of the world, a state of "pure perception" in Schopenhauer's terms. More importantly, it makes plain that the imagination is liberated in conjunction with the will, not subordinated to it as in Coleridge's view, but rather it seems to co-operate with it in such a fundamental way, in the poems I propose to discuss, that they become a single creative force—which might perhaps best be described as "poetic will." Hardy's moments of transcendence are therefore very different from those of Wordsworth and Coleridge. They are not vague stirrings—"a sense sublime of something far more deeply interfused," as in "Tintern Abbey"—nor an attempt to reach beyond the material world to an ideal state as in "Kubla Khan." Instead they register the achievement of meaning; they assert the joy of being here and now and Hardy constantly seeks to establish poetic structures to capture this.

It is important to insist on the positive quality of the poems I wish to consider because J. Hillis Miller again overstates his case, it seems to me, when he argues the corollary of his remark about Hardy's passivity—that in Hardy "the act of coming to self-awareness does not lead to a recognition of the intrinsic quality of the mind [but] is a revelation about the outside world, a recognition of the mute detachment of external objects." On the contrary, Hardy's visionary poems are fundamentally a record of self-discovery and a celebration of meaning and value and this is a process in which the obstinate facts of the external world are internalized and transfigured. Indeed, the intrinsic quality of the mind is the overt subject of the title poem of *Moments of Vision*. Working in co-operation with the poetic will, which functions intermittently when the universe is in equilibrium, sometimes in the depths of night or in the moments before death, the imagination, symbolized as a "magic" mirror which is both passive and active, has the power not only to transfigure the outer world but to "[throw] our mind back on us, and our heart,/ Until we start." It penetrates the inmost recesses of consciousness "like a dart," making us "such a breast-bare spectacle see/ Of you and me." This poem displays Hardy's profound sense of the relation between true selfhood and moral identity which is also evident in his reply to the charge of pessimism so often brought against him—that it constituted only "'questionings' in the exploration of reality" necessary as "the first step towards the soul's betterment."[13] His position is the opposite of, for instance, Dostoevsky's Kirilov in *The Possessed* who cries, "If God does not exist, everything is allowed." Because, in Hardy, the poet transcends himself not towards God but towards man, the achievement of being brings not only enormous freedom but also responsibility, both to himself and to others. Like Schopenhauer, whom he often quotes as a philosopher of hope, Hardy stresses the central importance of loving kindness in human relations; he affirms the fundamental human values of love and fellowship. And because it thus overcomes alienation and despair, Hardy's finest poetry also embodies a sense of profound joy.

As Donald Davie has pointed out, there is no clear line of development in Hardy's work.[14] His major visionary poems occur sporadically throughout his career and they do so because the unfettered operation of his poetic will was a rare accident, dependent on his sense of equilibrium in the universe. This feeling permeates "The Darkling Thrush," for instance, a poem of the highest imaginative order. Apparently a modern lament for the death of God and of Nature, the poem employs a universalized and visionary landscape to record the end of place and time—"The land's features seemed to be/ The Century's corpse outleant," the frost is "spectre-gray," the clouds form a "crypt" and the wind provides a "death-lament"; even the "ancient pulse of germ and birth/ was shrunken hard and dry,/ And every spirit upon earth/ Seemed fervourless as I." This awful nullity, which is developed by the image patterns of the first two stanzas, is mirrored in the consciousness of the poet himself. The century's outleant corpse makes a parallel with the poet who "leant upon a coppice gate" the "weakening eye of day" creates a metaphor for the darkened vision of the poet, while the tangled bine-stems scoring the sky "Like strings of broken lyres" is a further image of poetic sterility. The poet stands in mute contrast to the joyous thrush, the only other inhabitant of this ghastly landscape and to the creative impulse of the bird's "full-hearted" song.

Hardy's central distinction between the poetic sterility of the man for whom the universe is dead and the thrush which experiences "Some blessed Hope, whereof he knew/ And I was unaware," appears to justify Hillis Miller's criticism of Hardy as a detached and passive observer whose poetry displays fundamental withdrawal from life. But this view does not do justice to the complexity of the poem. Here, as in several of his visionary poems, Hardy inhabits the world of the poem not only as a neutral spectator, but also as an active participant. This duality of experience is embodied in the structure of the poem, which creates a profound connection between the two inhabitants of its desolate world, the nihilistic poet and the optimistic thrush. Of course the thrush has a richly symbolic function; on one level its instinctive song represents the natural world's anticipation of spring and regeneration; it is also a universalized symbol of humanity; but fundamentally, "aged . . . frail, gaunt, and small," like Hardy himself, the thrush functions in the poem as its governing symbol for the continued creative activity of the poetic will, which is still at work below the level of conscious thought and which is free to operate because the temporal frame of the poem crystallises a moment of poise in the universe. Like the poet, who is both observer and agent, the thrush creates his essential self by means of an act of will; he has "*chosen* thus to fling his soul/ Upon the growing gloom" (my italics)—a defiant action which images his attempt to transcend the way he has been "thrown" into the world in an existential sense. The thrush's affirmation of the sheer joy of being in the present moment and the accompanying sense of significance is given peculiar force by the poem's terrible context of non-being and by the awful irony of the poetic "persona's" inability to grasp the meaning offered. Nevertheless, its song of ecstatic optimism, an unwitting act of loving-kindness, forges a contact between itself and the poet, creating a sense of his solidarity with all living things, and because the thrush also represents the enduring connection between the poet and his creative imagination the poem is allowed to stand as a courageous celebration of the poetic will and of the possibility for the survival of undeceived joy in a world of dissolution.

Hardy also turns to his own life in order to explore the way in which the achievement of a sense of personal value is contingent on the perfect interrelation of time and place. "The Self-Unseeing" records a moment in his boyhood when he danced in the parlour to the music of his father's violin, while his mother sat by the fireside. Such moments, Hardy stresses, must be seized and utilized because, as he bleakly admits in this poem, the opportunity frequently passes unrecognized. This particular moment was unusually propitious because, as Hardy demonstrates, it was a moment of perfect universal balance. Here time, which is always the chief threat to the attainment of joy through self-definition, is disciplined, harmonised and humanized by music and dance. As the insistent repetition of the word "here" suggests, place is of fundamental importance in the process, not only because limited space and the present moment are the only contexts we have to create our integrity, but because for Hardy place contains both past and present and therefore has the almost magical power to suspend time. Place is concretely realized by the "ancient floor" and, paradoxically, by the images of feet walking and dancing, which frame the poem and reinforce the dominant image of stillness, of time annihilated by place. But the potential amount of transcendence is lost because the actions of the man, the woman and the child are involuntary. Listening to the music they enter a hypnotic state of euphoria, which is emphasized by the heavy alliterative effect of the final stanza. The woman muses, rapt, staring into the depths of the fire, the man plays his violin in isolated abstraction, while the child dances "in a dream." Passive and self-regarding, they are firmly linked with the "dead feet" at the opening of the poem, with time outside of place, time the destroyer which they apparently have controlled but which in truth obliterates them. That the moment described is one of sheer escapism rather than fulfilment is evident in Hardy's indulgent description of the cosiness of the scene; the warmth of the fire, the cliché of emotion in the phrase "glowed with a gleam" and the ironic undercurrent that runs through the too emphatic "Blessings emblazoned that day." Ostensibly connected by time, manifested in music and dance, they fail to realize that what connects them fundamentally is place, the "ancient floor" on which they act and which symbolizes a deeper and more sacramental relation of human lives. Visionary moments like this, grasped, offer unparalleled opportunity for people to transcend themselves by unifying acts of love, but in denying what links them they only confirm their human isolation and as Hardy unflinchingly records, the pleasure that they have gained is won at the cost of turning their faces away from a profounder reality.

By contrast, the achievement of genuine human fellowship is presented dramatically in "At the Railway Station, Upway," a poem in which once again Hardy's strange sense of special moments of equilibrium permeating human affairs is strongly in evidence. The station is an area of stasis where time is suspended as people occupy a limbo between trains and where different lives come together and then diverge without achieving any significant connection. The three figures waiting on the platform, the innocent young boy, the police constable and the handcuffed convict, create a universalized image of the human condition, but Hardy is fundamentally concerned to suggest the possibility of its transformation. The child's instinctive pity for the convict and the contrasting complacent indifference of the worldly constable establish perspectives of irony and sympathy which by the poem's conclusion have been transmuted into a unifying mood of common human charity. The boy's spontaneous act of loving-kindness in playing his violin to cheer the criminal creates the grounds for the convict's transcendence of both the boy's pity and the constable's indifference. His strange, apparently ironical singing about freedom is not sheer bravado, but a profound act by which he creates a sense of his own particular momentary value. Hardy employs the apt coinage "grimful glee" to describe the singular mood in which his stern assertion of will paradoxically produces a deeply felt liberating energy. What the moment reveals is the "*other side* of common emotions," the joy that lies beyond despair, the transcendence that can be achieved only through an awareness of tragic experience. What is more, the convict discovers in the same act not only an inner freedom, but a new sense of human responsibility. His song is also a kindly response to the boy's overwhelming need to feel that he has somehow helped the suffering man. And through the song the convict achieves solidarity not only with the boy, imaged in the music which they share, but also with the constable, imaged in their exchange of smiles which negates the corresponding earlier image of the cruel manacles. Subjection has been replaced by fellowship and the poem's dominant tableaux—the boy playing his violin and the handcuffed convict singing of freedom to the constable on the station platform between trains—establishes a complex and powerful symbol of the human will triumphantly wresting significance from the tragic absurdity of daily experience.

Hardy wryly defines his own sense of alienation from the modern world, with its illusory promises of purpose, action and progress, in the splendid visionary poem, "Old Furniture." It is a deeply personal poem in which Hardy, although aware that "the world has no use for one today/ Who eyes things thus—no aim pursuing!" nevertheless courageously asserts the absolute value of his own mode of vision. Indeed, the poem is organized by its many images of perception—"see," "eye may frame," "I see," "Who eyes things thus," "Creeps to my sight"—as Hardy enacts a magical resurrection. Time is brilliantly encapsulated by place and although the past is shown to be progressively and irretrievably past, the poem bears no trace of corrupting nostalgia because the co-operation between place and the eye of vision, which both perceives and half-creates in Wordsworth's phrase, makes the pasts of all the generations simultaneously present. Hardy's juxtaposition of the living candle-flame and the cold mirror which reflects it creates a factual yet visionary image for the simultaneity of the warm hands of the past generations and the shiny, dark solidity of the furniture which they caress. Although the poem's emotion is carefully controlled by Hardy's use of homely language and by the quiet, intimate tone, there is a magical effect created by the imaginative fusion of object and vision. Insensate things come alive at the moment of vision through the co-operation between delicate images of wraith-like movement—hands "dallying," the flickering reflections of the candle flame, the "foggy finger" moving with "tentative touches," fingers "dancing"—and the static, inert solidity of objects like the clock, "this old viol" and "that box."

For Hardy the neutral objects of the material world are given meaning as they are stamped by people's creative existence and he lovingly recreates in the vision the way people's identities have been captured in the almost sacramental "relics of householdry" around which their daily lives were built. He celebrates their love of domestic warmth (the box for tinder), punctuality and order (the finger putting the clock right) and harmony (the music of the viol), simple acts of human assertion which were once defined by place but which have been apparently obliterated from the surface of things by time. Yet the values which they won from their futile routine are available to the eye of vision and are given in the poem a permanent value outside time. Hardy's identification with the past generations stresses his profound feeling for the continuity of human life, which is evident, for instance in "Heredity" or "In Time of 'the Breaking of Nations,'" but in "Old Furniture" his resurrection of the dead is fundamentally an act of pure loving-kindness and while it emphasizes his isolation from the past as well as from the present, it creates at the same time a deeper sense of human solidarity.

Hardy's manipulation of time so that place is allowed to symbolize both past and present also has a liberating effect. It allows human actions to be redefined and revalued. As the generations live again, Hardy gives new meaning to their lives and they in turn bestow on him a surer sense of being. Hardy thus creates his own spiritual values in the face of the awful inexorability of time by a supreme act of poetic will. Indeed, the controlling image of this marvellously delicate poem is that of the poetic will at work, waxing and waning like the viol bow receding and advancing and the fact "glowing forth in fits from the dark" until inevitably it falters and, like the linten cinder, it "goes out stark." But not before there has been an achievement of knowledge, the recognition of human fellowship, the apprehension of beautiful lives, of meaning grasped, with an accompanying spiritual renewal.

Hardy's special, almost primitive sense of place is central to his visionary poems because for him place contains all time and preserves the significance of human actions, which can then be apprehended by the poet in a state of "pure perception." This awareness is the controlling force behind some of the poems which focus on the loss of his wife, Emma. In that moving poem, "At Castle Boterel," for instance, in which Hardy records his visit to a landscape he had once rambled over with Emma, he feels that the very place exudes her presence. The fact of Emma's existence transcends time because the "primaeval rocks" record "that we two passed" and it is this that gives life to the visionary phantom who remains on the slope long after they have both gone. Another of their favourite haunts, the waterfall in "After a Journey," fulfils a similar function and the revelation of Emma's continued existence gives Hardy the courage to assert that "I am just the same as when/ Our days were a joy, and our paths through flowers." The best example of this imaginative process, however, is the third poem of this series, "The Phantom Horsewoman," in which Hardy employs a similar technique to that which governs "The Darkling Thrush." He separates the poet, described from the ironic point of view of a detached observer, as a man in a "care-worn craze," from his description of the operation of the poetic will itself. As in "Old Furniture," Hardy draws attention to the uniqueness of his imaginative process by setting it apart from the modern world of scepticism and rationalism. What he presents in the first three stanzas is the conventional view of visions as simply illusions manifested to the insane in unlikely places, obsessive fantasies associated with their pasts that often root them to the spot. People like the observer speculate about the crazy man's vision as a "sweet soft scene," a "phantom of his own figuring." This description is coloured by pity because the vision is felt to be purely subjective and to bear only a limited meaning and value. And this is intensified as the stark reality of Hardy's bleak universe is captured in the dominant image of the desolate shore on which the poet stands staring at the empty waves.

But the separation which Hardy makes between the "persona" of the first three stanzas and the vision created by the poetic will in the final stanzas is his means of holding in tension the horror of the empty universe, imaged by the vacant sands and the bewildering sea mist and the achieved joy of the meaning of being there, symbolized by the moment of vision itself. The final stanzas remove the duality of the observer and the poet to allow immediacy of vision, no longer "drawn rose-bright" but hard and clear, as Hardy creates Emma in defiance of the terrible void of her absence. She is outside time and place but she inhabits the place and moment of his vision as she "draws rein and sings to the swing of the tide." Reality and vision are united in the final stanza because Hardy only achieves this moment by facing life squarely. Although Emma is beyond time, the poet himself is not, he is "toil-tried,/ He withers daily"; and similarly life and death are held in careful balance in Hardy's description of Emma as a "ghost-girl-rider." Hardy's vision is not offered as a metaphysical reality, as Tom Paulin suggests,[15] nor is he withdrawing from life. In "The Phantom Horsewoman" Hardy captures starkly the horror of a desolate universe and the awful finality of death, but he also bravely affirms that life is neither absurd nor futile if by a positive act of poetic will he can resurrect Emma, if she has a living presence in his being which gives a continued meaning to his life.

In Hardy such moments as these are won by the mind itself, for only the mind can give meaning to reality. Hardy's moments of vision are created out of lived experience and their fundamental commitment to life gives them a universal validity. This wholeness of life, mind and art is perhaps best seen in the final poem that I wish to consider, "During Wind and Rain," in which Hardy draws once more on his memories of Emma, this time of her family home in Cornwall. In some respects it is a puzzling poem on first reading and critics have responded to it in various ways. Basically, the poem is divided into four discrete, beautiful moments of vision which embrace human fellowship and harmony as positive joys, each of which, however, is undercut by a cruel refrain which reminds the reader of the inevitable passing of time and of mortality. A straightforward approach to the meaning of the poem is to see this division as marking a simple structural irony of the kind which operates in *Satires of Circumstance*. The vision of domestic harmony on a winter evening in the first stanza, with its magical co-operation between fact and imagination, is contrasted with the falling leaves. In the second stanza the family's instinct to combat the burgeoning of the natural world in the spring, by clearing the moss in order to make way for human concern is contrasted with the threatening spring gales and the malevolent storm birds. The domestication of nature is significant in the third stanza as a context for human fellowship, imaged by the sacramental breakfast under the summer tree, but it, too, finds its destroyer in time which rips the "rotten rose" from the wall. While in the final stanza the family's removal to a "high new house," symbolizing their courageous attempt to re-define their humanity in different places, puts their achievement of a poised, assured selfhood in jeopardy, like their furniture on the lawn exposed to the autumn rain. Time, present in the rhythm of the seasons, co-operates with place and with human lives, yet it also carries a threat, a reminder of the inherent futility of even their noblest actions.

One view of the poem is that Hardy simply offers two distinct perspectives and allows them to stand in silent commentary on each other. Another interpretation regards these moments of vision, incomplete as they are, as having greater vividness, more impact and significance than the negative images of the refrains. But a clue to a more fruitful approach to the meaning of "During Wind and Rain," in my reading of it, is given by its title, which is an echo of Feste's song that concludes *Twelfth Night*, a song which is itself both a profound recognition of the fundamental absurdity of the universe and a beautiful celebration of human life and values. Hardy's poem, I suggest, achieves a similar transcendence. In "During Wind and Rain" the moments of vision are not created in opposition to, or even in ignorance of, the waste and futility of life; nor are those poles of human experience permitted to stand in mute dichotomy; rather the terror of a meaningless universe is incorporated into the poem, not simply as a structural unity, but into each discrete moment of vision, subtly qualifying it and becoming part of its statement. This becomes evident if one pays close attention to Hardy's superb technique. His breaking up of the elaborate symmetry between the four stanzas by his metrical variations in the last line of each stanza suggests how, for the neutral observer, each idyllic moment is dissolved by a harsher reality. Yet the cluster of images conveying the delicate world of the poem also contains within it this ineluctable force of dissolution. The beautiful image in the opening stanza of the candles "mooning each face," both factual and visionary, includes within it the suggestion of decay, for even as they illumine the gathering the candles are burning out, and the moon is itself a powerful traditional symbol of change. Similarly, the springtime vision of the second stanza comprehends the creeping moss which remains an enduring threat to human significance; while in the third stanza the sea, which can be glimpsed by the breakfasting group, is also a potent symbol for the mutability of life and experience. And finally, the furniture left in the open air on the lawn makes a poignant image of human vulnerability and frailty. The moments of vision themselves thus include a strong sense of an indifferent universe, of dissolution as inevitable and of human action as ultimately absurd. But this knowledge, which permeates the places in which they choose to act, is shared by the inhabitants of the world of the poem. The careful symmetry of these stanzas is the formal correlative of the way in which they nevertheless impose order and beauty on the flux of experience. Their awareness of a terrifying nullity at the heart of things is transcended by actions which celebrate love, fellowship and the sheer joy of being, which displays a powerful sense of achieved selfhood, of purpose, adventure and gaiety.

To some extent the current uncertainty about the value of Hardy's poetry derives from the critical tendency to regard his work as exemplifying his "philosophy." But Hardy, like Wordsworth and Coleridge, developed a significant part of his thinking from mature reflection upon his poetic experience. Indeed, this informs both the prefaces to his poetry and his personal writings. And as I have been arguing, a more fruitful method of approaching his work than that of simply applying his ideas to his poetry is to consider how his poetic art illumines his thought. From this point of view, Hardy's well-known discussion of the relation between the Universal Will and the individual will, which is often regarded as the linchpin of his thinking, is not simply an abstract formulation of his view of a deterministic universe, but is also the result of a subjective analysis of his own poetic experience. Read in the context of those poems I have been considering, Hardy's assertion of the possibility of the liberation of the will and his insistence on the transfiguring power of the imagination explain how some of his finest poems came to be written. These moments of vision which, I think, lie at the centre of Hardy's poetic genius, offer a positive response to the modern experience. They rescue life from futility; they assert the significance of human values; they embody a strenuously achieved, undeceived response of profound joy and they reaffirm in a new form the continuing romantic ideal of transcendence.

NOTES

1. Geoffrey Thurley, *The Ironic Harvest: English Poetry in the Twentieth Century* (London: Edward Arnold, 1974), p. 32.
2. *Ibid.*, p. 34.
3. Tom Paulin, *Thomas Hardy: The Poetry of Perception* (London: Macmillan, 1975), p. 36.
4. Paul Zietlow, *Moments of Vision: The Poetry of Thomas Hardy* (Cambridge, Mass.: Harvard University Press, 1974), p. 10.
5. As early as 1868 Hardy had proposed to write a volume of poems on this subject. See Florence Emily Hardy, *The Life of Thomas Hardy* (London: Macmillan, 1962), p. 58.
6. See Wordsworth's Preface to *Lyrical Ballads*, ed. R.L. Brett and A.R. Jones (London: Methuen, 1965), pp. 244-45.
7. *Life*, p. 114.
8. *Ibid.*, p. 185.
9. Coleridge, *Biographia Literaria*, ed. George Watson (London: J.M. Dent, 1956), p. 173.
10. J. Hillis Miller, *Thomas Hardy: Distance and Desire* (Cambridge, Mass: Harvard University Press, 1970), p. 22.
11. Hardy, Apology to *Late Lyrics and Earlier* in *Thomas Hardy's Personal Writings*, ed. Harold Orel (London: Macmillan, 1967), p. 53.
12. Hillis Miller, p. 4.
13. *Personal Writings*, p. 52.
14. Donald Davie, *Thomas Hardy and Modern British Poetry* (London: Routledge and Kegan Paul, 1973), p. 28.
15. Paulin, p. 138.

Love in the Poetry of Thomas Hardy

DEEPSHIKHA KOTWAL

It is often assumed that Thomas Hardy took to writing poetry in sheer disgust at the hostile reception given to his last novel *Jude the Obscure* in 1895. Richard Carpenter, on the contrary, tends to believe, "the writing of novels was only a long hiatus from his real metier."[1] This view seems more acceptable when we realize that Hardy continued to write poems for more than thirty years after the publication of *Jude*. Disgust alone could not have inspired such a long and fruitful innings. In fact, he continued writing poetry even while he was busy with his novels although he did not publish any of his verse during this period.

The vast volume of his work and its quality assure Hardy's place as a poet of repute. Yet many influential critics like H.C. Duffin, F.R. Leavis and R.P. Blackmur, among others, have denied Thomas Hardy a place among the greats of English poetry. Duffin is of the opinion: "From the point of view of literary value it is probable that no one of the eight volumes of Hardy's poetry is worth a single chapter from one of his major novels."[2] Other critics have consigned his verse, except for a handful of Wessex poems, to the dust-heap of "astounding balderdash." However, with the brickbats has come praise from poets as diverse as Edward Thomas, Siegfried Sassoon, W.H. Auden, C. Day Lewis, Dylan Thomas and Philip Larkin.

It is obvious, all of what Hardy wrote was not equally good because of his habit of reprinting pieces on the level of Sunday Supplement "poetry page" and at times even below that. The discerning reader has to dive deep into a sea of triviality to come up with the genuine pearls of his poetic craft. The problem is heightened by the fact that though thirty years separated the first volume of his poems from the last, there is very little variation in their subject and style. Still, he left behind very little juvenilia as he scrupulously revised all that he penned. It becomes rather difficult to ignore any of his poems and to quote Dylan Thomas, "you've got to read the whole damn lot!"[3]

Alexander Pope stressed the manner in which the poet expressed his subject. Thomas Hardy, on the other hand, believed, like Wordsworth and Matthew Arnold, that the subject of the poem was more important than the poet's treatment of it. Leslie Stephen's dictum that the poet should "touch our hearts by showing his own" fits Hardy's poetry like a glove. As a poet, he wanted to look "steadily at his subject" and avoid the "jewelled line in poetry."[4]

Hardy's ability to look into the heart of a thing allowed him to fashion a poem out of any human experience whatsoever. Middleton Murry in an essay on Hardy's poetry says, "The great poet remembers both rose and thorn, and it is beyond his power to remember them otherwise than as together."[5] Hardy's poetry touched every conceivable topic under the sun. He wrote about people and the vagaries of human character, about nature, seasons, places, birds, animals and plants. His poems about ideas included speculations about God, war and love.

Love and woman interested Hardy above all other subjects. Regarding the subject of love, Hardy "has explored almost every possible phase and has wrought permutations and combinations on each."[6] Nearly two hundred of his poems, over a fifth of his total output, deal with love. Hardy's treatment of love makes these poems highly intense, sensitive and human and they constitute the ultimate touchstone of his genius: "The basic themes of his love poems are . . . infidelities . . . the inevitable loss of love, the destructiveness of time, the implacable indifference of nature, the cruelty of men, the irreversible pastness of the past."[7]

Hardy's vision of a world in which a freak determinism is at work lends itself to an ironic view of life. Samuel Hynes has defined the poetic pattern of tensions in Hardy's work as antinomial. It works as "thesis (usually a circumstance commonly accepted as good—marriage, youth, young love, the reunion of husband and wife) which is set against antithesis (infidelity, age, death, separation) to form an ironic complex which is left unresolved."[8] Irony provides the artistic tension required to lift Hardy's work from the level of mediocrity to that of greatness.

Hardy found love a fit subject for study because the irony of life was nowhere more apparent. It is fate which shapes the destinies of lovers, drawing them together, or separating them. It throws wrong persons together and prevents the fulfilment of love. Hardy believed that love exists, but it comes for a while and is then lost: "In Hardy's love poems the ring the lovers hope for rarely brings gold, only sadness."[9] He accepted the incompleteness of love as a fact of life. If the lines of love-poetry in Donne, such as "For God's sake hold your tongue, and let me love,"[10] suggest the joy of mutual and contented passion, Hardy's keynote is nostalgia for a love which is lost, frustrated or illusory. In the autumn of his life, Hardy attempted to recast the thoughts of love to which his fancy had turned in youth. If Donne's poetry talks about Eros Triumphant, Hardy's poems reflect Eros Defeated."[11] His poems may lack the sensuality of Donne but even the most tragic of his poems reflect the passion of days long past:

> Lit by a living love.
> The wilted world knew nothing of.

It is this feeling which provides a leitmotif to his later work, and it seems to grow stronger as Hardy grows older.

Trevor Johnson has classified Hardy's love poetry into three parts: (1) *Early love poems*—mostly dated 1866 or 1867; (2) *Mature love poems*—comprising a small number of poems which can be ascribed to a particular woman; and a large number which give no clue to the lady who seems to be a blend of his imagination as well as reality; and (3) *Poems about Emma*—at least a hundred of his love poems are dedicated to his first wife, Emma Lavinia. Donne and Milton, too, have paid tribute to their dead wives but "there is nothing in all literature to compare with Hardy's elegiac commemoration of Emma, of which what is now the most celebrated part appeared, as Poems of 1912-13, not long after her death; to be supplemented by a steady stream of others until Hardy's own death in 1928." (199)

The elegiac tone which is the keynote of his best love poetry is obvious even in the early love poems like "Revulsion" and "Neutral Tones."

> For winning love we win the risk of losing,
> And losing love is as one's life were riven
> It cuts like contumely and keen ill-using
> To cede what was superfluously given.

Or

> With nothing left of me and you
> In that live century's vivid view
> Beyond a pinch of dust or two.

Both the stanzas reiterate the deceptive and ephemeral aspect of love. The "winter day," "sun and white," "the starving sod," "the grin of bitterness" and the "grayish leaves" of "Neutral Tones" bitterly evoke the lesson that "love deceives."

The following lines from the poem "In the Night She Came" is not a celebration of love's immortality but its cruel defacement at the hands of Time:

> And in the night she came to me,
> Toothless, and wan, and old
> With leaden concaves round her eyes,
> And wrinkles manifold.

Poems dedicated to the love of his youthful years, Tryphena Sparks, are retrospectively sad. In "Thoughts of (Try)Phena at News of her Death," images of laughter and hope reflect the depth of Hardy's feelings for Tryphena in the first stanza:

And in vain do I urge my unsight
  To conceive my lost prize
At her close, whom I knew when her dreams
  were upbrimming with light,
And with laughter her eyes.

But the melancholic imagery of the last stanza reinforces the ironic tension visible in Hardy's best work. The thesis of the celebration of young love is followed by the antithesis of separation and loss of that love at the hands of cruel Time. The poet does not have even a lock of Tryphena's hair or a letter from her as a reminder of the time they shared as lovers:

  Thus I do but the phantom retain
    Of the maiden of yore
As my relic; yet haply the best of
    her—fined in my brain
  It may be the more
That no line of her writing have I,
  Nor a thread of her hair,
No mark of her late time as
  dame in her dwelling, whereby
  I may picture her there.

The titles of his poems and the images and metaphors used in them are not normally those which we associate with the delicate nuances of love. Hardy talks not about a lover's rendezvous but "A Broken Appointment":

  You did not come,
And marching Time drew on, and
  wore me numb.

The lovers do not meet on a clear, star-spangled, moonlit night or on a lazy afternoon by the grassy banks of a soft-flowing river. Their meeting is rudely disturbed by "A Thunderstorm in Town" and the pelting rain ruins her "new terra-cotta dress." The lovers take shelter from the downpour inside the cosy confines of the hansom. He tries to make the best of a bad situation by snuggling up to her. Incidentally, that very moment the rain stops and ruins what could have been an intimate expression of their love:

Then the downpour ceased, to my sharp sad pain
And the glass that had screened our forms before
Flew up, and out she sprang to her door:
I should have kissed her if the rain
Had lasted a minute more.

A "minute more" is a grim reminder of the easy oscillation between meeting and separating, between love and frustration.

Images from the cemetery and death abound in his work and many of the poems have morbid titles such as "A Death Day Recalled," "In Death Divided," "The Phantom Horsewoman Lament." "Your Last Drive" associates the grave with a peaceful resting place where you are "past love, praise, indifference, blame" and can rest at ease after the struggles of life. The association of Death with a peaceful last drive in the countryside recalls Emily Dickinson's personification of Death as a gentle courteous suitor who will take her for a leisurely drive in his carriage:

And on your left you passed the spot
Where eight days later you were to lie,
And be spoken of as one who was not;
Beholding it with heedless eye
As alien from you, though under its tree
You soon would halt everlastingly.
I drove not with you . . . Yet had I sat
At your side that eve I should not have seen
That the countenance I was glancing at
Had a last-time look in the flickering sheen,
Nor have read the writing upon your face,
I go hence soon to my resting-place; . . .

It is ironical that Hardy's impassioned verses written for Lavinia were never seen by her except for one or two poems. Hardy's tribute is a retrospective of the happy time he spent with Emma in Cornwall, the many aspects of their not so idyllic marriage and his subsequent sense of loss and loneliness at her death.

"When I Set Out for Lyonnesse" is a poem which begins on a note of loneliness and concludes on a note of sheer joy. It is a tribute to the power of young love and romance:

When I set out for Lyonnesse,
A hundred miles away,
The rime was on the spray,
And starlight lit my lonesomeness. . . .

When I came back from Lyonnesse
With magic in my eyes
  All marked with mute surmise
My radiance rare and fathomless, . . .

The poems written between 1912-1913 are a record of his "haunting by two ghosts, one the spectre of remorse now made futile by death, the other the phantom of lost love."[12] Hardy visits the old haunts and relives the happiness of youth at the ripe old age of seventy-two. The replay of a happier past gives him the strength to come to terms with his sense of loss. In a conversation with his friend, A.C. Benson, Hardy remarked: "The verses came; it was quite natural. One looked back through the years and saw some pictures; a loss like that makes one's old brain vocal."[13]

In "Under the Waterfall" the poet recalls the minute details of a picnic he shared with Emma long years ago by the waterfall. Trivial details like the "basket of fruit and wine," the glass they had both drunk from, how he tried to rinse the glass in the water and it slipped away, the hot August afternoon and even the cool touch of the water on their hands are vividly recalled from the shroud of time. This proves how memorable the day was for the poet and the solace it provided to him in his old age:

Whenever I plunge my arm, like this
In a basin of water, I never miss
The sweet sharp sense of a fugitive day
Fetched back from its thickening shroud of gray.

"Beeny Cliff" and "At Castle Boterel" echo the sentiments of "Under the Waterfall." In "Beeny Cliff" the poet laments that though the beauty of the cliff is still intact the woman who is associated with it is no more:

The woman now is—elsewhere—whom the ambling pony bore,
And nor knows nor cares for Beeny, and will laugh there never more.

In "At Castle Boterel" the poet is conscious that he is moving towards his final rest and he takes one last poignant look at a well-remembered scene:

I look and see it there, shrinking, shrinking,
I look back at it amid the rain.
For the very last time; for my sand is sinking,
And I shall traverse old love's domain
Never again.

The permanence of the "primaeval rocks" of the castle is contrasted with the fleetingness of love and mortal life:

Primaeval rocks form the road's steep border,
And much have they faced there, first and last,
Of the transitory in Earth's long order;
But what they record in colour and cast
Is—that we two passed.

The analysis of Hardy's love poetry can be concluded with a poem which seems to say it all. It deals with Emma's sudden and unexpected death. Hardy feels like a lover who has been betrayed by his beloved. It is the age-old lament of the lover that the beloved has gone where he cannot follow her:

Why did you give no hint that night
That quickly after the morrow's dawn,
And calmly, as if indifferent quite
You would close your term here, up and be gone
Where I could not follow
With wing of swallow
To gain one glimpse of you anon!

The ironic twist of fate is complete; Emma is gone forever without telling him or giving him a hint that her time is up. It seems destiny has had the last laugh at love.

NOTES

1. Richard Carpenter, *Thomas Hardy* (London: Macmillan, 1976), p. 153.
2. Henry Charles Duffin, *Thomas Hardy: A Study of the Wessex Novels, the Poems and the Dynasts* (Delhi: Anmol, 1991), p. 347.
3. Trevor Johnson, *A Critical Introduction to the Poems of Thomas Hardy* (London: Macmillan, 1991), p. 3.
4. *Ibid.*, p. 47.
5. J.M. Murry, "The Poetry of Mr. H" in his *Aspects of Literature*, qtd. Johnson, p. 53.
6. James Granville Southworth, *The Poetry of Thomas Hardy* (New York: Columbia UP, 1947, rpt. 1966), p. 24.
7. Carpenter, p. 161.
8. *Ibid.*, p. 162.
9. Southworth, p. 26.
10. John Donne, *The Complete English Poems*, ed. A.J. Smith (Harmondsworth: Penguin, 1971), p. 47.
11. Johnson, p. 171.
12. *Ibid.*, p. 217.
13. *Ibid.*, p. 218.

"The Thing Signified" in *The Dynasts*: A Speculation

WILLIAM E. BUCKLER

Despite differences of perception and emphasis among the critics of *The Dynasts*, critical orientation toward the poem's "outlook" has been essentially ideological, centering on the nature of the poem's metaphysics and the degree of Hardy's intellectual assent to the monism figured in the Immanent Will. An interest centered in these matters has naturally, perhaps, led critics to assume that, when Hardy spoke in his preface about "the thing signified," he was pointing the reader's attention toward such ideologically ordering concepts. But if one assumes that these ideological issues, being so large and reiterative a part of the simulated drama itself, are aspects of "the insistent, and often grotesque, substance," then he is forced to look further for "the thing signified."

That Hardy meant to unveil, at least fleetingly, matters somewhat different in kind from ideological or metaphysical perception is surely suggested by the vibrations he sets in motion by phrases like "scenes laid 'far in the Unapparent'": the "older, more invidious, more nervous, more quizzical" unhappy perplexity of the modern "meditative world": the "Riddles of Death Thebes never knew." Such phrases induce, not analytical poise, but experiential disquiet. And even experiential disquiet has to be transformed to cosmic terror the more we reflect upon the perpetual bombardment of awarenesses to which we have been subjected throughout *The Dynasts*. We, *homo agonistes*, have certainly been treated to some harsh lessoning in the course of the poem: that we are without any control over our lives, the puppets of an unconscious energy that evolves morally valueless patterns; that even our most magnificent representatives—our greatest heroes—are no more significant, historically perspected, than the most minute insect on the most mutable leaf; that our dynasts, remnants of the old order and restored monitors of our social and political lives, are conspicuously incompetent, even though we of the masses, are still in life-and-death service to them; that there is likely to be little correlation between the truth of our perceptions and the ardor with which we hold them; that people alter their perceptions of reality hardly at all even in the face of the most harrowing and relevant experiences. It would be an intimidating programme of human diminution if it were coherently articulated by a centered authority in the poem, and even as a cluster of possibilities with which the reader spectator, as ultimate judge, must deal, these perceptions of the human situation in the universe dislocate most of the traditional devices and structures by which we have sought to give ordered and self-satisfying expectations to our world.

Perception in its infinite aspects, how people suppose and state fact, is perhaps the central exploratory awareness upon which *The Dynasts* turns. But one aspect of human perception, intimately related to man's sense of anxiety in his universe, is so inevitable a dimension of experiential reinforcement that it is insinuated into the reader's consciousness in a relentless way. The poet-designer of the piece is determined to maintain the integrity of *The Dynasts* as an aesthetic structure, but he is also insistent that the reader spectator be brought face to face with all the realities of war. Those realities go far beyond the hellish horrors and lurid rituals of eyeball-to-eyeball death-dealing. They include pageantry, gamesmanship, power-broking, the basic concepts of alliances and jealous regard for national borders, the balance of power, the establishment of new and the maintenance of old dynasties, and so forth. The fragility of such arrangements and the confrontal consequences of their collapse keep even older civilized centers of the world poised on the brink of war; and ancient discontents and a ruler's personal ambitions may alike upset the precarious balances and draw clusters of nations into conflict.

Hardy realized, of course, that it was beyond any writer's capacity to affect directly the international arrangements that seemed to increase the likelihood of war, but he knew too that it was not the people at the top of the social scale (the dynasts themselves) who were likely to suffer war's actual brutalities. War was induced by dynasts, but fought by soldiers; and soldiers at the very lowest echelon were likely to be the greatest bearers of war's devastation with the least access to such spiritually compensatory roles as leadership and individual charisma. Hence, the lowliest foot-soldier became generally the genuine victim of the games dynasts play. Like the cavalry horse itself, he could find least reason to justify his wounds. This awareness of the penetrating irony of those who had the least to gain suffering the most became a way of perceiving the hellish disproportion and madness of war and the object of a special sort of literary endeavor.

To the perceptual possibility of an abrupt and all-pervasive diminution of human significance is thus added a massive demonstration of raw, undeniably real human pain, brutal and unreasonable. Man emerges as negligible, largely deluded, and tortured. It is a crushing perceptual cluster capable of casting over the human prospect a terrifying light.

Further, one's attempts to define "the thing signified" by *The Dynasts* demand that he weigh in the significant accumulation of symbolist images of absurdity in the poem, oblique suggestions that are inexhaustibly disturbing. The poem's apprehensive tone is so keenly ironic that its potentialities as a grand spectacle of the absurd are insistently present throughout: the poet-designer could have screamed with grotesque laughter at almost every turn. Hardy chose a different aesthetic center: he counterpointed the manifest examples of absurdity with equally manifest examples of genuine degree of heroism, pathos, fidelity, high purpose, and authentic tragedy. Hence the very tangible strain of the grotesque in the piece is serious rather than light, tragic rather than comic.

The images of absurdity are numerous and very real, functioning within an aesthetic medium in which the discrepancy between reality and perception or between perception and perception constantly threatens the consciousness with absurdity of mind-blowing proportions. An all-pervasive discrepancy of this sort is that between men's sense of themselves as responsibly engaged in a moral contest called life and Years' visualization of them as simply particles of vitalized matter "writing, crawling, heaving, and vibrating in their various cities and nationalities"—their habitats and sub-species. A more localized but quite grotesquely absurd discrepancy is implicit in George III's capricious response to Pitt's request for the personal relief and national unity of a coalition government: he thrusts himself like a colossal anachronism between the exhausted Pitt and his frustrating but fortitudinous efforts to create in Europe a sufficient international counterpoise to paralyze Napoleon's aggression. It is dynasties like George III's that are at stake, yet the King prattles on about the strains of his own office, "Our just crusade against the Corsican," the divine right of kings, the soundness of reasons never in fact thought of, climaxing with a royal petulance: "Rather than Fox, why, give me civil war!/ Hey, what?" (I, IV, I, 67-68) At the end of their totally deflating conversation, Pitt makes polite reference to a "curious structure" outside, to which the King replies as follows:

> It's but a stage, a type of all the world. The burgesses have arranged it in my honor. At six o'clock this evening there are to be combats at single-stick to amuse the folk: four guineas the prize for the man who breaks most heads. Afterwards there is to be a grinning match through horse-collars—a very humorous sport which I must stay here and witness; for I am interested in whatever entertains my subjects.

The flatulence of the King's reply in juxtaposition to Pitt is itself disquieting, but the succession of images that George unwittingly releases become symbolist implants of absurdity: (1) life is a stage (2) on which men are paid for breaking the most heads (3) after which people play the amusing sport of grinning through horse-collars. It is inexhaustibly disturbing because of the wry truth of it, the piquant irony of the context in which it is released, and the essentially unmediated imagery from which it draws its memorableness.

The reader may shudder at the full reverberations set in motion by this scene between Pitt and George III, but the cumulative effect of such images of absurdity is greater than the sum of them individually; and they do darken as the poem progresses. The story of how the crew "broached the Adm'l" reveals a considerably darkened image of absurdity. The broad humour with which the FIRST BOATMAN tells how the crew of the "Victory," when they "brought the gallant hero home," "fairly saved their lives" by puncturing his casket and drinking him dry—that is, consuming the alcoholic spirits in which his body was being preserved on the long journey home—is counterpoised by the inevitable realization, however delayed, that a cadaver thus preserved would release into the preservative its body wastes (residual excrement, urine, semen, and a host of body chemicals and stored substances), thus converting the broad humour intended by the teller into a symbolist image of a grotesque and psychically distressful sort. The dark side of this image is then deepened in the direction of the authentically tragic by the song that closes the fifth act, "The Night of Trafalgar," in which images of futility sweep over images of heroism:

> Dead Nelson and his half-dead crew, his foes from near and far,
> Were rolled together on the deep that night at Trafalgar!
> The deep,
> The deep!
> That night at Trafalgar!

These symbolist implants accrete rapidly. An indelible image is imprinted on the mind when, at Austerlitz, Napoleon quite capriciously and "with a vulpine smile" has the battery turned on the frozen lake which 2000 Russians are crossing: "A ghastly crash and splashing follows the discharge, the shining surface breaking into pieces like a mirror, which fly in all directions. Two thousand fugitives are engulfed, *and their groans of despair reach the ears of the watchers like ironical huzzas.*" (I, VI, IV, 121, emphasis added) Even the mirror metaphor is symbolic since it reflects the multifarious tragedy that will be served up to Napoleon in his Moscow adventure; and the description of the Russians then in turn mirrors *his* action here: "My God, they are Scythians and barbarians still!" (III, I, VIII, 349) That Pitt should receive the news of Austerlitz while he is in the Picture Gallery at Shockerwick House having highly cultivated talk of Gainsborough and Sir

Joshua Reynolds, Churchill and Quin stuns the nerves with a penetrating awareness that Pitt himself points up. Against the elegant perpetuation motif of eighteenth-century literary and artistic decorum is set Pitt's total sense of personal dissolution:

> So do my plans through all these plodding years
> Announce them built in vain.
> His heel on Europe, monarchies in chains
> To France, I am as though I had never been! (I, VI, VI, 128)

One of the most complex symbolist images imprinted on the mind is that of the war as perspected by a group of English deserters in a house-cellar on "A Road Near Astorga." The grotesque humour with which the scene is projected by the several deserters cannot disguise the bizarre low to which their world has degenerated, nesting as they are in wet straw among dead or drunk or naked men, women, and children and looking out upon a civilization in reverse motion—"dying downwards," as it were. What they see is horses falling from exhaustion, being pistoled in the head; soldiers who have pillaged being executed by lot; people who have died in transport being laid out beside the road with "some muddy snow scraped over them": a momentary display of soldierly behaviour in absurd pantomime. This is what, from inside the English ranks, the war looks like—a complex image burnt deep into the reader-spectator's consciousness without authorial interpretation or judgment.

Walcheren represents a different kind of nadir to the English. That it is authentically historical in no way detracts from its massive metaphorical quality: one of the inevitable dimensions/ possibilities of war is that one may, like the speaker in "Hap," have to forego the satisfaction of a combatant, may have to forego one's personal Prometheanism for lack of an available tyrant. One is perhaps fairly reminded of the soft, nerveless, pithless, misty world of Lotosland as an ironically reversed analogue: the narcotic-laced Lotos-eaters crave a death-in-life state, while the soldiers sinking into the sediment of Walcheren, hiding toward an inertia-point of human misery, crave but the chance to "yield their lives" in fair fight within sound of the echoes of "the aggressor's arrogant career." It is the most haunting error of English strategy, and it is the victims' fear that

> Our country's chiefs, for their own fames afraid,
> Will leave our names and fates by this pale sea
> To perish silently! (II, IV, VIII, 251-52)

But of course the most devastating images of a grotesque absurdity are implanted in Napoleon's Russian campaign (III, I); and there, if anywhere, we can expect to find a revelation, however oblique, of "the thing signified."

The first scene of Part Third, in which massive anxiety is projected, functions at two very different levels—that of the *dramatis personae* and that of the reader-spectator, the latter having gradually learned through the literary procedures of the piece to translate even its denotative action into symbolist awareness. Napoleon himself is the primary dramatic personage in the scene, so what we are essentially faced with is Napoleon's view of himself versus our views of him. That he is somewhat shaken though defiant, is overwrought and has lost his fine-tuning, begins to see history as closing in on him, feels fated even against his "better mind," but faces his gloom in a spirit of grim irony—these aspects of his self-hood we perceive and can believe that he perceives them too. But there are dimensions of our awareness that he does not share, and these move the experience of the scene for the reader-spectator to a deep ironic level. Napoleon is beginning the long slide toward moral and psychological shabbiness, and he is blinding himself to glaring contradictions in his self-projection: his naughtiness toward the Russian sense of destiny countervenes his own oft-repeated claim of a manifest destiny; he attempts to equate the disastrous strategy of invading Russia at an inopportune time of the year, wholly his wilful error, with the need to lesson Russia in French insuperability; he falls back upon the "force" that moves him "inexorably" to offset the sense of ominous foreboding that has enveloped his psyche. But it is the images induced by the scene that scarify the mind. Napoleon's version of the "Malbrough" air projects his self-serving return after abandoning his troops starving and freezing in Lithuania, while Sinister's revision of the same air projects the chaotic destruction of half-a-million men "*dead and buried*"—at least till the coming of spring! This is then immediately followed by an image of the "Christ of war" shrinking, shrinking to the aspect of a doll while the heavens burst with thunder and lightning and torrents of rain as if a divine dispensation were in fact ending. It is a literary realization worthy of Aristophanes.

The scene in "The Open Country between Smorgoni and Wilna" (III I, XI, 357-59) that closes the Russian sequence is widely recognized as the nadir of horror represented in *The Dynasts*, and it deserves that recognition because of the literary manner Hardy brings to it. The symbolist technique is complete. "These stricken shades in a limbo of gloom" perambulate as tattered skeletons (scarecrows) in merciless wintry desert of which there is no beginning and no end, no alpha and no omega. Like Dante's limbo-inhabitants, they are without hope, and they move about like iced automatons building their bivouac fire and having their meal of horse and rat. Word that Napoleon has abandoned them drives them variously into paroxysms of "grief, rage, and despair," some sobbing like children, some becoming wildly insane. The "Mad Soldier's Song" becomes their aria of ironic salvation since they have reached a state of being that has finally exceeded pain as ordinarily understood. Then they gather in their physical exhaustion for the ultimate symbolist tableau of *The Dynasts*: the last survivors of the Grand Army gathered around the bivouac fire, pressed close for shared body heat, cindered in front, caked hard with frost in the back, with the tears on their cheeks "in strings of ice." Thus they are found by Kutuzof and his men; thus they are left to be buried by the falling snow. And the reader-spectator is spared intrusion in his awed contemplation of the scene.

What happens within this symbolist envelope provides the chief key to "the thing signified" by *The Dynasts*.

It should be noted that, when Napoleon arrives at Moscow, he has been seriously depleted: the ardors of the march and battle-butchery have already destroyed three-quarters of his army. As he says, "And it was time." Thus he is ill-prepared, in physical or psychological resource, for the failure of expectation that Rostopchin and Kutuzof have prepared for him. Here he is, the supreme European, face to face with Asia, and Asia has prepared a bag of "foul tricks" for him: "My god, they are Scythians and barbarians still!" For Napoleon to arrive, after such hardship, at an abandoned Moscow is as bizarre as for Marlow, in Conrad's *Heart of Darkness*, to witness a French man-of-war firing into the continent of Africa; it is surreal, defying comprehension by the highly coded European mind. It is a "crazed act," an "infernal scheme" which some "Satan" has devised. This Europe-Asia dichotomy is made explicit, in Hardy's oblique, ironic way, on Napoleon's journey to Elba. He says to Bertrand, "Yes—all is lost in Europe for me now!" Bertrand replies, "I fear so, sire." Then Napoleon: "But Asia waits a man,/ And—who can tell?" (XXX, IV, VI 420) And just before this (III, III, II, 383), the poet-designer has noted, "Nationalities from the uttermost parts of Asia here meet those from the Atlantic edge of Europe for the first and last time."

This climactic revelation—that for the coded European mind to look into Asia is to look into a vast mystery, as incomprehensibility, with which it is not prepared to cope—is a perception that has haunted the twentieth century. Hardy suggests it somewhat circumspectly, to be sure; but it is highly significant as one of a cluster of perceptions that draw us to the terrifying conclusion—perhaps "the thing signified" in *The Dynasts*—that the modern European is possessed of a whole repertoire of strategies for coping that are simply irrelevant to the things to be coped with; that his reality is a preferential disposition, not the true truth: that beyond the painted shell of his privately packaged universe there are "deep wells of nothingness" with which he has no capacity to deal. It is a frightful vision, and if one takes Hardy's epic analogy seriously, *The Dynasts* spells the doom of modern Europe as surely as the *Iliad* spelled the doom of ancient Troy.

But Hardy does not seem to have been inclined to translate these dire imaginings into a voice *in propria persona* and to assume the role of a modern vates. Like his own, the preceding, and the following generations of poets, he was "dramatic," "personative," creating structures in which truth was not authorially mediated but authentically explored through the aesthetic placement of a reader-spectator who is not infallible in a position analogous to that of an author who is not infallible watching a protagonist who is not infallible. Such structures could be as comparatively simple as the dramatic lyric in sonnet form entitled "Hap" or as epically direct, dramatically complex, and aesthetically inexhaustible as *The Dynasts*. But the mark of their modernism, being attitudinal, is the same. The modern artist has no obligation to dismantle the past, however anachronistic it may have become; indeed, the modern artist, as Arnold said, does not deal in pastness or presentness, but in relevance; he makes the past and the present creative bedfellows to the degree that he makes his individual talent and his inherited literary traditions organic. Thus both modernism and the modern artist are in a perpetual state of becoming. Like the Immanent Will, in many ways a fit analogue to the artist right down to the unconscious center of his creativity, the modern poet-designer is an instrument of creative evolution, his aim "to alter evermore/ Things from what they were before" (III, VII, VIII, 518); or, to translate this into words from Hardy's preface to *The Dynasts*, to adopt as one's single aim "the modern expression of a modern outlook."

Thus the modern poet puts a premium, not on action, but on awareness: consciousness-raising (spiritual transformation, imaginative elevation) is the goal to which everything else he does is subordinate. His faith is not in social arrangements or in political or religious creeds but in metaphors and myths because they are his instruments of metamorphosis. The imagination, he knows, is an organic part of everyman; and the cultivation of the imagination, for which the poet-designer has special gifts, is an organic cultivation promising organic (and hence permanent) results. Every dimension of man's consciousness—from day-to-day perception to loving-kindness to cosmic symbolism—is dependent on the state of cultivation of that man's individual imagination.

What we have in *The Dynasts*, then, is a frightful vision set against an irrefragable faith. The *vrai verité* of a universe that very quickly outstrips rational comprehensibility (a universe centered in the consciousness as well as in the cosmos) is juxtaposed to an aesthetic way of ordering reality, a way exemplified by both *The Dynasts* and its analogue, the *Iliad*. At the time Hardy published his epic-drama, the *Iliad* and *The Dynasts* constituted, for the moment, a literary frame, an alpha and an omega of sorts, of man's imaginative efforts to deal with his woes and to establish, at least suggestively, a symbol of reconciliation to his frightful condition. That symbol became literature itself, *The Dynasts* and all those instruments of imaginative awareness, from Homer and Aeschylus and Sophocles to Dante and Shakespeare and Shelley, through which man has been enabled to perceive imaginative coordinates in what would otherwise be a chaos both within and without. Like Shelley, in whose *Defence of Poetry* he found the text, Hardy seems to have endorsed Tasso's perception—*Non merita nome di creatore, se non Iddio ed il Poeta* [*No one deserves the name of creator, except God and the Poet*]—with this fundamental difference: that by the time Hardy wrote *The Dynasts*, the poet stood alone.

It should be clear from the foregoing that anyone who does not know *The Dynasts* simply does not know Hardy. To ignore his epic-drama is to ignore his efforts to create a truly monumental work, to wed his individual talent and his keen sense of contemporary spiritual ambience to the most ancient theory and practice of the Western literary tradition, to convert history into myth and thus to place the nineteenth century in Europe in the literary pantheon of the Indo-European ages. It is to ignore, too, a fine literary achievement that, in retrospect, is more and more seen as the twentieth century's prototypical literary formulation, the aesthetic structure that gathers in the fright and the fragments, the pulverizations and the importunities, the inheritances and the alienations—the epic, narrative, dramatic, lyrical, elegiac, symphonic, panoramic, picturesque, impressionistic, grotesque, symbolist artistic expectancies and despairs of "these disordered years of our prematurely afflicted century." Hardy brings to bear on the literary procedure of the poem his complete literary repertoire as he tries to create a massive artistic structure in which there is a place and function, not only for the sweeping panoramic spectacle, but also for the thousands of bits of individual dramatic role-playing, in high and low alike, that go to make up a densely textured, Breughel-like, vibrant representation of life. And he does this, in what must be called a grand literary paradox, Homerically rather than Miltonically: he overleaps the whole Christian experience in literature and finds his analogical mirror in a literary text that, as Hardy read it, did not depend on "an indivisible and regular system, which occupies *the whole extent of the believing mind*," but is "composed of a thousand loose and flexible parts."

The Dynasts represents, in a quiet new degree, a breakthrough from systematic ideology to genuine metaphoric awareness, even from a closed system used metaphorically to a metaphoric open-endedness in which one's own system-making can undergo fundamental restructuring and renewal. It is authorially non-judgmental as a literary work, and in it even the soul-warts of representative modern men are allowed to surface and show. It is a work that creates a massive collision of individual "systems"—some austere and disciplined, some soft-headed and limply sentimental, some conscientiously researched, some got up on the run and for the occasion—for the singular purpose of exposing in the raw and in the mass modern man's perceptual resources and perceptual techniques; and against these are set relentless exposures of man's perceptual needs if he would hope, with anything like the "complete rationality" necessary for human survival, to reconcile himself through his individual consciousness to his cosmic situation.

Twentieth-century poets have long since recognized that Hardy had discovered in his long dramatic poem a "modern expression of a modern outlook" that was eminently usable by pursuers of their craft. Twentieth-century critics have been slower—perhaps because they have been imaginatively duller, perhaps, because they have felt no need, in the pursuit of their craft, for the recognition. Nevertheless, it has been an unfortunate critical short-sightedness, allowing one of the pedestal documents in modern literary transmutation and definition to lie gathering dust in the full but glazed sight of all.

The critic who presses *The Dynasts*, however belatedly, upon the attention of the student of the twentieth century's imaginative life must be cautioned by Hardy's judgment that for a certain type of reader, his poem was unsuitable—specifically the reader "unwilling or unable" to participate along the co-creative lines designated. Reversing the implications of Hardy's astute judgment here, one can perhaps identify the type of reader for whom *The Dynasts* is most suitable. He is a reader who knows that a literary experience worthy of our best efforts is a complex and strenuous activity demanding full use of the enriched resources of writer and reader alike; that, with few exceptions, it is an experience that must be repeated several times before he gets a practiced feel for the individuality of the work being assayed and the literary traditions upon which it is drawing; and that the experience is its own end, the exercise of some of the most refined and pleasurable resources of his consciousness for purely organic reasons having little to do with political or cultural or philosophical direction or wisdom. For such a reader, *The Dynasts* should be an extraordinary adventure. An ambitious poem monitored by a pervasive awareness that poetry itself has become the chief instrument of order and significance in a godless modern world, Hardy's "Iliad of Europe" has an open aesthetic center out of which hundreds of individual poetic structures emerge in an incremental but flexible surfacing of varied human efforts to systematize reality through or in response to language. These poetic structures in turn become metaphors of human reality (perceivers perceived perceiving) within a symphonic magnitude of complex variations that absorbs these individual poetic structures into a densely configured awareness of epic proportions and significance. The historical subject—a decade of Pan-European struggle—is translated into a modern myth having a genuine analogue in the *Iliad*; the human subject—how people suppose and state fact or the head-games people play with reality—is gradually enriched through poetic technique in this mythohistorical structure until ultimately two of the most insistent subjects of both historical and modern man come to dominate the poem and, through their interlocking, define its central concern: war and peace, perception and truth.

How well Hardy sustains such a challenging concern in the working out of his literary procedures is ultimately a judgment to be made by the individual reader; but obviously to anyone who thinks that he sustains it superbly, every other item in the Hardy canon will be seen in literary magnitude and importance as secondary to *The Dynasts*.

NOTE

All quotations from and references to *The Dynasts* have as their basis *The Dynasts: An Epic Drama of the War with Napoleon*, by Thomas Hardy (New York: St. Martin's Press, 1977). This is a reprint of the text of the edition issued by Macmillan in 1924 with the same consecutive pagination throughout, and quotations used have been checked against the 1924 text. Passages are identified by Part, Act, Scene, and page and are given in parentheses in the text as appropriate.

Index